THE INTERNATIONAL
PSYCHO-ANALYTICAL
LIBRARY
No. 105

THE INTERNATIONAL PSYCHO-ANALYTICAL LIBRARY

EDITED BY M. MASUD R. KHAN

No. 105

THE MEANING OF ILLNESS

Selected Psychoanalytic Writings

by

GEORG GRODDECK

Including his correspondence with

SIGMUND FREUD

Selected, and with an Introduction, by

LORE SCHACHT

Translated by GERTRUD MANDER

LONDON

THE HOGARTH PRESS

AND THE INSTITUTE OF PSYCHO-ANALYSIS

1977

Published by
The Hogarth Press Ltd.
40 William IV Street
London WC2N 4DF

*

Clarke, Irwin & Co. Ltd.
Toronto

British Library Cataloguing in Publication Data

Groddeck, Georg
    The meaning of illness: selected psychoanalytic writings. – (The inter-
national psycho-analytical library; no. 105).
    Bibl. – Index.
    ISBN 0–7012–0422–2
    1. Title   2. Freud, Sigmund   3. Schacht, Lore   4. Mander, Gertrud
    5. Series
    616.8′917′08   RC509
    Psychoanalysis – Addresses, essays, lectures

Photoset, printed and bound
in Great Britain by
REDWOOD BURN LIMITED
Trowbridge & Esher

Contents

Introduction

Looking back over his life at 64, Groddeck wrote:
I run a sanatorium which is visited by people who do not find help in other places. Sometimes I am lucky with these difficult cases, sometimes not. I am a pupil of Schweninger, who was, perhaps, the greatest doctor of the last century. Following in his footsteps I suddenly found myself, without knowing it, faced with the necessity of evaluating unconscious processes in the treatment of organic diseases. When a few years later I came upon Freud's works I had to give up the idea that I was a discoverer myself, not without a struggle. For it became apparent that I had first read about these in a notice in the daily paper *Rundschau*. The only achievement I can claim for myself with some justification is the introduction of a knowledge of the unconscious into the treatment of all patients, and particularly those patients who suffer from organic illnesses, and that I am as aware as Freud that psychoanalysis is a world-wide affair and only partly a medical affair and that its tie-up with medicine is a disaster. I do not have a title, but there are people who love me and I have insights which make my life harmonious in so far as that is possible at all. I cannot send a prospectus of my small clinic – 15 rooms – where I am assisted by my wife, not only in the household. There is no prospectus. My charges are adjusted to the means of my patients, in the treatment I rely on my head and on my hands and on the view that every patient has his or her own illness and that the person who wants to help them has to practice the saying: nil humanum a me alienum esse puto (I believe that nothing human is strange to me) and also on the exhortation: Children, love one another! I have patients of all kinds; I am not a specialist, but a general practitioner with the knowledge and experience gathered in an active professional life. And I may perhaps be allowed to say that I have not forgotten during my life as a doctor that man's true profession is to become a human being.[1]

1

This is an extract from a letter written by Groddeck to Hans Vaihinger, Professor of Philosophy, on May 8, 1930, in which he also discussed his father's doctoral thesis 'De morbo democratico nova insaniae forma', and argued that Nietzsche had probably known it.

Walter Georg Groddeck, born on October 13, 1866, the youngest son of a physician, in Bad Kösen, grew up in a household where the memory of his maternal grandfather, the literary historian Koberstein, was held in high esteem and where up to the Seventies of the last century many well-known scholars of German literature used to meet. From childhood on he knew that he was going to be a doctor, too, by his father's wish.

When his father lost his money in 1881 through a series of miscalculations, the family moved to Berlin.

I barely scraped through the final exams of my grammar school in March 1885 because I was an unruly schoolboy and my teachers were less satisfied with my conduct than they were with my knowledge. I was to study medicine, and as my father did not have the means to finance my studies at a university and was favourably impressed by the medical training course offered by the army since he knew one of our best military doctors, Oberstabsarzt Villaret, the intention was to send me to one of the military medical schools. When I arrived in Berlin where my father was working as a slum doctor I was told that I had applied too late and would not be able to start until the autumn. . . . In order not to waste all that time I put myself down for a lecture course in Chemistry; if I remember rightly I went three times and one of the lectures I remember clearly, it was about arsenic; but my father believed that the most useful thing I could do was to sit in on his consultations with his patients. Under the pretext of making notes and writing out prescriptions on his dictation I was assigned a chair next to his desk from where I was able to watch all that was happening. These were the early days of the general health insurance scheme, my father had applied to be a general practitioner in the scheme and day in day out there was now a constant stream of bakers, bricklayers, and other workers pouring into his consulting rooms and seeking to confirm their admission into the scheme. This was quite an entertaining experience for me, my father loved talking to these people and asking them questions about their lives and their opinions, and I acquired some insight into working-class life and into the struggle between the employers and the people who were only considered hands working for the firm; important as this was for my personal development, there was something else that influenced me even more though I did not know how to appreciate it at the time: I got to know the medical profession not by meeting sick patients, but by meeting healthy people. This proved to be of invaluable importance to me . . . At that time moreover, the event occurred that jolted me out of my dreamlike existence and gave my career its decisive direction: my father had a stroke while treating patients.[2]

Apart from the influence exerted by his father Groddeck's medical career was shaped decisively by his meeting with Ernst Schweninger as a student and by later becoming his assistant.

Schweninger (1850–1924) had achieved fame as Bismarck's personal physician and held a teaching post at the Kaiser Wilhelm Universität in Berlin from 1894. His method of treatment was based on the idea that the doctor was merely the catalyst who starts off the therapeutic process. He was opposed to the use of drugs and specially favoured diet, hydrotherapy, and massage. After finishing his tour of duty as a military doctor, Groddeck went to Baden Baden to become the assistant of Schweninger whom he had known since his student days. In 1900 he set up a clinic of his own there. Because his reputation quickly spread beyond Baden Baden he soon established a flourishing practice. His domestic life was less happy at first – his marriage in which there was a child ended in separation, and because of the difficulties he had in obtaining a divorce he had to wait until 1923 before he could get married a second time, to his Swedish assistant, who had worked with him since 1915.

Groddeck began to write. Apart from articles on medical questions, he contributed to the arts page of the *Frankfurter Zeitung* and even wrote novels later on (*Ein Frauenproblem*, 1903; *Ein Kind der Erde*, 1905; *Die Hochzeit des Dionysos*, 1906). He was also interested in social problems and gave regular talks at the workers' community centre in Baden Baden. He also initiated the founding of a consumers' cooperative.

In his essay 'Georg Groddeck als Sozialreformer und Mensch' (Georg Groddeck as social reformer and human being), Michael Pichler writes:

> In Spring 1912 the consumers' cooperative that could be considered Dr. Groddeck's work was able to open its first shop. But the enterprise had yet to be put on a firm basis, since the business community was trying its hardest to prevent it from succeeding. The doctor always thought up new ways and followed them in his own thorough fashion. For example, he hit on a very effective publicity method. He announced a series of talks on the theme: 'Health and Sickness', held in the Bletzer Brewery, at first in a small room nicknamed 'cigar box' on account of its shape. There was only a small group of friends of the doctor's and members of the consumers' cooperative in the beginning. But the first talk proved so interesting and fascinating that the second talk drew such crowds that the cigar box was full to capacity. For the third talk the garden room had to be used, and all the following talks were so well attended that all the available chairs in the building had to be brought in to seat the audience. The series proved a great and lasting success, not only for the doctor, who was pleased by it, but also for the consumers' cooperative. The discussions which followed every lecture made these evenings particularly interesting. When the series came to an end after twelve talks there was general disappointment. The talks were published in 1913 as a book by Hirzel in Leipzig, under the title *Nasamecu* (Natura sanat, medicus curat – nature heals, the doctor cures) and subtitled 'Der gesunde und kranke Mensch' (The healthy and sick person).[3]

The book *Nasamecu* marks the transition between two phases in Groddeck's life, the phase during which he was Schweninger's pupil, and the phase in which he tried to be Freud's pupil. The book is written, on the one hand, in homage to his teacher Schweninger whose therapeutic principles are commemorated in the title (Natura sanat, medicus curat). It contains, on the other hand, a criticism of psychoanalysis which Groddeck at the time knew by hearsay only. In 1913 Groddeck at last began to read Freud, *The Psychopathology of*

Everyday Life and *The Interpretation of Dreams*. On May 27, 1917, he decided to write Freud a letter. This turned into a long letter, the longest he ever wrote to Freud; in it he outlined his main ideas in a systematic and lucid way such as he hardly ever achieved again, and he asked Freud whether he should consider himself a psychoanalyst or whether he was going beyond psychoanalysis. Freud's answer came quickly, on June 5, 1917:

> ... I understand that you are requesting me urgently to supply you with an official confirmation that you are not a psychoanalyst, that you do not belong to the members of the group, and will be able to call yourself something special, and independent. Obviously, I am doing you a service if I push you away from me to the place where Adler, Jung, and others stand. Yet I cannot do this; I have to claim you, I have to assert that you are a splendid analyst who has understood for ever the essential aspects of the matter. The discovery that transference and resistance are the most important aspects of treatment turns a person irretrievably into a member of the wild army. No matter if he calls the unconscious 'It'. Let me show you that there is no need to extend the concept of the unconscious in order to make it cover your experience of organic illnesses. ...

This is the beginning of the remarkable relationship between Freud and Groddeck in which Groddeck insisted on calling himself Freud's pupil without really playing the part. The fact that he never gave up his own opinions, particularly the concept of the It which he had found a long time before he met Freud and which he put forward with self-confidence, did not prevent Groddeck from revering Freud as the great master; he even seemed to long for permission to revere him. The ideas of Freud's which he used and applied in his work remain essentially limited to those mentioned in his first letter to Freud, namely the ideas of the unconscious, of transference and of resistance. Yet his admiration of Freud went far beyond this:

> Allow me in conclusion to say something about Freud. His work, his discoveries of the unconscious, of resistance and transference have been compared to the discoveries made by Copernicus. This may be a useful comparison for scholars.

But he did more for us as human beings. He discovered that apart from the human languages of sound and gesture there are hundreds of other languages a thousand times more important and true than the former, means of communication which bring people closer to each other. In the context of world history Freud did something that can only be compared to the work of the founders of religion if we have to make a comparison at all. He taught people new ways of understanding one another, he brought them closer together, he built a thousand bridges across the gap that separates human beings from each other, he gave to those who followed him a newer, deeper, happier, more childlike way of living, a new kind of loving and a new kind of believing. To know is to doubt, to believe is not to doubt. In science Freud forced us to doubt and re-examine everything we thought we knew up to then. In our personal lives he brought us a belief, the belief in loving one another. He increased in us the ability to get to know each other which results spontaneously and inevitably in a greater human love and respect for others, it reduces the compulsion to lie, offers the possibility of a greater freedom of living and reduces anxiety. I am glad I know him.[4]

Unique in the relationship between Freud and Groddeck is the fact that Freud continued to show interest in and concern for Groddeck's writings until Groddeck's death in 1934, that he defended him against other analysts and gave his permission to publish his works in spite of the reservations he had against them or mentioned about them to other people. An example is the following passage from a letter to Oskar Pfister, dated February 4, 1921:

I energetically defend Groddeck against your respectability. What would you have said if you had been a contemporary of Rabelais? Poor Rank will have to be my scapegoat more often now.[5]

Pfister wrote back on 14 March:

I understand very well that it is impossible for you to think otherwise. The state of mind that leads you to encourage Groddeck is exactly the same as that which made you the discoverer and pioneer of psychoanalysis. But, with the best will in the world, I cannot adopt your view, as indeed you do not expect me to. But there is a big difference between Rabelais and Groddeck. The former remains within his role as a satirist and avoids the error of putting himself forward as a savant. Groddeck, however, wavers between science and belles lettres . . . .

To which Freud replied, on 23 March:

. . . I was delighted with your remarks about Groddeck. We really must be able to tell each other home-truths, i.e. incivilities, and remain firm friends, as in this case. I am not giving up my view of Groddeck either, I am usually not so taken in by anybody. But it does not matter.[6]

Of the psychoanalysts such as Ernst Simmel, Karen Horney and Frieda Fromm-Reichmann who came to admire Groddeck, Sandor Ferenczi enjoyed the most lasting friendship with him. Suffering from severe nephrosclerosis, he had become a patient of Groddeck's on the advice of F. Deutsch in 1921.[7] He was soon able to go home with all his symptoms cured, and used to take regular 'therapeutic holidays' with Groddeck in Baden Baden.

Many analysts were critical of Groddeck and yet on the occasion of Groddeck's sixtieth birthday there was an article in the *Internationale Zeitschrift für Psychoanalyse* by Ernst Simmel, who writes, among other things:

When we think of Groddeck as members of the International Psychoanalytic Society we remember the day when he first appeared in our midst in person during the conference at The Hague. He went up to the platform and announced: 'I am a wild analyst.' He was right. Yet one should understand the word 'wild' in a way that is different from the usual meaning of a psychoanalyst who launches into therapy with mentally ill patients without any training let alone a trace of understanding for the spirit of psychoanalysis. Groddeck may call himself wild – as a member of our movement who owes his training to nobody except himself. He may be called wild because of his passionate nature which wants to help where others have resigned or are hiding their impotence behind the mock techniques of exact diagnostics. His nature is the source of that 'wildness' which has enabled him, a fanatic of the art of healing, thanks to his unique gifts, to apply success- fully Freud's discoveries about the unconscious psyche in the fight against organic illnesses. Groddeck's wildness is also the courage to pursue singlemindedly one goal, it is the ab- solute truthfulness which he sees embodied in Freud. Groddeck's wildness is also the hatred with which he fights the old fashioned medical practices by which, before Freud, the doctor was placed in the centre of the healing situation instead of the patient, out of a kind of medical narcissism. We believe that a wildness of this kind should not be criticised, particularly when it is accompanied by such blessed innate artistic gifts as in the case of Groddeck.

While we psychoanalysts are busy and have to be busy learning everything Freud discovered and keeps on dis- covering in psychoanalysis and discussing and teaching these things in our 'school', i.e. in our societies, while we have guidelines and have to set guidelines for our therapeutic ac- tivity, Groddeck can do without these because his extensive work with organically sick patients is without parallel so far. He uniquely fits the distinction made by the philosopher Georg Simmel between artist and scientist: 'The scientist sees because he knows, the artist knows because he sees.' We know or seek to know what we can get by learning. Groddeck sees and knows without making this detour.[8]

In 1934, Groddeck left Germany on the advice of his friends in order to escape arrest by the Gestapo. He had an invitation from the Swiss Psychoanalytical Society to give a talk. He gave the talk 'Vom Sehen, von der Welt des Auges und vom Sehen ohne Augen' (Vision, the World of the Eye and Seeing without the Eyes).[9] A few days later he died in a clinic in Knonau, Swit- zerland, having suffered his first heart attack in 1930 and another one shortly before his trip to Switzerland.

GRODDECK'S WRITINGS

Groddeck's writings contain an extraordinary wealth of ideas which are sometimes formulated very briefly, almost aphoristi- cally, or illustrated by one clinical example alone, until they get taken up again in a later work. Because of this peculiarity, ideas

8

may appear in a fragmentary form in several essays without ever being dealt with extensively elsewhere. Groddeck's thoughts seem to have been in permanent flux although most of the time they were concentrated on one and the same basic idea, his concept of the It. Yet there is not the consistent arguing out of an idea nor the construction of a coherent theoretical system.

Groddeck's style is of such brilliance and beauty that one is inclined to present him in an introduction like this through his own words mainly, in order not to mispresent or dilute and fragment the specific quality of his thought. Yet occasionally there is a marked discrepancy between his brilliant exposition of ideas and passages in which he seems to get lost in a labyrinth of etymological derivations by which he hopes to justify and confirm his speculations. The present selection consists mainly of his theoretical and psychoanalytical writings, leaving out, among other things, his psychoanalytical novel *Der Seelensucher* (The Seeker of Souls), 1921, and his biographical essays.

In the following pages I shall outline Groddeck's most important themes in the sequence adopted for this book.

ORGANIC ILLNESS

Groddeck claimed to have come to the psychiatric and psychoanalytic treatment of patients with chronic organic illnesses by way of being a practising physiotherapist, and he has often been called the founder of psychosomatic medicine. This is an honour he would probably have shrugged off since he was keen on showing that there was no basic difference between organic and mental illness. In his first letter to Freud he outlined his main ideas about the nature of organic illnesses and put forward the suggestion that

> the distinction between body and mind is only verbal and not essential, that body and mind are one unit, that they contain an It, a force which lives us while we believe we are living.

Encouraged by the interest Freud showed in him, he wrote and published the essay 'Psychic Conditioning and the Psychoanalytic Treatment of Organic Illness' (pp 109–31 below) in the very same year; it was reviewed by Ferenczi in the *Internationale Zeitschrift*; and contains the following remarks. The It can choose the soul or the body, it manifests and makes itself understood not only in dreams but also in the physiognomy, the behaviour or in a serious organic illness.

It may set up conditions in which the pathogenic agent becomes effective, if it considers that an illness will serve a purpose (p. 112 below).

The It ties a person down, if necessary, it saves him by illness from dangers of a more serious nature than danger of life can ever be, it forces him to certain activities by certain disabilities, to rest through heart disease or tuberculosis (pp. 115–16 below).

Groddeck maintains, for instance, that headaches are one of the most widespread and well-known methods used by the It to immobilise thoughts and drives, that short-sightedness can serve as a means to spare a person the sight of objects unbearable to him and, conversely, that the long sight of the elderly helps them symbolically to make death appear far off.

The idea of illness being of use to the person suffering from it, even enabling him to express himself or to understand himself, is put most lucidly in the essay 'The Meaning of Illness' (pp 197–202 below). Yet it is not restricted to organic illness alone:

We have become very careless in our use of the label neurosis and have completely lost sight of the fact that illness is not an evil in itself but always a meaningful process and not infrequently brings out forces which are only effective within the context of being ill.[10]

Groddeck differentiates neither between organic and mental illnesses nor between health and illness. For him health is only one form of It manifestation. The It decides on whether a person is ill, healthy, or recovering from an illness. Thus Groddeck's conception of illness has to be understood in the context of his efforts at understanding the great unknown, the It:

For me, the question of psychogenesis does not exist. Illness is a sign of life, and even the most celebrated scholar knows nothing about the causes of its origin and as little about the causes of its disappearance. One can only fantasize about that. Since the terms 'psyche' and 'physis' are used in medicine without any further thought, since it is impossible to get human thought habits away from their beaten tracks, I thought up the term It. I liked the indefiniteness about it – X would have been too mathematical, and X, moreover, demands a solution, my It, however, suggests that only a fool would try to understand it. There is nothing there to understand. Yet since the It is the most important thing about people, everybody who uses it says: we do not understand anything about life, we can only live it. All definitions are thus made null and void, they have nothing but a momentary meaning, are only justified in so far as they are useful. One cannot build on definitions as if they were foundation stones, and it is not the task of science to construct since the structure of life is there and is indestructible unless it changes by itself. Everything is changeable, therefore definitions are changeable, too, and the more so the wider their frame of reference. The time has come either to do away completely with the words soul and body or to redefine them.

So far I cannot find any meaning in the word psychogenesis.[11]

GRODDECK'S CONCEPT OF THE IT

In his early book, *Hin zur Gottnatur* (Towards God Nature), Groddeck wrote in 1912 already:

There is no such thing as an I, it is a lie, a misrepresentation to say: I think, I live. It ought to be: it thinks, it lives. It, i.e. the great mystery of the world. There is no I.[12]

'The great mystery of the world' is also called 'Gottnatur' (God Nature) by Groddeck, an expression he got from Goethe:

What more can man gain from life
Than have God nature revealed to him:
How it turns matter into spirit
How it makes the creations of the spirit live on.[13]

In his Christmas letter of 1922 Freud writes:

I think you got the It (in a literary, not an associative way) from Nietzsche.

11

Groddeck himself writes retrospectively, in a letter to a doctor patient dated June 11, 1929,[14] that he used the term the It 'in connection with Nietzsche and for reasons of convenience'.

From the first, Freud refused to understand the It in the way in which Groddeck wanted him to see it. Already in his first letter to Freud Groddeck went so far as to say that the It, as a force by which man is being lived even if he believes to be living himself, manifests itself as much in his thoughts and emotions, his organic and mental illnesses, as in the external appearance of man, and he drew attention to the fact that Freud's concept of the unconscious had to be widened in order to allow the psychoanalytic examination of physical illness. Freud's answer was: 'There is no need to extend the concept of the unconscious in order to make it cover your experience of organic illnesses.'

Groddeck cannot give an answer to the question, what is the It? He contents himself with distinguishing the various manifestations of the It. Thus the Ego, consciousness, any human expression of life, be it physical or mental, healthy or unhealthy, are all manifestations of the It.

After reading the first chapters of Groddeck's work, *Das Buch vom Es* (*The Book of the It*), Freud wrote on April 17, 1921:

I understand very well why the unconscious is not enough to make you consider the It dispensable.

And, at Christmas 1922:

Do you remember, by the way, how early I accepted the It from you? It was a long time before I made your personal acquaintance, in one of my first letters to you. I made a drawing there, which will soon be published in almost the same form.

On March 25, 1923, after the publication of *The Book of the It* Freud congratulates Groddeck and continues:

The work, moreover, argues the theoretically important point of view which I have dealt with in my own forthcoming work *The Ego and the Id*.

Groddeck, after receiving Freud's *The Ego and the Id*, which was published in the same year as his own *Book of the It*, set about answering in a highly critical way on May 27, 1923, 'as godfather, present at the christening'. In the comparison he uses there he calls himself the plough, Freud the farmer who is ploughing:

> The plough, which has finally through hard experience come to the conclusion that it is not an Ego, tends to consider the concept of the It as an illusion produced by the It. At least it cannot decide to do without the assumption that every cell has its own consciousness and thus possesses independent discharge. The Ego, in its opinion, is apparently not even able to control the motility of voluntary muscles, much less that of the intestines, kidneys, heart, or brain. In doing this it does not deny the Ego or the Super-Ego. Yet they are merely tools for it, not existing entities. I have the impression that the farmer remains in the region of the so-called psyche, at least for the time being, and can perhaps ruin a number of ploughs without producing a big harvest. In other words, the plough considers the farmer a little obstinate. But then it only has the brains of a plough.

Before writing this letter to Freud, Groddeck apparently allowed some time to pass, as he had written to his wife on May 15, 1923:

> *The Ego and the Id* is pretty, but quite uninteresting for me. In reality it was written to appropriate secretly loans made by Stekel and me. And yet his Id is of only limited use for the understanding of neuroses. He ventures into the realm of organic illness only in a very sneaky way, with the help of a death instinct or destruction drive taken from Stekel and Spielrein. He disregards the constructive aspect of my It, presumably to smuggle it in next time. Some of it is quite amusing.

In a later work, 'The It and Psychoanalysis', 1925, Groddeck writes, among general ideas about the conference mania of his (and our) time:

> The beginning of man who is the object of my scientific inquiries, is fertilisation. Whatever originates there I call the It of man. This term aims to describe the uncertain, uncertifiable nature of this entity, the miracle. . . . To study and

13

understand this It that builds up our personality according to a completely planned blueprint, that gives it consciousness, the illusion of thought and reason, and an ego-awareness, imprints the notion of guilt and punishment into it, builds cathedrals as well as houses on sand and castles in the air, teaches us to love and to invent murder weapons, is one of the oldest pre-occupations of man. One could say he never did anything else. All our efforts and all our strivings are directed towards this It. And in order to study it scientifically, methodically, we have to observe its manifestations and learn the language it speaks. . . . When one reads Freud attentively, without preconceived notions and without bothering about repressions, one soon discovers that his concept of the psyche is the same as mine, namely of a manifestation of life, and emphatically not the system 'conscious' which so far it has been held to be, but the system 'unconscious' and, absolutely dominating both, the It. Freud knows that this psyche is not the opposite of physics, not at all, but only another form of life. In order to know this it does not need his verbal assurance, it can be read between all the lines of all his works published so far. For him there is just as little division between body and soul as there is for me and every human being. But for the purposes of his profession as a specialist of mental illness he named these things in different ways, more appropriate to his purposes, and confined himself apparently to the fields of neurosis and psychosis. But he really believes in the It as does and did and will do everybody, in the past, the present, and the future.[15]

Freud, for his part, writes on June 18, 1925:

Everything from you is interesting to me, even if I may not follow you in detail. I do not, of course, recognise my civilised, bourgeois, demystified Id in your It. Yet you know that mine derived from yours.

In 'Traumarbeit und Arbeit des organischen Symptoms' (The effects of dreams and of the organic symptom), 1926, Groddeck writes:

Freud honoured me by drawing attention to me in his book *The Ego and the Id* as the person who was the first to use the expression 'the It' and said that he had taken it over from me. This is true, except that the term 'It' as used for my purposes was unusable to him and he turned it into something different from what I meant. As far as I can see he chose the expression in order to illustrate his ideas about his conception of what he calls topic. Yet he has not changed the nature of psychoanalysis with it, neither adding nor subtracting anything. It remained what it was, the analysis of the conscious and of the repressed parts of the psyche. But the It cannot be analysed whether it is Freud's Id or mine which share a common name, any more than can Ferenczi's Bios.[16]

In order to point up the difference between Freud's and Groddeck's conceptions, English translations of Groddeck's 'Es' use the word It in contrast to Id for Freud's 'Es'.

A later discussion of the It in which Groddeck – pointing out other important themes – stresses the bisexuality of man, his use of symbol and of language as particular manifestations of the It, is found in his last book, *Der Mensch als Symbol* (Man as Symbol).

In the ten years since I last put forward some hypothetical thoughts on the human It nothing has happened that would induce me to give up this often tested approach or to make decisive changes in my ideas about it. I maintain the position that everything human is dependent on this infinitely mysterious entity and I also persist in maintaining that nobody can fathom the depths of the It. And yet I can say a few things about those manifestations of the It which have not received much attention so far. I also consider it necessary to emphasise that the Ego is one of these manifestations. In the *Book of the It* I explained to the best of my ability what I mean by this.

Another form of the It which is more accessible to me I want to call the dual nature of the It. All human life can be seen as simultaneously male and female, child and grown-up.

The It, moreover, manifests itself as independent and as mutually dependent in the life as a whole as in the parts of a living human being's existence, or, in other words, there is apparently a similar relation between the whole human being and the cell or even smaller entities, the tissue, the individual organ or part of the body as was expressed by the terms macrocosmos and microcosmos in former times to describe the universe and its parts. And finally the symbol as manifestation of the It permeates all human life.

My attempt at examining all these manifold forms of the It was prompted by a rather singleminded and idiosyncratic pre-occupation with works of art and language, apart from the pressures of everyday life and work.

The term 'unconscious' is not synonymous with 'It'. Unconscious material was originally conscious at some time, the unconscious presupposes the existence of the brain. Yet the It exists before the formation of the brain, the brain is an instrument of the It by which it opens up certain rather limited areas of existence to our thought for unknown reasons while taking care that the brain deludes us into believing all sorts of strange notions which are peculiar to man, such as the belief in an I. I repeat: It and unconscious are two totally different concepts – the unconscious is a part of the psyche, the psyche a part of the It. Thus psychoanalysis is not identical with an examination of the It. The It is man himself in all his vital minifestations and as such it is neither freely accessible to psychoanalysis nor to any other method of examination, yet there are ways which lead us very close to the It and the best of these, the closest approach to the target, is psychoanalysis.[17]

Groddeck discusses human bisexuality in many of his writings. He discovered that, although bisexuality plays an important part in analytical theory,

yet it is not seen as one of the fundamental phenomena, as the focal point of all human existence and thought. Bisexuality has been talked about for quite some time, to be sure, and the woman's desire to have male sexual organs and to behave like a male sexually and in other ways, and the man's desire to be a woman, to conceive, be pregnant, give birth are important issues in the theory and practice of interpretation of the unconscious. Yet the assumption remains that a man is a man and a woman a woman. The curious thought that in reality

16

man is without female attributes and woman without male, that it is possible to be all man or all woman, creeps into this line of thought and the impression is that the whole thing is rather indecent and could or should be overcome. The possibility that man is female-male and male-female is repressed.[18]

Groddeck's conception of the symbol can only be understood in the context of his interpretation of the It as he himself kept emphasising:

And finally the symbol as manifestation of the It permeates all human life.[19]

Groddeck considers man's compulsion to symbolise to be an expression of the It and not of conscious thought. Conversely, all conscious thought and action is an inevitable consequence of unconscious symbolising. Groddeck's dictum that man is lived by the It is parallelled by the other dictum that man is lived by the symbol, from his very beginnings. While the grown-up has difficulties in gaining insight into the interaction between the symbol and the It, the child has this insight spontaneously.

We are compelled by the repressive forces of human life and of our man-dominated environment (education etc.) to fantasize about the real. Originally we are not dealing with the world of objects, but with symbols. So far little interest has been shown in the methods by which the new-born child learns about his environment and in his reaction to it. If I try to imagine what I might have experienced in the womb, I come to the conclusion that I must have considered everything that belonged to my world as a part of my own self; the self and the environment of the self were one and the same thing. This symbolic way of thinking may be changed somewhat by the event of birth, but judging by the behaviour of babies in their first months of life I have to assume that the infant still thinks largely in symbols during the main learning period of his life, the first hours, days and weeks: a spoon is not a spoon to the child but a hand, a door not a door but a mouth, a bed not a bed but a womb, etc. Our conscious and unconscious thinking never rids itself completely of these early notions – which are retained almost unchanged by primitive cultures. Until the end of our lives our understanding is tied to the symbol. No matter how rational we are we cannot help it: a window will remain an eye, a cave a mother, a pole a father.

We also see man and his parts in symbolic ways as we did when we were children. Once we knew from experience that the head is a whole and a part at the same time, an independent and a dependent entity, that man is a symbol for the head and that the head is a symbol for man. The symbol does not describe the similarities between two objects; in the symbol two objects are thrown together, they become one. Because we think and feel symbolically, are, in short, tied to the symbol as to something belonging to human life, it is possible to look at everything in human existence symbolically.[20]

With this conception of the symbol as part of the whole and as a key to 'the mysteries of human life'[21] Groddeck takes up thoughts he had already in 1912 about an idea of Goethe's:

He (Goethe) showed science a new way, the way to see the part in the whole, to conceive of the apparent whole as a symbol of the universe, to see symbolically the whole world in a flower, an animal, a pebble, the human eye, the sun, to recreate from this flower, to renew, to explore the world of objects not analytically, but by taking it in as a whole.[22]

It was not without good reasons that Groddeck entitled his last, unfinished book, *Man as Symbol*. He had announced it in a letter to Freud on February 7, 1932:

It is a book in which the idiosyncrasies of language and fine art are used to prove how close the connections between symbol and life have always been. Medicine, particularly in the first part, will only be loosely linked to it, yet at the same time I want to discuss the influence of the symbol on the whole of the organism and its individual parts – either in a volume on its own or in individual pamphlets.

One of Groddeck's favourite themes was *seeing*. The 1917

18

essay 'Psychic Conditioning and the Psychoanalytic Treatment of Organic Disorders' (pp. 109–31 below) already contained a discussion of the psychodynamics of seeing and explored the causes of near-sightedness and long-sightedness. He chose the same theme for his first talk to the Psychoanalytic Society during the congress at The Hague (see his letter to Freud, September 11, 1920). The last lectures he gave before his death in Germany, England, and Switzerland were on the subject of seeing that interested Groddeck all his life. The manuscript of these, written down in 1932, had the title 'Vision, the World of the Eye, and Seeing without the Eye'. As early as 1917 he wrote:

> The ancients thought of the poet as blind; and it makes sense that his eyes have to look inwards.[23]

Groddeck's ideas about seeing centre in man's ability to combine the rational exploration and understanding of the world with an almost mystical experience of inner vision. He himself combined in his personality an inclination for accurate clinical observations of surprising vividness with a constant search for inner truths – he is scientist and philosopher in one, as Lawrence Durrell, in a brilliant essay written in 1948,[24] presented him. Groddeck talks about two essential ways of seeing:

> The outside-inwards way of seeing is the one which is normally called vision. The inside-outwards way of seeing is the dreamer's, the visionary's way. This phenomenon is also present in normal vision, and seeing is thus a mixture of external and internal images.[25]

GRODDECK, THE DOCTOR

Groddeck thought of himself first and foremost as a doctor who strives to cure his patients. In 1917 he announced firmly that he was not interested in constructing a theory but in doing therapeutic work:

> Our task is less that of thinking up valid theories than of finding working hypotheses that are of use in treatment.[26]

In a letter to Freud, dated April 1923, he rejects any claim to having disciples and maintains that his talent is essentially 'one for treating patients'. Later, in his memoirs, he calls it his 'need to be a doctor'.[27]

But who does the curing? Groddeck is deeply convinced that it is not the doctor but the It. For Groddeck the doctor is less of a therapist and more of a servant. The word treatment may lead the doctor to assume that he can determine and guide the process of healing. But in reality it is the It that decides on that:

> As the It uses something from the environment as a cause for an illness, so it takes something from the environment to cause recovery when it wants to manifest itself in a state of health. It treats itself. . . . There is thus no right or wrong treatment. This and this alone explains the reason why most illnesses cure themselves without a doctor, why many people recover more readily when treated by an old shepherd or clairvoyant or magnetopath than by a university professor.[28]

I shall quote from another essay in which Groddeck discusses his ideas of therapy:

> (1) I consider the psychoanalytic method not as *the* method but would like to say that every method is right and that I myself use any method that works no matter what name or technique it may follow.
>
> (2) I almost never depend solely on the psychotherapeutic method in its widest sense in my treatment though I always use it. I know that this reduces the value of my experiences for others and that I would feel in the dark, too, if I didn't find a balance in the wealth of my experience. In the long run I believe that the It is the point to tackle in treating both mental and physical illness, and that this It can use a laparotomy or a dose of digitalis in a psychological way and suggestive or analytic approaches in a physical way.
>
> (3) . . . my 20 years of psychoanalytic activity have taught me to believe that efforts at making repressed material conscious may often have a therapeutic effect, yet as often such results do not occur and conversely there are many cures without any attempt at treating unconscious or repressed material. It is a question of convenience whether a specific case is tackled by analytical or by other methods.[29]

Massage, the exploratory touching of the body, was always

an essential aid to easing the symptoms of illness for Groddeck. Hermann Graf Keyserling[30] describes in the chapter on Germany of 'Spectrum of Europe' his impressions of Groddeck as a physician and as a human being:

The greatest magician among the psychoanalysts and without doubt the most important human personality of them all was Georg Groddeck. I met him in Sweden in 1924 and was immediately fascinated by his veritably diabolical face that looked at me as if from a fiery furnace of hell and yet was so full of deep goodness. My heart went out to him in an almost maternal way, for I felt the enormous vulnerability of this soul which protected itself by spikiness and play-acting. As long as he lived he came to Darmstadt regularly and never in my life have I had better praise than from Groddeck in a letter shortly before his death: 'You are the only person who never hurt me. I am grateful to you for this.' We got to know each other because of Groddeck's promise to cure me within a week of a recurrent phlebitis with boils which other doctors had believed not curable. I travelled to Baden Baden to Groddeck's clinic and lo and behold the wounds healed, the swellings on the leg disappeared, and at the time of writing I have not had a relapse. Groddeck's treatment resembled his appearance, it was a kind of carefully directed hellish pain. My leg literally boiled, and his special kind of massage during which he conducted an analysis based on my expressions of pain was a technically controlled form of torture. Yet in the case of patients who found him congenial Groddeck achieved miracles. As an analyst Groddeck was the most incredible catalyst such as I have never considered possible. He said hardly anything. Yet all that needed to be liberated in me came spontaneously to my mind in his presence. I owe to this meeting with Groddeck the first insights into the deeper significance of my mother experience. It is difficult to describe in detail what it was that made Groddeck's Wei Wu so magical. On the whole it probably was his own completely relaxed naturalness. With all this he was, of course, like all analysts I know, an unresolved analytical case, yet otherwise he possessed a genuinely Lao Tse-like elusiveness. Because of this he couldn't help being a liberating agent for other

21

people; in his presence I found one image after the other pouring into my consciousness – and yet Groddeck had hardly asked a question.

Groddeck sums up his attitude when he says:

> My task is not to teach, it is not to help, to give or take responsibility, the doctor's profession is only concerned with the moment, the doctor has to be, not to act. The more his being is stressed the more the doctor *is* instead of *does*, the easier it will be for the patient to use him. For us it is not a matter of 'we ought to' but of 'we are'.[31]

One is reminded of the essay 'Language' (pp. 248–63 below) when Groddeck mentions to Freud, on October 17, 1920, the ancient wisdom 'that words put chains on thought', and already in 1912 he discussed the possibilities and the limitations of language critically. He had called language the 'vehicle of culture', and yet he had also pointed out how impossible people find it to give words to their essential experiences, and had further argued that in language the falsification of truth begins. This essay from Groddeck's pre-analytical period is of special interest because it contains or hints at themes which Groddeck took up again in his later writings. Here we find the beginnings of his idea of the It and his closeness to Goethe's thoughts. Groddeck here talks about his great reverence for the poet which is important for his later literary work. The inclusion of this essay at the end of this selection may help us trace Groddeck's thought back to its origins.

WRITINGS WHICH COULD NOT BE INCLUDED

... People are so stupid that they expect one still to remember at the end of a lecture what one said in the beginning. They do not want to know that the human mind is mobile and yet this mobility is the only thing of interest. I enjoy jumping from subject to subject since I have become too stiff to jump over physical obstacles. ...[32]

As I said in the beginning, Groddeck had the ability to introduce and deal associatively with several subjects in the framework of one essay. Only a full reading of his work will thus do justice to the wealth of ideas scattered through its pages. In this selection some very important articles had to be left out, for instance the essays in his house journal, *Die Arche*, written for the patients of his clinic, in which he tries to elucidate organic symptoms, organic processes by applying psychoanalytic techniques. These clinical papers are concerned with the following organic illnesses in particular: headaches, arteriosclerosis, the formation of kidney stones, and constipation.

Furthermore, Groddeck's highly original writings on literature and the fine arts unfortunately had to be left out of this selection. They consist of a first series of literary lectures on Ibsen's plays which Groddeck gave around 1910 in Baden Baden and in which he concerns himself particularly with the interpretation of female characters (see Freud's letter of October 28, 1917 and Groddeck's answer in November). In his later works on artistic themes Groddeck tries to prove that the It manifests itself not only in sickness and health, but in language and gesture too:

Every year the belief – or rather superstition – that psychoanalysis is an affair for doctors, that it is a kind of psychiatric treatment which should be used for the patients' best, is growing in strength. I consider it a necessary duty to fight against this erroneous belief by lecturing and writing, for if this opinion becomes prevalent – and unfortunately there are many people who defend this position – the world would be deprived of the most precious thing Freud gave it. The study of the unconscious – which is a possible translation of the term psychoanalysis – is an affair of all mankind and its use in medicine is only a small fraction of all that this study consists of. In order to make this clear I chose the four pieces of literature mentioned in the announcement – the *Ring of the Nibelungs, Peer Gynt, Faust,* and *Struwwelpeter* – as material for my talks, and in order not to make people think that I was dabbling in aesthetics I called these pieces textbooks. Yet this does not mean that I intend to give a course in psychoanalysis, with the help of these textbooks. Psychoanalysis cannot be taught, for the simple reason that it is innate in all of us, that it is a human ability like seeing or hearing. I rather feel like a bookseller who is asked for his advice about what books to read in order to be informed on this or that subject, a question which is indeed often put to me, because of the interest in psychoanalysis. And I must say that none of the current textbooks will inform you as easily, simply and thoroughly about the nature of psychoanalysis as will these four works of literature.[33]

The *Ring of the Nibelungs* turns into a textbook on the Oedipus complex. On *Faust* he writes, in a summary, that it is a confession and understanding of the fact that human beings are lonely and each a world to himself. The famous German children's book *Struwwelpeter* he considers a complete collection of all symbols, and a sensitive presentation of the childish mind as a description of the dual world in which the child is living, as an evocation of the irrational world which grown-ups find almost inaccessible.

In his essay on *Peer Gynt* he discusses the concept of the self. This essay is perhaps the most personal work of Groddeck's. He identified so deeply with the Peer Gynt character who turns into a 'troll' that, as the author of *The Book of the It*, he signed the letters to his lady-friend Patrick Troll.

The essay attempts a confrontation of I and Self. In the course of this it arrives at a definition of the Self which is based on the conception of the It. Groddeck had insisted in many previous articles on man's duty to confront his self. In 1926 he wrote:

Our time uses the words selfish and egocentric as if it were the biggest character weakness to possess one of these qualities or to cultivate them. I have no right and no inclination to go into the moral and ethical implications of selfishness, but as a physician I have to say that I find it horrifying how little people care for themselves, even the so-called selfish and egocentric persons, and they least of all since their lives are usually a permanent escape from themselves; it may be right to assume that they serve their ego or what they consider their ego, yet this ego-serving is in reality the result of a great fear of their selves, a turning away from the self, from their deepest emotions. For the doctor's work it would be desirable if people showed more interest in themselves, in the manifestations of the It, for the mute and yet so insistent entreaties of their innermost soul which strives desperately to get a hearing and clamours for attention in a thousand ways, in actions, dreams, and the symptoms of illness, and I would think that these phenomena which the doctor can see so clearly, deserve to be examined by the moralists, too, for a change.[34]

A year later Groddeck argues that the child is much nearer to self-knowledge and points to the developing ego-consciousness as an obstacle to self-knowledge:

Know thyself! Formally speaking this is an advice, an admonition to strive for self-knowledge, but in reality it is merely a confirmation of the fact that a person who knows something about himself is a special tool in the hand of the universe, of God Nature, that he has special gifts and potential for action similar to those which all human beings possess at a certain age, i.e. during childhood. Children are the best teachers and if you do not become like children you will not enter the kingdom of heaven. Self-knowledge is not knowledge of the Ego, but knowledge of our Self, our It. For me, there is no doubt that as long as the human Ego-consciousness is still weak man knows more about his Self, his It, than from the moment onwards when he uses the ominous word 'I'. This word is like a pair of spectacles, an indispensable unavoidable pair of spectacles which forces us to see everything, particularly our Self, in distortion or embellished and which was given to us by God Nature in order not to be like God.[35]

Since Groddeck developed his ideas on Man's attitude towards his self in the Peer Gynt essay at particular length, I would like to quote from it some more:

Peer Gynt can regard his 'self' as an object, he can 'vaere dig selv'; he can also 'vaere sig selvnok'. If we try to translate the 'vaerl dig selv' we must not say: 'Man, be thyself!' but 'Man, be a thou, a thou to thyself, or, by all means, be a self to yourself. Stop being an "I".' Try to confront yourself the way a child does. Make yourself a part of the great whole, the universe. Deal with yourself on the basis of the knowledge that you are not an 'I', but a 'thou'. If the oft-repeated words 'dig self' are taken in this sense, all the difficulties of interpretation fall away, since Ibsen allows Peer Gynt to speak of his self or thou (though this is not the same thing) instead of his 'I'. It is, of course, not possible to make this clear in a stage representation, it would become too clumsy, yet one can learn to understand it at home and then the performance will not lead one astray. Yet as it is at the moment the play does not make sense.

It should be obvious to everyone that the self is not identical with the ego, for the ego is something entirely personal and in essence illusory, something existing only in our own imagination. It comprehends only a very small part of a man. The self on the other hand is the whole man. We all know it, yet none of us lives in accordance with our knowledge, for we are all under the spell of the ego idea. . . .

We all fancy we must have a core at the centre, something that is not merely shell; we would like to hold within us some specially aromatic kernel, to be a nut which holds the eternal, the sacred. And we do not realise, cannot realise, that we have in fact no kernel, but are ourselves, from the outermost peel to the innermost minutest leaf, that the peel self is our own self, that we are onions. But in the onion every leaf is its essential nature. The onion is genuine right through, and it would be bad, rotten, if it tried to grow a kernel different from the rest, and to destroy the peel as though it were something false, something apart from its onion nature. Peer understands this at first only intellectually. His heart wants to despair, his heart is keen on being a whole man, a man with a kernel.[36]

GRODDECK AND PRESENT-DAY PSYCHOANALYTIC RESEARCH

Groddeck was seminal in many ways. There are, first, his ideas about the nature of organic illness and about health, about therapy and the importance of resistance in this, and his ideas about psychoanalysis as an important instrument in research. Yet there are many other themes which Groddeck discussed that are topical again, for instance the importance Groddeck assigned to the good relationship between mother and child. In this context it may be interesting that Groddeck insisted on man's need to play. In a letter to the woman who later became his wife he wrote:

> It is quite unimportant what we play with as long as we play, and people who cannot play, who long for unobtainable playthings instead of making a living doll from a handkerchief, are rather stupid. Those who like their own stupidity may keep it, in God's name. Everybody should have his own pleasure. (6.4.1916)[37]

The possible role of psychoanalysis in obstetrics Groddeck mentioned to Freud in his letter on November 8, 1923:

> There is still a lot to be learnt about the mother's and the baby's psyche as well as about the practice of obstetrics.

It entirely depends on the reader how Groddeck's ideas will strike and possibly affect him. Some may be irritated if not repelled by many of his more abstruse thoughts and by the way he jumps from idea to idea. This reaction would be nothing new; it recalls the indignation and criticism which Groddeck aroused on his first appearance at the International Psychoanalytical Congress in The Hague, in 1920.

Groddeck's importance to psychoanalysis is manifold. Through his encounter with Freud he has become a part of the history of psychoanalysis. What is particularly remarkable is that Freud continued to encourage and support this very ingenious and original thinker and therapist in spite of the personal difficulties the correspondence testifies to. Clearly Freud's genius was able to understand and tolerate the very different genius of Groddeck.

It is important to keep in mind what Groddeck's real intention was:

> It is more advisable to initiate than to exhaust a theme. This, at least, is the way my talent works.[38]

The writings collected in this anthology are chosen from the four volumes of Groddeck's writings published by Limes Verlag: *Psychoanalytische Schriften zur Literatur und Kunst* (1964), *Psychoanalytische Schriften zur Psychosomatik* (1966), *Der Mensch und sein Es* (1970), and *Der Mensch als Symbol* (1973).

Der Mensch und sein Es contains, apart from the correspondence between Groddeck and Freud, further letters by Groddeck, twenty articles from the 1920's, mostly published in *Die Arche*, a magazine for the patients in his clinic, and finally some biographical writings and essays. The volume *Psychoanalytische Schriften zur Psychosomatik* contains essays which had been published before, in psychoanalytical or psychotherapeutic journals or in *Die Arche*. There are also a number of unpublished works, whose titles were chosen by the editor of the German edition. The volume *Psychoanalytische Schriften zur Literatur und Kunst* contains writings from Groddeck's pre-analytic period, from his analytic period, and finally extracts from Groddeck's last book, *Der Mensch als Symbol*, which was published in full in 1973.

The editor thanks Vision Press for permission to reprint V.M.E. Collins' translation of 'Clinical Communications' and 'Massage and Psychotherapy' from *The Unknown Self* and *Exploring the Unconscious* respectively. Special thanks to the editors of the German editions, in particular for being able to use the footnotes and comments to the correspondence between Groddeck and Freud.

With the exception of the letters from Freud to Groddeck dated 5.6.1917, 8.2.1920, 25.3.1923 and 21.12.1924 which were published in English in *Letters of Sigmund Freud*, 1873–1939, edited by Ernst L. Freud (London, The Hogarth Press, 1961; New York, Basic Books) the correspondence between Groddeck and Freud is published in English for the first time in this volume.

A number of biographical details were taken from Carl M. Grossman *The Wild Analyst* (New York, George Braziller, 1965; London, Barrie and Rockliff).

LORE SCHACHT

NOTES

1. Letter to Professor Hans Vaihinger, May 8, 1930, in *Der Mensch und sein Es*, pp. 125–6.
2. 'Erinnerung an den Vater' (Memories of my father), *Der Mensch und sein Es*, pp. 400–02.

3. *Der Mensch und sein Es*, pp. 421–2.

4. 'Das Es und die Psychoanalyse nebst allgemeinen Ausführungen zum damaligen wie heutigen Kongresswesen' (The It and Psychoanalysis with general remarks about congress mania then and now), *Psychoanalytische Schriften zur Psychosomatik*, pp. 161–2.

5. *Psycho-Analysis and Faith: The Letters of Sigmund Freud and Oskar Pfister*. Translated by Eric Mosbacher (London, The Hogarth Press). p. 80.

6. *Ibid*, pp. 81–2.

7. See Groddeck's letter to Freud, December 4, 1921.

8. *Internationale Zeitschrift für Psychoanalyse*, 1926.

9. See pp. 172–196 below.

10. 'Lebenserinnerungen' (Memoirs), *Der Mensch und sein Es*, p. 271.

11. 'Vom Unsinn der Psychogenese' (The Nonsense of Psychogenesis), *Psychoanalytische Schriften zur Psychosomatik*, p. 164.

12. *Psychoanalytische Schriften zur Literatur und Kunst*, p. 28.

13. Was Kann der Mensch im Leben mehr gewinnen,
Als dass sich Gottnatur ihm offenbare:
Wie sie das Feste lässt zu Geiste verrinnen,
Wie sie das Geistgezeugte fest bewahre.
Johann Wolfgang von Goethe.

14. *Der Mensch und sein Es*, p. 120.

15. *Psychoanalytische Schriften zur Psychosomatik*, pp. 154–9.

16. *Psychoanalytische Schriften zur Psychosomatik*, p. 209.

17. *Der Mensch als Symbol*, pp. 5–6.

18. 'Das Zwiegeschlecht des Menschen' (Human bisexuality), *Psychoanalytische Schriften zur Psychosomatik*, pp. 256–7.

19. *Der Mensch als Symbol*, p. 6.

20. *Der Mensch als Symbol*, p. 7.

21. 'Vision, the World of the Eye, and Seeing without the Eye', p. 175.

22. 'Language', p. 252 below.

23. 'Psychic Conditioning and the Psychoanalytic Treatment of Organic Disorders', p. 115 below.

24. *Horizon* magazine (London), vol. XVII, No. 102, edited by Cyril Connolly, June 1948.

25. 'Vision, the World of the Eye, and Seeing without the Eye', p. 174 below.

26. 'Psychic Conditioning and the Psychoanalytic Treatment of Organic Disorders', p. 128 below.

27. *Der Mensch und sein Es*, p. 267.

28. 'Das Es und die Psychoanalyse . . .', *Psychoanalytische Schriften zur Psychosomatik*, p. 218.

29. 'Über die psychische Behandlung der Nierensteinbildung' (Psychiatric Treatment of Kidney Stone Formation), *Psychoanalytische Schriften zur Psychosomatik*, p. 218.

30. See Groddeck's letter 18.12.1924, Freud's letter 21.12.24, Groddeck's letter 13.6.1925 and Freud's letter 18.6.1925.

31. 'Erziehung' (Education) *Der Mensch und sein Es*, p. 154.

32. Letter to Frau von Voigt, his later wife, 10.4.1916.
33. 'Der Ring' (The Ring), *Psychoanalytische Schriften zur Literatur und Kunst* p. 135.
34. 'Verstopfung als Typus des Widerstands' (Constipation as a type of resistance), *Psychoanalytische Schriften zur Psychosomatik*, p. 185.
35. Erziehung (Education), *Der Mensch und sein Es*, p. 252.
36. 'Peer Gynt', *Psychoanalytische Schriften zur Literatur und Kunst*, pp. 182–8.
37. *Der Mensch und sein Es*, p. 101.
38. *Psychoanalytische Schriften zur Psychosomatik*, p. 388.

I

Correspondence with Sigmund Freud[1]

Baden Baden, May 27, 1917

Dear Professor,

Please allow me to begin by expressing my warmest thanks for all that I have learnt from studying your works. The need to express this gratitude turns into a duty because I published a book in 1912[2] in which I expressed a rash judgment on psychoanalysis; on closer inspection it can be seen that my knowledge of psychoanalysis was then based only on hearsay. It would not be necessary to assert that this unforgivable mistake was due to my own ignorance – that would not make it any the less – were it not for one interesting event in the history of my conversion.

In 1909, three years before the publication of that book, I started treating a lady patient, and the observations I made with her forced me to pursue the same ideas which I later learnt to be those on which psychoanalysis is based. I can assure you with all truthfulness that this patient had never even heard the word psychoanalysis, and I believe I could claim almost the same for myself. Through her I first learnt of the peculiarities of infantile sexuality and of symbolic action and soon, in a few weeks in fact, I was confronted with the concepts of transference and resistance – I have only recently learned the terms transference and resistance – both of which became almost automatically the main aspects of my treatment. The pleasure of discovery kept me in a trance that lasted for several years. Testing my findings against other case material and the events of daily life proved an exciting experience.

The more I shed my initial reticence to communicate my views to other people, the more often I was confronted with the name Freud as that of the pioneer of similar ideas. As I had entertained all my life, against much evidence to the contrary, the wishful thought that I was a creative thinker, I resisted the

31

knowledge of having, in a mysterious way, acquired and digested somebody else's ideas. My attack in 1912 was thus launched from a position of prophetic envy, so to speak. In 1913 I saw your *Psychopathology of Everyday Life*[3] in the window of a bookshop. I bought it together with *The Interpretation of Dreams*[4]. The effect of these books was so disturbing that I did not finish them, though I was aware of the fact that I deprived myself of an extraordinary enrichment of knowledge and life.

In the course of the following years, because of time-consuming psychiatric treatments, my practical work piled up to such an extent that I had to find a new way out of the dilemma. I had the idea of giving talks to my patients in the sanatorium in order not to waste time on telling every individual patient about the general basis of my ideas. This really worked out well. Moreover, people were so impressed that I decided to write down and to publish the freely delivered lectures. This plan was made in October 1916. Suspecting dimly that something was wrong with my apparent invention, I took up your books again and was led from them to a thorough study of all the psychoanalytic literature that had not been silenced by the war. One of the consequences of my belated honesty is this letter, which is probably primarily an attempt at self-justification.

Yet the wish to publish the results of many years of work in some form or other is still there. There is, however, one difficulty which I have not yet solved. After reading your papers on the history of psychoanalysis I began to doubt whether, according to your definition, I could count myself a psychoanalyst. I do not want to call myself the member of a movement if I am in danger of being rejected by the leaders of the movement as an intruder who does not belong to it, and this is why I want to ask you to give me a few more moments of your time and read this letter.

I arrived at my, or should I say your, views not by studying neuroses but by observing complaints which are commonly called organic. I owe my reputation as a doctor originally to my activities as a physiotherapist, more specifically as a masseur. For this reason my circle of patients is probably different from that of a psychoanalyst. Long before I met the above-mentioned patient in 1909 I had become convinced that the distinction between body and mind is only verbal and not essential, that body and mind are one unit, that they contain an It, a force which lives us while we believe we are living. Naturally I cannot claim this idea for myself, either, yet it was and is the basis of my activity. In other words, from the first I rejected a separation of bodily and mental illnesses, tried to treat the individual patient, the It in him, and attempted to find a way into the unexplored and inaccessible regions. I am aware of the fact that I am at least close to the mystical approach, if not actually engaged in it. And yet simple facts force me to continue on this way.

So far psychoanalysis, if I understand it rightly, uses the concept of neurosis. But I suspect that for you, too, this word represents the whole of human life. It certainly does so for me. The It, which is mysteriously connected with sexuality, with *eros* or whatever you chose to call it, shapes man's nose and hand as well as his thoughts and emotions; it expresses itself as much in pneumonia as in cancer or in a compulsion neurosis or in hysteria; and heart failure or cancer caused by It activity are as much the object of psychoanalytic treatment as are hysteria or neurosis. There are no basic differences that force us to attempt psychoanalysis here and not there. It is rather a practical question, a question of personal judgment that decides where psychoanalysis treatment should stop. I use the expression treatment because I do not believe that the doctor's function should extend beyond treatment; it is not he who brings about the cure, it is the It.

And this is the point where I doubt whether I have the right to call myself a psychoanalyst publicly. It is not possible, while advancing such ideas, to use a terminology that differs from the one you have developed. It cannot be replaced, and it suits my purpose, too, if the concept of the unconscious is enlarged. In the *Internationale Zeitschrift,* however, you expressly restrict the meaning of the unconscious. If one extends this meaning, as one must when considering the psychoanalytic treatment of so-called organic illnesses, one goes beyond the frontiers laid down by you for psychoanalysis. In this event I shall have to add a section to my projected book dealing with the confusions in my relation to psychoanalysis, and this will most probably not be understood. It would not be a question of expanding Adler's theories but rather of proving that organic complaints have the same origin as functional disorders.

I am afraid that I have not made myself completely clear when I talk about my It as shaping the individual, causing it to think, act, and fall ill. The matter may become clearer if I mention a few examples.

A woman patient wakes up in the morning with a badly swollen upper lip; the swelling is due to Herpes rash. In answer to my question when it started she gives the previous day as the date, and my visiting hour as the time. During that visit I jokingly told the patient, whom I have been treating for years for polyarthritis, that her lips were too thick and this meant that she had repressed a passionate desire to kiss. An hour after establishing this the swelling of the lip disappeared. This prompt reaction can certainly be called hysterical, too. But then one has to call all sorts of things hysterical, among others her polyarthritis that led to a double-sided patella luxation. Her case history would be too detailed to tell in this context in full, but it shows that her It created her polyarthritis in order to prevent her from running away. In the last few years I have followed carefully the various deteriorations and improvements of her joint complaint and have been able to effect some changes in the condition of her joints by stirring up and removing resistance against myself.

In the case of another lady, whose condition I have observed for years, I was able to bring out and remove a latent phlebitis by a similar kind of psychological experimentation. I have also gathered experience in the field of obesity and slimming and of child growth. Of interest, too, are changes in the size of the nose which can be influenced psychologically. The reaction of the mucous membranes to the influence of psychological repression in the form of colds, bronchial catarrh, diarrhoea etc. is well known; its psychoanalytic treatment produces astonishing results.

I would like to quote a few more examples. One of my patients suffers from retinal bleeding. Strangely enough, this always happens in autumn. It emerged that this highly intelligent yet totally uneducated patient – he taught himself to read and write at 18 – had every day in his childhood seen a blind man of whom the villagers said that he had lost his sight on account of a blasphemy. The patient had completely forgotten that at the age of nine he had thrown stones at a wooden statue of Christ placed at the exit of the village. How strong the effect of this forgotten event must have been can be gathered from the fact that the patient fainted after communicating this bit of information. There were, moreover, oedipal and castration complexes which hardly need to be enlarged upon. Since then there has been no bleeding for five years, except once very slightly on the day before he was drafted into the army, at a crossroads, opposite a crucifix. It became apparent, moreover, that the man had again completely forgotten his childhood experience and that even my reminding him of it could not revive his memory of it; it only came back a few days later.

In this connection I will make some observations on a blepharitis which was linked with masturbation complexes. The analytical treatment of a fairly sizable goiter was successful in so far as the left side of the goiter disappeared completely, the right side by about three quarters.

Finally I want to mention a patient whose It produced syphilis symptoms, very characteristic rashes, ulcers on the penis and neck, sore throat and a positive Wassermann test. Everything, including the Wassermann (the name was a contributory factor, by the way) disappeared in the course of the psychiatric treatment. The case is doubly interesting because during the treatment the It produced temporarily, for hours or days, temperatures of 40 degrees C. when certain names were mentioned or certain ideas revived. The patient suffered from sclerodermia, too, for which I had treated him 20 years ago. The revival of this process at a time when I was already aware of the It's activities made me think of treating the matter by analysis. The result was a cessation of the process and a complete healing of the newly affected areas. The analysis, moreover, uncovered the history of the origins and development of his sclerodermia in a way that I found convincing; it had started on the left leg and was connected with the attempt to squash a younger sibling in his mother's womb. The love for his own and other people's legs played a decisive part in this. Later, under the influence of repressing sadistic and pregnancy fantasies, the arms and the skin of the belly were affected too.

35

I hope I may assume that you, dear Professor, will understand from these hints that I intend in my book to put forward the idea that all human illness, like all human life, comes under the influence of an unconscious and that in this influence sexuality can always be traced, at the very least. I can well imagine that you might disavow anyone who held such a theory as somebody who does not fit into the psychoanalytic circle in your sense of the term were he to call himself a psychoanalyst. I do not want to expose myself to this. I would be very grateful to you, therefore, if you could let me know what you think of this. I shall adjust my position accordingly and, in the book, give a clear description of what excludes me from the official school of psychoanalysis.

I would have to do this publicly, if you told me that I am going beyond the limits of psychoanalytic practice. Yet personally, even though I came to psychoanalysis by a way other than through your writings, I shall always have to consider myself your disciple whose respect and gratitude I beg you not to reject.

Yours truly DR. GEORG GRODDECK

Vienna, 5.6.1917

Dear Colleague,

I have not had a letter for a long time which so pleased, interested, and stimulated me as to make me drop the politeness due to a stranger and adopt analytical frankness in my answer to it.

I shall therefore make the experiment: I understand that you are requesting me urgently to supply you with an official confirmation that you are not a psychoanalyst, that you do not belong to the members of the group, and will be able to call yourself something special, and independent. Obviously I am doing you a service if I push you away from me to the place where Adler[5], Jung[6] and others stand. Yet I cannot do this; I have to claim you, I have to assert that you are a splendid analyst who has understood for ever the essential aspects of the matter. The discovery that transference and resistance are the most important aspects of treatment turns a person irretrievably into a member of the wild army. No matter if he calls the unconscious 'It'. Let me show you that there is no need to extend the concept of the unconscious in order to make it cover your experience of organic illnesses. In my article on the unconscious which you mention there is an inconspicuous footnote: 'We are reserving for a different context the mention of another notable privilege of the *Ucs*.'[7] I shall tell you what was not mentioned here: the assumption that the unconscious act exerts an intensive, decisive influence on somatic processes such as conscious acts never do. My friend Ferenczi[8] who knows about this has a paper on pathoneurosis waiting to be printed in the *Internationale Zeitschrift* which is very close in its ideas to yours. The same point of view even caused him to undertake a biological experiment for me which is to demonstrate that a consistent application of Lamarck's[9] theories of evolution turns into a conclusion of psychoanalytic thought. Your new observations are so much in keeping with the arguments contained in this paper that we can only wish that at the time of our publication we will be able to refer to your ideas as already published.

Thus, while I would like to hold out both my hands to you to receive you as a colleague, there is only one disturbing circumstance, the fact that you have not managed to overcome the trivial ambition of claiming originality and priority. If you are so sure of the autonomy of your acquisitions why do you still need originality? Anyway, can you be sure in this respect? You must be 10 or 15 or perhaps 20 years younger than I am (1856). Could you have absorbed the main ideas of psychoanalysis in a cryptomnestic way? In a way similar to my discoveries relating to my own originality? What's the use of struggling for priorities against an older generation?

I regret this point of your information particularly since experience has shown that an untamed ambitious individual sooner or later jumps up and turns into an eccentric to the detriment of science and of his own career.

I liked the examples you gave me from your observations very much and hope that much of it will survive the test of strict investigation. The whole field is not at all strange to us, yet examples like that of your blind man have never before been given. And now the second objection! Why do you jump from your beautiful basis into mysticism, cancel the distinction between mental and somatic, commit yourself to philosophical theories which are not called for? Your experience does not take you any further than the realisation that the psychological factor is of an unimaginably great importance also in the origin of organic diseases? Yet does it cause these illnesses by itself, does this invalidate the distinction between mental and somatic in any way? It seems to me as wilful completely to spiritualise nature as radically to despiritualise it. Let's leave it its extraordinary variety which reaches from the inanimate to the organic and living, from the physical life to the spiritual. Certainly, the unconscious is the proper mediator between the somatic and the mental, perhaps the long-sought 'missing link'. Yet because we have seen this at last, should we no longer see anything else?

I am afraid you are also a philospher and of the monistic inclination which discards all the beautiful differences in nature in favour of the temptation offered by unity. Can we get rid of differences like that?

I would, of course, be very pleased if you answered me. In any case I am very interested to know how you will take my letter which may sound much more unkind than was the intention on which it is based.

Yours truly FREUD

June (?) 1917
. . . .

I would like to add a few words about the unconscious (the It). If I understand the matter correctly, researches in the psychoanalytic field have so far led people to derive from the unconscious important aspects of human life in religion, language, art, technology, daily life, in physiology, and pathology. Yet there is still, at least apparently, a contrast between the unconscious and consciousness, as if there were two forces at work. Even in psychoanalytic circles many phenomena of life are apparently still claimed as pure products of consciousness, as if the unconscious had nothing to do with them. I am of the opinion that consciousness is merely a form of expression used by the It; that everything which happens in human life (animal and plant life is as irrelevant to my purposes as inorganic life), that ultimately everything is created by the unconscious. Consciousness is merely a tool of the unconscious, serving essentially similar purposes of communication as language or gesture. It often seems to me also as if the unconscious wants us to preserve our feeling of omnipotence by way of consciousness, and is playing a very gay yet also very cruel game with us, i.e. with itself. It will never be possible to uncover the connection, but occasionally the observer succeeds in seeing something that looks like the face or the hand of the unconscious. The connections between choice of profession and the unconscious have been pointed out. Yet somebody's way of walking, posture, movements, and the shape of a hand often enough betray our conditioning by unconscious forces. Pavlov's experiments[10] produced some dark hints as far as digestion is concerned; we have known about it for quite some time with regard to breathing, heart beat, pulse, and the digestive juices, and the Abderhalden experiments[11] show us the direction in which medical chemistry somehow gets involved with the unconscious. I am surprised that the question of the conditioning of consciousness is avoided again and again, and that this avoidance is called exact science while it is really exact stupidity. Surely there is nothing to be lost by asking whether thinking takes place outside the context of everything else, whether we think, act and are formed out of our own, somehow extra-wordly omnipotence, or whether we belong to the circle of natural phenomena and are lived by the will of forces which we can see quite well in reflection. Psychoanalysis is not afraid of going back to prenatal times and it is right to do so. Yet why does it always and persistently cling on to the organ of the brain, and why does it not want to see that *ceteris paribus* semen and ovum always produce hands, eyes, brains? Surely there is no question of consciousness and conscious intention here. And if the unconscious manages this, then perhaps it will also be able to bring on a corn or guide a gesture of the hand or change the human chemistry in such a way that it becomes vulnerable to germs. Just now, an airship is passing over my house; does it merely look as if it were a giant *membrum*, is this only a symbolic association of thought, or was the unconscious perhaps at work and created something in its own image which consciousness claims for its own, in self-mockery? 'Like a beautiful silver bird', a woman's voice calls out. Isn't this a joke?

I do not consider myself a monist; when I am honest with myself I notice that I take pleasure in the colourful interaction of all forces without always realising. Yet when I perceive that the word science too is nothing but a game, I do not let myself be persuaded that it is all seriousness. And when I have grasped the fact that ovum and sperm make up the whole of human life including its sciences then I am no longer prepared to be pushed back into the well-defined boundaries of a stupidity which cannot see that life exists before the brain. Occasionally I am tempted to take somebody by the ear and show him an embryo. I also imagine that it is as important and as intoxicating to go in search of the unconscious as it is to count and recount the fibres of a muscle or to copy out of old books that there are tubercle bacilli. That the frontiers of science and mysticism get blurred for me in the process, as do the frontiers of body and mind (which, for the Greeks, in their heyday, did not exist, by the way), I do not consider a disaster, certainly not for me, because it interests me, and not for my patients, for I help them as far as I am able to, like other doctors, and as for what happens in the world at large I do not consider myself important enough. I shall probably not go off on a wild goose chase, because I am too much bound up with practical things; everything with me ultimately gets channelled into the treatment of patients. And with regard to this I work on the hypothesis that the It makes people ill, because it is pursuing some purpose which it finds useful. When a person has bad breath, his unconscious does not want to be kissed, and when he coughs, it wants something not to happen, and when he vomits, it wants to get rid of something harmful, and when there is a corn, I invariably find a painful spot underneath the corn which the unconscious wants to protect by horny skin. And when somebody gets gout in the legs it can be proved that he has a reason for walking carefully in order not to stumble over something; and when somebody loses his sight then he has merely taken a little too far a habit of the It, which is not to notice most things. For it is not true that we always see merely a fraction of what we could see; the It does not allow us to see, to see consciously what is in front of us. Yet it does not prevent the waves of what we do not see from affecting the retina and thus affecting us 'reflectorially'. Reflectorially, is anyone not laughing? You must have found as often as I have that the object we see, but do not perceive, is an obstacle to the well-being of our subconscious.

My letter has grown immensely long. Yet I must first thank you once more for yours. It told me what I hoped it would. And thank you even more for everything else, for what you are and what you are doing.

Yours most sincerely GRODDECK

Esorbato, 29.7.1917

Dear Colleague,

Your letter reached me and interested me very much. I sent it on to Ferenczi and had to wait rather a long time for its return, which is the reason for my answering it late.

I believe that you should consider yourself somebody who is close to us inspite of the fact that your position on the question of the distribution between the somatic and the mental is not quite ours, and you should help us in our work. Our journals are open to you. We would be pleased to have contributions from you, perhaps some preludes to your more substantial works.

In expectation of these and with best wishes for the continuation of your work

Yours sincerely FREUD

Baden Baden, 3.10.1917
Sanatorium Groddeck

Dear Professor,

My answer to your kind letter was delayed because I wanted to send you at the same time a pamphlet[12] which only reached me today. Essentially this is a repetition of what I have already told you in my letters. Yet it may interest you a little to see these fruits of your suggestions.

I thank you for the invitation to contribute to your journals occasionally. I shall certainly make use of this. Today merely some remarks to while away the time. First on the subject of male pregnancy. Recently I treated a gentleman who suffered from gout. One morning he complained of a new attack. It had started right at the beginning of a walk. He could not remember whether he went straight to the street or through the park first. Associations: Park – Parkin, the name of a hair growth product which his brother used; as a student he himself used a brown hair growth oil, his landlady was angry because the bedding had brown stains. Question, whether he ever dirtied his bed. He laughs and tells me: after his wife had given birth a second time, which lasted a whole night, he had dreamed the following night that he had to push something out of his body, he had pushed and pushed and when he woke up the child was lying between his legs, in the form of a stool. The gout attack passed quickly when the association bald head-empty purse (*kahler Kopf-kahler Beutel*) had been found and analysed.

In the latest issue of *Imago*[13] there is a paper by Levy[14] on the story of paradise. The interpretation of apple as breast is probably right; as important, perhaps more important, is the apple as symbol of the behind (Italian *mele*). In German apple is quite commonly used with this meaning. Even more striking is the peach (peach cheeks) particularly for the eye. The snake is closely related to the tree (*Baumstamm* = tree trunk, *Stammbaum* = pedigree). The iconographical representations of the Fall of Man offer a rich field. Herr Levy misses the most interesting bit of the curse, the interpretation of 'it shall bruise thy head, and thou shalt bruise his heel' (limpness *post coitum* and stork's tale). Ferenczi talks about hoarseness in the *Psychoanalytische Zeitschrift*. I have a lot of material on this subject and want to draw attention to the fact that people get hoarse – for ever, too – when they have got something that can only be told in whispers, a mysterious complex which, on one unconscious level, they want to communicate, while on another they struggle against it. Stopping in the middle of a sentence belongs to the same syndrome – or stopping in the middle of a word while writing. Very interesting are the voice changes from soft to loud during conversation. In childhood complexes the voice usually goes up for individual words only.

To qualify information by means of interjections such as

'isn't it?', 'I believe' (German: *ich meine, ich* (I) and *mein* (my)) is also popular.

If you could make use of a collection of small human traits like these I would have a try.

Yours truly G R O D D E C K

P.S. In case you think that Ferenczi or any of the other gentlemen would be interested in the pamphlet I would gladly send one to them. I do not know their addresses, however.

Vienna, Octover 7, 1917

Dear Colleague,

Many thanks for sending me your paper[15] which I found interesting and important in spite of the reservations you know. I shall find room for your paper in the *Internationale Zeitschrift*.

Yours most sincerely F R E U D

Vienna, October 7, 1917

Dear Colleague,

I gratefully accept your offer to send me more copies of your paper. My copy went to Ferenczi (Budapest Hotel Royal) who is going to report on it. I would like to have a second copy for myself, and a third one should circulate in the group in order to get people interested in your work.

The contributions which you promised will be accepted readily and printed as soon as the present difficulties are over. It would seem to me particularly to the point to have a short manifesto (in line with your latest work) which presented to the readership of the journal what is new and surprising about your experience, and which would introduce you yourself most effectively. You know that my interest in your lists of observations is great, and I am only uncertain about the appropriate length.

With sincere regards Yours F R E U D

Vienna, October 28, 1917

Dear Colleague,

I acknowledge receipt of the offprints of your paper which I shall circulate in the group. Ferenczi has already sent in his report on it.

Your interesting remark[16] on the analysis of *Rosmersholm*[17] has prompted me to reread the play and discuss it with my only assistant at the moment, Dr. Sachs[18]. We agree that we cannot give in to you. Everything seems to speak against the notion that Rebecca West's confession is fictitious. Sachs believes that this would cut off the play's vital nerve. I believe that the honest excitement of the passage where she explains how one is pushed further and further against one's will in such a way speaks against your assumption. To get Rosmer over the bridge is a symbol of an aim and not in itself an aim for which one might give one's life. It is merely meant to imply that he brushes aside his wife's suicide. His impotence can certainly be established, yet Ibsen did not bring it up again, did not make it the centre of his play.

Today I saw a lady of 44 who wanted psychiatric treatment, yet I had to diagnose multiple sclerosis (neuritis in the past, bladder trouble . . .). I have sent her away, yet I am now asking you whether you could take on a case like this in which there is strong evidence of a psychological influence.

With kind regards FREUD

Baden Baden, November 1917

Dear Professor,

Many thanks for your kindness. I am willing to have a try with the lady patient you mention. The costs are, all inclusive except for heating 25–35 Marks a day according to the size of the room. This includes treatment.

So you haven't changed your views about Rebecca West.[19] Now I am merely curious to know how you explain why Rebecca listens to the conversation between Rosmer and Kroll, and why she tells Kroll that he knows who wrote the anonymous letters. Ibsen was too careful in his works to let us assume that he had introduced both just for fun. I have found that with Ibsen's writings one always comes up against new problems, both aesthetic and psychoanalytic, with every new reading. In recent years I have gained the impression that he makes fun of mankind in the most astonishing way. Nora[20] in particular is a good example of that. This apparent suffragette lies to a degree which normally one only comes across in lecture rooms, and she sermonises her husband, whom she knows to be drunk, in private in a way which would only be justified if the circumstances were quite different. It is a malicious mocking of the public which, as we know, thoroughly fell for it too.

Similarly in *The Masterbuilder*,[21] *The Wild Duck*,[22] and, above all, *Rosmersholm*. The play's vital nerve is in my view not altered by my interpretation, the entire play merely appears in a new light and the pathos is changed into dramatic irony. As soon as he notices the disproportion in Ibsen between means and results one realises, I believe, that he does not write bourgeois plays but comedies. He probably knew this and was thoroughly familiar with the silent laughter of the ironist. It is an ironical tragedy that a splendid woman like Rebecca should perish because of the milieu of Rosmersholm and a 'noble human being'.

With warmest wishes,

Your ever loyal disciple GRODDECK

Baden Baden, 19.10.1919

Dear Professor,

By the same post I am sending you a manuscript[23] which I called a psychoanalytical novel in a fit of whimsy. The book made its obligatory round of the publishers and was in turn sent back to me with polite rejections and thanks. I have now given up hope of finding somebody who might publish it, yet I would like you to have a look at it before it disappears for good. Maybe Ferenczi, too, might be interested, and have a glance at it. I would be happy to reward him for his kind criticism of my pamphlet[24] with a few hours' happy reading.

In my provincial isolation I do not hear anything about the happenings in the outside world. My rumour-mongering bookseller maintains that *Imago* and the *Psychoanalytische Zeitschrift* have died. Is that true? I had got so used to this pleasure, yet for months now I have been unable to get a copy.

With all best wishes I remain

Yours gratefully GRODDECK

Baden Baden, 31.1.1920

Dear Professor,

May I ask you to return the manuscript of my novel? I have entered into negotiations with a publisher again, probably without result, yet I want to have another try. The book seems to produce displeasure everywhere, at least I interpret your silence as a sign of dislike.

While preparing my talks[25] for publication I came across some which deal with the subject of *Moses*, Book I[26], others on *Struwwelpeter*[27] and on a few Klinger pictures[28]. If you could use these for *Imago* I could send them to you. But perhaps you have material enough on hand.

With all best wishes I remain
Yours most sincerely G R O D D E C K

Vienna, 7.2.1920

My dear Colleague,

Your paper arrived, it is as inventive and original as everything you write. If you would like me to I could confirm everything essential in it from my own experience. We shall put it into the journal. I hope it is merely the precursor of other contributions.

As for your novel, may I make the suggestion that the choice of a less whimsical[29] title might help its publication?

Yours sincerely F R E U D

Vienna, 8.2.1920

Dear Colleague,

I shall have your novel returned in the next few days by our publishing house. But you are wrong: I liked it. In parts I was most amused. The characters of old English humourists are well-drawn. In one respect it seems to us to resemble that model of all humorous novels, *Don Quixote*. The hero turns in the author's hands into something more serious than was originally planned. I admired your talent for graphic description, which is unusual, particularly in the railway scenes.

Now I do believe with you that the book will not be to everybody's taste. So many clever, frank, and playful ideas are not easy to digest. And yet you should try and have it published. Worse products have been published in the name of analysis.

Contributions of yours to *Imago* will always be welcome. At the moment, we have not got any paper but we are trying to get some.

Yours sincerely F R E U D

Baden Baden, 2.3.1920

Dear Professor,

Your letter made me very happy. The novel is now on its way to the publishers, I hope it will be printed. I am making use straightaway of your invitation to contribute to your journals. Neither the Bible nor *Struwwelpeter* materialised, however, but the sulphurous smoke[30] may find its admirers, too. Will you please decide for yourself whether it is to be *Imago* or the journal. I have the impression that the article, earthy as it is, hovers between the sublimity of *Imago* and the earthiness of the journal.

With sincere gratitude and loyalty
Yours ever G R O D D E C K

Baden Baden, 7.4.1920

Dear Professor,

Under the influence of the news that the hell article[31] is to appear in the journal, I have written something new. If it is of no use I beg you to excuse my eagerness.

As for the novel, I have to report that it has been rejected once again. Rejections are not accompanied by detailed reasons, they start with high praise of the first part and end with the verdict that the analytical part breaks up the artistic form and therefore destroys the whole. The latest publisher even maintained that I am losing myself in crass materialism. I shall continue to shop around. The fact that you mentioned the work in your last letter gave me back my courage. The question of a title is always difficult. I will cast around for something else. But I am not very hopeful. Everybody who reads it is somehow brought up against his own repressions and then resistance starts.

I am writing an article on symbolism[32] which is meant for *Imago*; but it is becoming long and will only appeal to a few people.

With warmest wishes
Yours ever GRODDECK

Vienna, 22.4.20

Dear Doctor,

Every contribution of yours is welcome. You have to get used to the fact that the editors of the *Psychoanalytische Zeitschrift* here value your importance. If we had money and paper our publishing house would put an end to your novel's perambulations.

I have one reservation about the most recent analysis you sent us[33] which I would like you to help me destroy. I believe I can recognise the half-ironical patient of your analysis; there cannot easily be two such people. He is also too well-versed in your way of printing and expression as well as with your article on hell. Now so far we have tried not to allow people to doubt the documentary character of an analysis. It would open the door to many abuses. Moreover, the semi-fantastic character of your analysis (the justification of which I personally recognise) might embarrass us vis-à-vis the public. Tell me what you think of this and whether you could preserve the core of this 'analytic delirium' in a thoroughly serious critical form for publication?

With warmest regards
Yours FREUD

Baden Baden, 27.4.1920

Dear Professor,

I do not know whether the changes in the article on the cross please you, but they certainly clear up to some extent what was incomprehensible before. And a few more words will show you what strange things happen sometimes. The analysis really happened as I wrote it down, yet it could only turn out the way it did because the patient is my stepson who has been living in my house ever since he was in his eighth year. He is gifted with a highly imitative, lyrical talent which might perhaps turn crea- tive one day. During the war he broke down with a grave neu- rosis and has been in treatment with me for the last two years with many interruptions. That he expresses himself like the hero of my novel is because he is jealous and embodies Thomas Weltlein[34] in nature for me. The imitation of my person which has obviously contributed a lot to Thomas Weltlein plays a large part in the symptoms of his neurosis and probably in their causes too. Treating him has its attractions and its difficulties because of the close ties. Perhaps one day I shall have time to write down his case history: it is characterised by neurotic com- plexes, which produced a series of boils on the face and back, and is a typical example of the condition which originally made me learn to analyse patients suffering from so-called somatic ill- nesses.

I tried to work out why I did not immediately claim my copy- right in the essential points, but invested my stepson with traits for which I am responsible and not he, even though he formally produced them under analysis. The revision shows you that this is due to the Christ myth. Something inside me warned me, but just as you sensed the distortion from the form of the article, so did some friends to whom I showed it. And I myself had an uncomfortable feeling about it. This has now gone since I have honoured the truth. I am very grateful to you for having taken this burden from me.

I would like to say something special about the article. The essential thing about it – for me at least – is its interpretation of the crucifixion. It struck me quite early on – probably in con- nection with an etching by Félicien Rops[35] – and for years I have been carrying it around with me, as well as lots of other ideas about the New Testament. I have decided to work it into the second part of Thomas Weltlein, which will probably remain unwritten, and to take it over into the revision of my talks. Meanwhile I was made impatient by the fact that, one after the other, my imagined discoveries were published by you and your colleagues, and this prompted me to write the matter down in this form. I am firmly convinced that in the next two years somebody will treat the Christ theme, and often I still find myself a prey to the priority madness.

Now it is merely a practical question for you and me whether the interpretation should be published in one of your journals or whether it is better to wait. You can tell how this matter preoccupies me from the fact that I first put it into the mouth of my stepson and that I am also hiding behind your back and burdening your journal with it. I believe this is obvious enough. Please, do not publish the article.

So now I have said it. It was not easy. Yet I am always satisfied once I decide to admit an unworthy action and to make up for it. I am glad that you are understanding.

Now I would like to say a lot of nice things to you, for instance that I am once again reading your books and enjoying them. And then that I am pleased to know somebody in Vienna who is interested in me, without knowing me, who tells me things while otherwise everything in the far distance is silent and I can only hear voices which are very near.

Would you be pleased if I joined one of the psychoanalytic societies? I won't quite fit, I know that already; yet I can say that I am easy to get on with.

Finally a word on my novel. I receive one rejection after the other. Would it be possible to publish it in the psychoanalytic publishing house if I myself bear the costs? But what about paper – if I am immodest, please forgive me. You have to take part of the blame for that because you are friendly to me and that is something new for me – at least on the part of doctors.

With warmest regards
Yours GRODDECK

Vienna, 9.5.1920

Dear Colleague,

What a strange mixture of guesses and mistakes! But now that you have made the matter all clear and tidy I want to ask your agreement after the event to my actions.

I have already handed on your valuable contribution to the editors of the journal.

By the way, isn't there an expression 'the son clings to the mother' or, as we would say, 'he is fixated on her'?

The offer you made me for the publishing house is tempting, of course. *If* we get paper we could consider the matter. But do you know how high the costs are these days? One sheet one Mark, i.e. about 20 sheets for 1,000 copies 20,000 Mark. Give me the good news that figures like these do not matter to you! Then I would make the suggestion that for the title you should simply use the name of the hero and underneath put: a psychoanalytic novel.

You ask if we would profit from having you for instance in our Berlin group. I would think so; one could then meet during our conferences (the next one is going to be held in The Hague, on September 8).

My warmest regards. You are right, there is very little good will in the world.

Yours F REUD

Baden Baden, 21 May, 1920

Dear Professor,

I gladly offer you my forgiveness after the event, am very grateful for the publication of my piece and only regret that your idea about 'the son clings on to the mother', and 'fixated' and *crucifixus* did not get into the article. If it is not immodest I would like to ask you to add it in a footnote.

I have applied to be admitted to the Berlin group. It would be good to meet you sometime, and The Hague is not totally out of my reach. For years I have considered asking you to be my very welcome guest here for a few weeks. Yet one has to wrestle with a wish like this before one can express it. Surely, one is allowed to harbour wishes.

Thomas Weltlein, a psychoanalytic novel – that's simple and good. Many thanks. That you might accept the novel for publication is such a welcome piece of news that I cannot rejoice enough. The question of money can be solved, though not from my own means; yet I have friends – particularly in Holland – who will help me and therefore as soon as there is a prospect of paper, I can deposit the 20,000 Mark where and how you wish. From my own circle of acquaintances I can reckon on a few hundred copies sold, so that even under the worst conditions the loss will not be too great for the backer. Would you like to have a try?

I have changed a few small details, but I believe that you will be pleased with the changes.

My work on symbols is resting at the moment. If it succeeds it will interest you, but the question is, will it succeed?

Warmest regards
gratefully yours ever GRODDECK

The Hague, 11.9.1920

Dear Professor,

Your question of whether I was serious in the contributions[36] I made to the congress has preoccupied me. I shall try and make myself clear to you.

When so-called healthy people are asked to look at the objects in their sitting-room and then to close their eyes and name the objects they generally leave some things out.

When one analyses why these specific things are not consciously perceived, it turns out that they are parts of repressed complexes. So there is a censor while we are awake.

If in the case of highly visual people the repressed complexes become too intense, censorship is strengthened and the eye is rendered short-sighted. If this is still not enough, the unconscious destroys the retina with bleeding.

The process is the same in a different field, like the formation of anti-toxins to overcome toxins, or like fever and pus formation to overcome infection.

When the repressions are resolved, censorship can be reduced and retinal bleeding is stopped. Ceteris paribus: when are you coming to Baden Baden?

Yours ever GRODDECK

Baden Baden, October 17, 1920

Dear Professor,

Instead of the article on symbols which I promised you a long time ago I am sending you something which arose out of the congress[37]. For me this attempt at sorting out the terminology is necessary because otherwise I shall be constantly misunderstood. After this test I hope to be considered worthy of the diploma of psychoanalysis and shall return, my conscience cleared, to my own gibberish which I find easier to handle and which leaves me the freedom to think what I must think. The congress had a rather unpleasant consequence for me. The old experience that words put chains on thought was confirmed to such an extent that my fear of technical terms and strict definitions has become even greater than before.

The article can perhaps be used in the *Zeitschrift*. Did Rank[38] tell you the title he has found for the novel? *Der Seelensucher* [the seeker of souls]. I like it, but I do not want to change anything without your approval. By way of explanation I must add that I introduced a story about a silhouette into the first chapter where Thomas Weltlein is called a seeker of souls which dominates the novel; the whole of the silhouette is printed on the title page. To make the acquaintance of Rank was especially pleasant for me. The few words he said during the congress expressed clearly and resolutely what he was thinking, and that is a gift I find interesting.

Otherwise I followed you round during the congress in a semi-trance; like somebody who is in love. And thinking back on this now I am glad that I am still young enough to have strong feelings, when it is worth while. My wish now is to be together with you once in peace. But the prospects are not favourable. I am stuck here and have to earn money and you are probably in a similar position.

Give my regards to Fräulein Anna[39] and whoever else is interested in having them, and warmest regards to you

from your loyal disciple GRODDECK

53

Vienna, November 15, 1920

Dear Doctor,

I am glad that we have managed to tear such a beautiful and honest article[40] from you. It has already disappeared into the editorial file and will leave it (hopefully) to be put into the second number of the new volume. Of course I know everything about your novel and approve of Rank's title. This moment a pretty cover illustration is being devised.

I cannot quite understand why you should feel a martyr because you had to accept our terminology. A residue of your first letter to me, a little bit of chalky dust from the gate through which you came into our little town! I said jokingly that you turned dogmatic and fantastic at the end of your fine, original, and freely sceptical article and invested our unconscious, which until then had been mutually understood though, thank God, provisional and indeterminate, with the most positive qualities from secret sources of knowledge. Now every clever person comes to a point where he starts to turn mystical, where his most personal thinking begins. But couldn't you perhaps change a few things in these last sentences, make a sacrificio d'emozione? It will be acknowledged with thanks.

Your words about the attractive prospect of a fuller exchange of ideas between the two of us have found a strong echo in me. Yet your resigned postscript is correct too. I am in the position of the Sybil of Cumae who wants more money for the last third of her wisdom than for the whole. I, too, am so impoverished that I have to sell the remainder of my working time and strength dearly; fortunately it is no longer a (full) third. The analogy also does not hold in that I do not meet any of the now so rare kings. Thus I gather money from colleagues and tradesmen.

With warm regards
Yours FREUD

P.S. My daughter is still in Berlin and will be pleased about your kind mention of her.

Baden Baden, 20.11.1920

Dear Professor,

Again I see from your letter how kind you are to me. The last sentences of my article[41] are not usable, if read *senza emozione*. I beg you to cut the whole paragraph and finish the article with the words: 'emerges, that the psychoanalysis of the organic has the same theoretical laws and practical results as the psychoanalysis of neurosis'.

The matter is thus deferred, yet it is not over and done with since without ado and quite cheerfully I can forego the accuracy here where it would be quite misplaced, whereas I shall have to find an outlet for my mysticism, without which I cannot exist, somewhere else. This brings me to a matter I have mentioned several times before. For some years now I have been hatching out a book which will set out calmly and lucidly what I am thinking. I plan to shut myself away for some months in winter and get down to this work, but I am afraid you won't be very pleased with it because there will be a lot of mysticism and fantasy in it. It will be good for my relationship with you, if nothing else, to have brought this sea monster to light. I feel like a child whom people believe to have been good while it is really planning to do all sorts of things it knows will not be approved of by its parents, and this is why I want you to get to know the work. It will decide whether you can continue to allow me among your ranks.

I am well aware that behind this fear of losing your approval there is the wish to be free again. Yet this wish will not have any influence on my work, particularly now that your letter has drawn my attention to the danger of *emozione*. The wish to be great is still there in me and sticks its head out where it shouldn't. Then I find it difficult to be silent, merely because one doesn't quite know whether what one says is right. Too often I have had the experience that things which only one person can say have remained unsaid because of excessive caution. And at 50 one can still utter a cheeky opinion that would appear impossible at 60, and as an unknown person one does not carry the fetters of a past and of having been an authority.

Perhaps I am mistaken and the book is not as dangerous as all that. In any case I beg you not to come to a final verdict about me yet as far as my medical activities are concerned. And as far as the human being Groddeck is concerned you won't get rid of him so quickly, because he won't let go. I have got a very tight hold of you and it would cost me a piece of my fur if I were shaken off.

I hope my protestations of love are not too monotonous. But I am really assured since I saw your understanding smile that personifies so accurately the saying: 'do not judge!'

With warmest regards and wishes

Yours ever GRODDECK

Vienna, November 28, 1920

Dear Doctor,

Thank you very much for the sacrifice at the end of your article for the *Zeitschrift*.

I understand well that you want to make up for it (the economic approach!) and am looking forward very much to the book you announced. Yet I do not at all share your threatened fears, rather I believe that we shall ask you to give us this heretical work too, if things continue to be all right for our publishing house. I am myself a heretic who has not yet become a fanatic. I cannot stand fanatics, people who are capable of taking their narrowmindedness seriously. By holding on to one's superiority and by knowing what one is doing one can do a lot of things which are against the tide. The courage you intend to show I like very much, too. Perhaps the latest little work of mine that has just appeared, *Beyond the Pleasure Principle*[42], will change my image in your eyes a little.

I, too, do not intend to give you up easily.

Warm regards

Yours FREUD

Baden Baden, December 31, 1920

Dear Professor,

With my compliments for the New Year I am sending you a somewhat mis-shapen article[43] for *Imago*. If nothing else, it is characteristic of my condition. In the first half everything is dense and well-structured, then it becomes threadbare and finally there are only a few connected strips enclosing enormous holes. The whole thing deserves the name 'product of laziness'.

Meanwhile the proof copy of *The Seeker of Souls* has arrived. Cover and title page are marvellous and the whole lay-out is dignified. I am very glad to see the fool run around in such good clothes. Now we have to wait and see what the world has got to say about it. I have not yet received your new work and shall thus be able to look forward to it a little longer. I wish I could somehow give you back part of the *joie de vivre* I have received from you. Yet I can only do what good boys do for their fathers, namely resolve to work well and prove worthy of them.

On Monday I shall go on holiday, for the first time in 6 years, to the Black Forest, a little house away from people, accompanied by my assistant only, without servant and without running the risk of seeing anybody. She will cook and I shall chop wood and sweep rooms; we shall roam about the forests, feed birds and deer and sleep a lot. And if the heavens are merciful I shall start the book on the unconscious. Something popular. A few years ago I had the urge to write it, now I have to force myself.

I shall not be able to collaborate on the children's book I was asked to by the publisher.

Outside the boys are setting off bangs and rockets and yet the night is as warm as if it were April. Every now and then the wind shakes the trees in front of my window and life is really very nice.

With warmest greetings as ever
in gratitude and devotion GRODDECK

Vienna, 9.1.1921

Dear Doctor,

Manuscript arrived[44], no scolding, clever and cheeky as ever. The 'fool'[45] looks good in his clothes. He will give pleasure to many people and anger many others. Ferenczi has asked to greet him[46]. Very envious of your forest journey, yet is there no other time of the year?

Warmest regards FREUD

Vienna, 17.4.1921

Dear Doctor,

It is Sunday and I am treating the day as a holiday by answering your letter.

The five letters[47] are charming, I have firmly decided not to let you go to another publisher. You are irresistible. Particularly when you talk about yourself. I must tell you that my daughter, who is so far the only reader apart from myself and who came back from The Hague somehow adversely influenced, has had the same impression.

Now I am very interested to see the sequel. Will you be able to melt the difficult material into a liquid flow again, and will you succeed, with all your capriccios, in making the piece of ground that you jump off from appear as distinctly? Your style is enchanting, your speech like music.

To talk about something more serious: I understand very well why the unconscious is not enough to make you consider the It dispensable. I feel the same. Yet I have a special talent for being satisfied with the fragmentary. For the unconscious is merely something phenomenal, a sign in place of a better acquaintanceship, as if I said: the gentleman in the havelock whose face I cannot see distinctly. What do I do if he appears without this piece of clothing? For ages now I have been recommending in the inner circle that the unconscious and the preconscious should not be opposed, but rather the coherent Ego and the repressed material split off from this. But that does not solve the difficulty either. The Ego is deeply unconscious, too, in its depths, and yet fused with the core of the repressed material. The more correct notion thus seems to be that the categories and hierarchies observed by us only apply to relatively superficial layers, and not to the depth for which your 'It' is the right name. Like this, perhaps:

We shall talk about it further when the little book (yours) is ready. I, too, would much rather talk than write. Yet how could we manage that? Could you get away for a few days in summer, to Gastein or wherever else I may be later?

You also said that I was getting away from eroticism. My next little paper will perhaps show you that in doing so I still take Eros along with me on my journey (*Group Psychology and the Analysis of the Ego*[48]).

With warm regards and in expectation

Yours ever FREUD

Baden Baden, May 22, 1921

Dear Professor,

May I start with a request? Do come here for a few weeks. Whenever it suits you. I know it is often tiresome to be somebody's guest. But one can really be at ease in Marienhöhe. Nobody is disturbed or allows himself to be disturbed. Like everybody else you will get your meals sent to your room and when you need company at meals or otherwise you can tell me and I shall eat with you. For years now I have spent the whole day there; my own house is nothing but a place to sleep in for me. The patients – there are never more than fourteen – you will not notice, nor is there a smell of iodine or medicine. And you will be in Baden Baden. I have seen much of the world, but there is no more beautiful spot than Baden Baden. I myself, a Prussian, emigrated here, and I have as little love for the South Germans as they have for me. But the scenery here is beautiful.

The only difficulty is that you will be with a lover. But I am still young in this, and I shall behave as I did in The Hague, when I was satisfied with seeing you and talking to you occasionally.

If my information is correct, you are accustomed to having your daughter with you. I hope she will be kind and accept my invitation and persuade you too. Please, give her my regards.

The words and the drawing of the repressed Ego and It have had their effect on me and will bear fruit. Thank you very much!

My writing stagnates a little. I have a woman patient who has been labelled heart disease and chronic kidney infection. High-grade dropsy and a strict Catholic. Initially the treatment went fairly well. Suddenly with the help of Sunday the water level rose, the pulse-beat became frighteningly weak, and urine secretion stopped for 36 hours. On Monday morning I discovered the reason for her resistance. At half past one the bed pan was full and by next morning she had passed three litres. Isn't that a nice story?

And another one. The woman patient in question had been infected years ago with gonorrhoea. The condition cured itself, yet supposedly some traces of salpingitis remained. Four months ago there was thick, yellow discharge again, without gonococcae, heavy pain in the left side near the fallopian tubes. Long-drawn out gynaecological treatment. The label chosen by a wise Englishman: septic endometritis and salpingitis, presumably therefore streptococci evidence. At one o'clock first analysis. Two hours later the pain had disappeared. Next morning some white discharge. Search for and find resistance. Since when discharge disappeared. Isn't that nice, too? If only other people decided to investigate whether the distinction between the organic and the neurotic is justified.

Dear Professor, do come here to Baden. You will certainly like it.

All the best and warmest wishes
Your loyal disciple GRODDECK

Vienna, May 29, 1921

Dear Doctor,

What a tempting prospect you open up to me! And how clever to ask my little girl, too, to prevent me from getting homesick! Of course, I have to say no. The rational reason is that this year's holidays are already planned and there is no room left for anything else. The real reason is different. Because I have lost my youth. If I were 15 years younger no devil could have stopped me from sitting on your neck for a few weeks and watching the kind of skills you are practicing, as I did – earlier on – with Bernheim[49]. But now I have to tell you frankly, and I am even confident that you won't tell anyone else prematurely: in reality one has only a single need in old age, a need for rest. It is a quite transparent calculation. Since I shall not be able to pick the fruit of this tree I shall not bother to plant it. Mean but honest. One does not want to learn anything new any more, but one also does not get any real pleasure out of old things either. In about 20 years you will understand me better and not think any worse of me then, when you remember that I subjected myself to fate without any illusions.

It is certain that I cannot be with you just to enjoy the charm of your company. I should have to go into the curious influences which you are studying. Yet there is also the transference of thought which demands to be let in and many other things generally called occult. The possibility of changing pathogenic factors by exchanging and adding sex glands etc. What one has achieved oneself is unfinished, fragmentary, provisional; one ought to have a second life in order to improve on it.

And yet it is not impossible that there may still be a gap in the schedule and that I may one day turn up unannounced as a visitor at your door. I hope travelling in Germany is a pleasure again. It isn't in this country.

It is not nice of your lady-friend[50] that she no longer urges you to continue the correspondence.

        With warmest regards and thanks

                            Yours FREUD

Baden Baden, July 2, 1921

Dear Professor,

Your letter left me with a slight hope of your perhaps turning up unannounced in my house. I am holding on to this and am delighted about it.

If this hope is not fulfilled I will have to be content with the prospect of the congress, but I do not know whether there will be one. The journals take a long time to get here.

The lady-friend[50] has taken your admonition to heart and persisted in pressing my belly until I had given birth to a couple more spiritual children. They will be sent on to you in the next few days. As I do not know how many letters you have got I shall start with No. 6 for good measure and send everything after it that is ready. In any case I have to ask you to consider the letters as temporary drafts. The material is so vast that I shall probably have to cut out a lot later.

In my practice I occasionally experience things that are worth communicating. Recently there was a case of endometritis with stinking pus discharge that had been treated for four years by English and Dutch gynaecologists. The patient had been infected with gonorrhoea – before the marriage – by her subsequent husband. The gonococcae have long since disappeared, the endometritis remained. The marriage came about against the will of her husband's family, ostensibly because he married far beneath his class. In the very first interview it became apparent that the patient produced the smelly discharge in order to answer every humiliation on the part of the husband or his family by the idea: 'I am not good enough for you, but your high-born son has infected me.' The symptom, which had lasted for four years, disappeared very quickly. By the way, it did so only by way of psychoanalysis (or the discontinuation of any kind of local treatment and physical treatment). The most interesting thing was that she had (apparently?) wished the infection onto herself through a horror of having children. Then behind all the other things there emerged an obvious and, I hope, now resolved Oedipus complex. Moreover I found here another demonstration of my old theory that an increase in weight implies symbolic pregnancy. The patient lost 11 kg in three weeks.

One of your patients is with me at the moment, a Dr. Veneziani from Trieste. I am keen to know what will become of him.

Occasionally I hear something about *The Seeker of Souls*. But nicest of all are the reactions of my most intimate friends to the book. They hide it carefully.

Finally I must express once more my hope that you will come here after all. The trip is expensive but no more uncomfortable than any other trip. Please, do come.

With all best wishes

Your loyal disciple GRODDECK

Bad Gastein, 29.7.1921

Dear Doctor,

Received further letters to your lady-friend and read them here in my holiday retreat. I particularly like your beginnings and the bits of self-analysis; you are really charming in this. You should sacrifice a few bad habits and change a few details which the analyst would disapprove of. For instance, it is inadvisable to look for deep meanings in the Mosaic story on the creation of man[51]. It is probably a deliberate priestly distortion of the old myths and thus the only known example of the origin of woman from man instead of the opposite (incestuous) relationship. As to the discussion of menstruation[52] the same self-righteous person demands that the complication and layering is taken into account. If a woman answers the man's visit by starting her period early then it is not merely the old sexual desire, but also a strong defence drive which uses the old and now obsolete approach. The exploration of strawberry urtikaria will merely cause offence – without clarifying anything etc.

As a warning example in the distance there is a certain W. Stekel[53], too unreasonable and with all very inconstant.

I would like to know what the composition, extent, and aim of the work will be like since I certainly intend to take it on. The fragmentary case histories of patients are crying out for more.

The undersigned will stay here until the 13th of August, and will then go to Seefeld in Tyrol.

With warm regards
Yours FREUD

Baden Baden, August 6, 1921

Dear Professor,

Gastein and Seefeld, there will probably be no time left for poor Baden. And I would so much like to have you here, if only to dissuade you from the gloomy prognostications with which you accompany my psychoanalytical career. For I probably have to assume that the allusion to Stekel implies some kind of worrying, though I cannot fathom its significance. Apart from his book on dreams[54] I do not know anything by him; a book on war phenomena I found so boring that I put it aside after the first two pages. I do not know, however, what happened between him and you. Yet you described him to me, and one of his characteristics I accept with pleasure for myself, unreasonableness; I am not inconstant, however. May I add a word of explanation concerning my unreasonableness. During my apprenticeship the words exact and objective played an important part. I myself never managed to be exact and objective in the way demanded of me, and because I wasn't I watched everybody in the field that interested me mainly, namely medicine, who boasted of possessing these characteristics. As I wanted to see the mistakes I saw them, and thus came to this curious overestimation of the subjective and the contradictory. From this developed a kind of exact paradoxicalness that resembles unreasonableness closely and in a certain sense is unreasonableness too. My definition of terms suffered most under this. In the beginning I tried to upset every one of them and this was not too difficult. Yet gradually I lost the ability of definition so that I have to try hard and understand the meaning of terms, and often enough I do not succeed. A barrier has grown up that blocks off quite a bit of the world for me. Yet the most important aspect of my inability to be reasonable is not that I carry on ad infinitum, but an inability to keep order within a limited area. As a schoolboy my cupboard was permanently in a mess with combs and sandwiches and schoolbooks living side by side. And this remained so. In other words I cannot see the demarcations between objects, only their fusion. This is a fault, but it is also a big advantage. Systematic minds need people like me in order to feel important, as the pinch of pepper that perfects the dish. In the last resort, my unreasonableness is probably due to my relations with my parents and siblings. We were brought up with an arrogant motto: 'There are good people, there are bad people, and there are Groddecks.' Between us and other people there is a barrier which cannot be overcome. But as an equivalent I have come to harbour the wish to ignore the incest taboos and to have no barriers between me and the Groddecks. You can imagine what a crazy knot of complexes this produced, since the incest taboos did not care for my wishes. In fact they have not been broken, as far as I know, yet it must have meant a lot to me that I alone remain alive from among all the members of my family. My poverty and recovery from illness can be dated by the deaths in my family, and it is particularly striking that after the death of the last Groddeck[55] I attached myself with all my power of feeling to a human being[56], and took her over since she reminded me daily and hourly of some member of my family, especially my sister[57] and my mother[58].

Forgive this long explanation, be nice to me, and have confidence in me. I shall revise the letters and try and cut out everything that might give offence. There will still be enough left to give me the satisfaction that someone or other will pronounce anathema on me.

In a few days I shall send you a further pile of letters to the lady-friend. The question of composition, extent, and aim I can only answer tentatively. There is no composition; my aim was originally to write a popular book on psychoanalysis which was to help in treatment. Meanwhile I have come to understand that books are of no use in treatment. Therefore I am writing without any aim, merely for my own pleasure and to help those people who like my way of writing to while away the time and draw them a little closer to myself by teasing them. The length can be more or less as I decide. Maybe you will tell me when it is enough.

I do not want to reread what I have written to you. It is very sultry and even though I am almost completely naked I am dripping with wisdom and sweat. I would prefer you to be here. I cannot resign myself to the thought that I shall not be given the pleasure of seeing your face opposite mine and of hearing your voice.

I recommend myself to your forgiveness and remain, as ever,

yours gratefully GRODDECK

Seefeld in Tyrol, 27.8.1921

Dear Doctor,

I acknowledge receipt and perusal of the third instalment of your letters to a lady-friend. As fascinating as the earlier ones, perhaps less whimsical. Because of its forcefulness alone this work should become known among the public, as it emphasises the real novelty of psychoanalysis, and it should break down prejudices and narrowmindedness and provoke violent outbursts of insult.

Cordially yours FREUD

Hildesheim, 23.9.1921

Hope you were pleased with substitute. FREUD

Were you? Ferenczi

Best regards, Dr. Rank

Ditto Abraham[59] Ernest Jones[60]

    Hanns Sachs   Eitingon[61]

Baden Baden, December 4, 1921

Dear Professor,

The letters to a lady-friend are now completed. I could continue a little while longer yet it seems to me enough for the first go. I am about to do some revision on them, shall try and cut out everything that is hostile and make them as readable as possible. A few of them I still like, yet overall I think there is too much irony. The talks from which they originated were full of enthusiasm and that seems to be hidden now behind the laughing mask.

Meanwhile Ferenczi has been here. I had a lot of pleasure from his visit and hope that he, too, liked me and my people. He promised to come again and I think he will keep this promise. Apart from the enjoyment we will get from his visit he can do with it, too. We profited a lot from each other.

So far I am content with the substitution. Yet it remains a substitution and does not exonerate me from the promise that I shall torture you incessantly until you come here in person. Baden Baden is worth a visit and neither Troll[62] nor I myself missed the opportunity of asking both the Ferenczis about Freud's wishes and needs. You cannot know what part this often dreamed-of fantasy plays in my life.

I shall send you the manuscript of the letters[63] ready for printing towards the end of the month. Printing can then be started at any time. For January and February I shall return to the wilderness again and shall start the second part of *The Seeker of Souls*. This will keep me busy for next year. Ferenczi's Critique made me very happy. He brought it along to Baden. Mrs. Ferenczi[64] came, too. The two women made friends and we still talk a lot about their visit.

In my practical activity I still find many surprises, and I hope I shall continue to make progress the more boldly I push on. The dangers of philosophising and of occultism are still with me. I have a tendency for the first, but occultism is taboo for me.

I am treating a lady suffering from arthritis deformans of both knee joints and from habitual patella luxation. I hope I will be successful. The main result so far is that I fell off my bike on my way to visit the patient and smashed my right knee. That brought me back to self-analysis and with striking success.

Ferenczi wrote that Baden Baden might be chosen for the congress in 1923. I would be madly happy if this came true and I do not believe that a more beautiful or comfortable spot could be found.

Dear Professor, accept for once my gestures of love and keep alive your kind interest in me.

Ever your loyal disciple GRODDECK

Vienna, December 29, 1921

Dear Doctor,

The delay in answering your latest letter is due to sordid everyday ἀνάγκη and has now had one result, namely that I can wish you all the best and most beautiful things for the coming year 1922, and for myself, at the same time, the restoration of omnipotence of thought so that my wishes will bear fruit.

I am most grateful for your repeated invitations to come to Baden Baden. It is good to know of an asylum where one could always go if one's strength should fail. Yet so far I am still pulling hard and am thinking of the English saying: 'There is still life in the old dog.'

Quite imperceptibly I have recently moved into old age, no longer write anything myself and instead read other people's manuscripts. Hardly treat any patients, but train analysts by self-analysis (one patient to nine students).

When the remainder of your manuscript arrives I shall put aside all others in order not to delay printing. I was very pleased by the news that our foolish friend did not have an accident but will continue to tell us about himself. Don Quixote also had a second part.

I hope this letter will reach you before you disappear into your lone- or twosomeness.

Sincerely yours FREUD

Baden Baden, Werderstr. 14, 30.12.1921

Dear Professor,

By the same post I am sending you the manuscript of the letters to a lady-friend which is now ready for printing. Only the 14th of the letters which you have not yet seen is interesting; it contains quite a detailed description of a curious case history.

Would you be so kind as to hand over the manuscript to Rank. I am writing to him at the same time. I am proposing three alternatives for the title; I like the middle one best. Perhaps you will think of something better or Rank may have another ingenious idea as he did with *Seelensucher* (Seeker of Souls).

I am delighted that the novel is going into a second edition. It makes me more determined to start the second part soon, especially since Polgar's review in the Berlin *Tageblatt*[65] will probably have an effect.

I shall disappear into the mountains until the first of March, but I am giving you my address in the bold hope that you might write a word to your distant admirer.

I hear little of what is happening among psychoanalysts. I am too far removed from Berlin. Occasionally Ferenczi tells me something, otherwise I am living out of the journals and my own experiences.

Troll tells me that she hopes to get your works for translation into Swedish. I know enough Swedish to help if necessary. We are both happy to be able to share some literary work after six years of analytical work together.

My practice this year has had some good results, for my own development as well. If this continues for a few years, you will be pleased with your most fantastic but most loyal disciple.

It is warm and good to live here, almost as if it were Spring already. We are in the middle of our going-away preparations, packing tins, blankets, crockery, and tobacco without which I cannot do. The books have been mailed and the paunch that has lost its shape is hoping to shed some fat. Habakuk, the tom-cat, and Fick, the canary, are coming along, too. Troll-Voigt has packed the cookery book and makes my mouth water with descriptions of Swedish dishes.

Why do I write all this to you? To tempt you to come here and, if you are not going to just yet, to make me imagine that you are at least thinking of me.

And now finally, best wishes for the New Year. All the best to you and your family

most sincerely your loyal disciple GRODDECK

My address is: Murberg near Sasbachwalden c/o H. Zink

Murberg, near Sasbachwalden, 1.2.1922

Dear Professor,

Like last year I am using the holidays again to read Freud. Or rather, in the first weeks I read Westerns and Marlitt's romantic novels[66], was bad-tempered, and slept a lot. Now, after a few long walks in the snow of the mountains, I am fit again and have convinced myself that I make books from individual sentences of your work like other people, too. I do not know if this is the right way to get myself to continue the fool book, but it is useful, in any case, as a corrective to my arrogance in other respects.

I take your silence regarding the letters to a lady-friend as a sign that you have quite a few objections to make or even that you disapprove in some important respects. Although I would be very sorry I would not consider it irreparable. The letter form allows all kinds of changes. This is the main reason why I chose this odd form of writing. I am expecting your criticism and shall make use of it in a later edition, which I consider possible, as I did with one of your objections. Personally I do not mind if my writings contain mistakes. I would only mind if you were angry about it. I shall then try and make amends.

I am struck by the fact that I have taken up the Dora frag-ment[67] again, and when on one of my recent walks I fell head first over some bits of rock I found a kind of explanation for this in the night. In the fragments from the analysis I talk about in the letters to a lady-friend the name Raabe[68] occurs. A schoolfriend of mine with that name broke his leg in a rocky landscape, similar to the place where I fell, and I thought of that the moment I fell. It was such a remote and desolate spot that I would probably have been eaten up by raven and fox (*Rabe und Fuchs*, the latter is the name of my holiday dog's owner). *Rabe* (raven) was near to my thought because a few days earlier I was visited by somebody in whose analysis the raven had played an important part ('What kind of a beggar is it? It is wearing coal black clothes'). In the letters, too, I arrived at Dora by way of Rabe. Yet here there is a new association. The schoolmate Raabe was friendly with my mathematics teacher Buchbinder, and his daughter was called Dora. He was nicknamed *Dragoner* (dragoon) which brought me to Drago, a name which occurs in the Genoveva legend. This legend has been on my mind recently, apparently in connection with an analysis, too. It was brought to my memory moreover by a Christmas present, Schwab's Popular Legends[69]. Schwab is also an important name for me, as the letters show, too.

You can see, my thoughts are preoccupied with self-analysis and with the letters. Thomas[70] is still very far away for me.

I have information for you with regard to the sexual theories of adolescence. I was consulted by a young man about impotence. It emerged that he had the idea at ten that for the conception of a child the testicle, the ovum, was pushed through the urinal tract, and he imagined that it must be very painful. And this idea, which persisted semi-consciously and remained uncorrected in the dark recesses of the soul in spite of better knowledge, seems to have been the main reason for his impotence. At least the man was with a girl the day after his secret had come out and he has been all right since then. – I send my best regards and wishes.

Yours ever gratefully GRODDECK

Murberg (Sasbachwalden), 12.2.1922

Dear Professor,

Dr. Rank wrote to me today that the letters to a lady-friend are being set up. I had told him for certain reasons of my own and because of certain words in your letters that I assumed that the book would not find complete approval with the publishers. He confirms this and suggests that I make extensive cuts and advises me where to cut. I accepted this advice gratefully and am hoping that this way something workable will be arrived at.

So far all is well, but I have used the opportunity to ask Rank what the publishers think of my writings and I would also like to ask you this question. What made me bold, strange though I felt as a determined subjectivist in the midst of objectivist believers, plagued, moreover with a chronic knowledge of my ignorance, what made me bold enough to express myself in public was your personal interest in my works. Now I am not convinced that this interest applies to the letters to a lady-friend, too, and therefore I want to ask you to tell me whether I have become a nuisance to you. I do not think it is probable that I shall stop on the way I have chosen, or even deviate from it. However bizarre they may be, the letters at least clearly show the direction in which I am moving. If this direction leads more and more into darkness and corresponds with the work of your disciples I would be pleased. I know nobody else but you to whom I could put a question which is important for me, namely whether the leaders of the psychoanalytical movement approve of or at least acquiesce in what I have written or what I shall write in the same vein. Be so kind as to give me an answer to it.

With best wishes I remain, as ever, your grateful disciple

GRODDECK

Vienna, 12.2.1922

Dear Doctor,

That you have taken the absence of an answer to your last but one letter (which had crossed mine) to mean criticism and dissatisfaction is understandable and yet far from the truth. I did not write to you because I am being eaten up by my scholarly and business correspondence, because I had house guests like Ferenczi and Abraham, because for weeks I have been suffering from a creeping, feverless kind of influenza and in circumstances like these one tends to put off the most intimate letters in particular. What you have heard or will hear of criticism and suggestions for changes from Vienna is not by me but by Rank who anyway possesses good judgment and is well disposed towards you. This does not mean that I have no criticisms to make, yet I would have been agreeable to let the respectable idiotic public have you with all your warts and originality and to ask them to take you as you are. It might, however, be better for you to let Rank influence you. My critical objections to your views emerged right in the beginning of our correspondence. That I do not share your pan-psychism which borders on mysticism but confess my agnosia much earlier than you; that I believe you despise reason and science too rashly and give too much honour to the university officials who you think are representative of both of them. That you seem to have preserved firm traces of former fixations etc. Yet all this I recognised as your personal right; it neither interfered with my pleasure of reading your writings nor made me go wrong in my estimate of your original discoveries and opinions.

Keep well in your present lone- or twosomeness.

Sincerely yours FREUD

Vienna, 16.2.1922

Dear Doctor,

Our letters crossed again! I am sorry if you have been doubting us for a moment. Yet 'fishing for compliments' is not like you. Please do not be unhappy! It is the others who desert me; when I am somebody's friend I remain so for a long time. I have enjoyed the letters to a lady-friend very much and would like to make up a variation on Goethe's words;

Of all the spirits which say yes
The clown is least burdensome to me[71]

Sincerely yours FREUD

Murberg Sasbachwalden, 19.2.22

Dear Professor,

Your letter would have made me even happier if it hadn't contained the news of your sneaking influenza. From this distance there is nothing I can do except think friendly thoughts.

This is doubly easy for me because for a few days I have been in possession of a lovely edition of your lectures[72]. The publishers have thus surpassed themselves and I was very happy that you let me have a copy. Many thanks for this and I hope you will get well soon.

In a few days my holidays are coming to an end. I haven't done any work, but I have collected all sorts of impressions of the forest and animals in winter and snow.

With best wishes
Your loyal disciple GRODDECK

Baden Baden, May 9, 1922

Dear Professor,

During the past few days I have experienced a little episode which I want you to know about. I have a young patient who is trying to work out an analysis of Aristotle in a way that corresponds with his own complexes. Every day this attempt brings nice surprises although coping with the dead language is quite difficult. When Aristotle mentions things that touch on his impotence and castration complex he starts talking and always uses the same expression τοθετι. The translators maintain that this is the same as Kant's *Ding an sich* and translate it accordingly. We agree that Kant invented the *Ding an sich* (which according to him is unknowable) on the basis of a castration complex which contains masturbation anxiety and hermaphrodite complexes. The *Ding an sich* would thus be the *Ding an* Kant, just as Luther's 'Man's heart is an obstinate and cowardly thing' and 'It is a good thing that the heart becomes firm' stand for the slackness and erection of the penis and establish most intimate connections with the heart. In the course of such a discussion my patient told me the following: he had just read something on degrees of accuracy in a book by Moskovsky, and Moskovsky was using the sea in his argument. (The patient has an unresolved Oedipal complex and curiously enough did not understand that he was talking of himself by way of association – *Meer = la mère* – while he was interpreting Moskovsky with my help.) According to Moskovsky there are four degrees of accuracy in the observation of the sea: first the shape of a sphere, then that of a rotating ellipse, then the shape influenced by moon and stars, fourthly a shape made of swinging atoms. In the analysis it now emerges that the first (chronologically the last) is the pregnant body, the second, lower-lying (chronologically earlier) is the rotating child, the third mating, the fourth the state before mating (moon = erection and slackening, atoms = semen and ovum). Thus in three there is erection, beginning of pregnancy (moon) and bustle of sperm after mating. The four steps are the four-legged animal in the riddle of the sphinx. Sphinx derived from σφιγγειν = embrace. Sphinx leads on to sphincter and the afterbirth.

I do not know whether the association sphinx-sphincter has ever been used in a literary way. Yet the four degrees of accuracy seem to me worth communicating to you. And above all I think it is good that for once an expert – which the patient is in the field of scholarly philosophy – should attempt an analysis of philosophical systems. As far as I am conversant with modern philosophers I find that, unlike pre-Aristotelian philosophers, they all suffer from Oedipal or impotence complexes connected with a striking avoidance of all symbols. My patient is himself a typical example: he recognises the symbol, yet he can only hold on to the knowledge for a second and at once changes it, after he has culled it briefly and with difficulty from the abstract concept, back into an abstraction. It is a parallel to Jung's alleged synthesis! Has this avoidance of the symbol, which I have come across several times as an obstacle to analysis and one that is difficult to overcome, ever been investigated in a specific case?

Baden has put on its best blossoms in order to join me in greeting you.

As always your grateful disciple GRODDECK

Vienna, June 1, 1922

Dear Doctor,

Apologies for answering on a postcard instead of with a treatise. I cannot keep you waiting any longer. I am snowed under with work. Your letter makes me think. In anaemic abstraction it is difficult to recognise anything, easier in the hallucinations of Kielholz, Jakob Böhme[73]. The avoidance of the symbol has not been treated generally, it is very obvious indeed with our 'educated' people. Symbols are about the most unpopular aspect of learning and science.

Sincerely yours FREUD

Baden Baden, 2.11.1922

Dear Professor,

The bearer of this letter, Herr Karl Kotthaus, Tegernsee, has made a collection of comparative physiognomy which seems to me worthy of the interest of the psychoanalyst. My judgment is however not impartial because the main idea that the appearance of the face as well as character and profession is determined by embryonic plasm is all too close to my own fantasies and because I have not had enough time to think about the question more thoroughly. Yet I am convinced that you will enjoy examining the pictures and am asking you to receive Herr Kotthaus if your time allows it at all.

With all best wishes
Your devoted disciple GRODDECK

Christmas 1922

Dear Doctor,

Are you astonished that I did not answer your interesting letter with all its information earlier, or can you understand that the date explains everything, the delay as well as making amends?

Enough, finally about to answer it I find that this is not a letter one can answer but one that should be talked about for several evenings, yet since such evenings cannot be had . . .

I was very sorry that you find it necessary also to avoid a psychoanalytic career. This explanation of your indeed unsuccessful paper[74] and your categorising my person as a mother figure, a role which I quite obviously do not fit, show clearly that you are trying to evade the father transference. In analysis the victims are forced in their vital interest to get involved and to accept what is useful in it.

Do you remember, by the way, how early I accepted the It from you? It was a long time before I made your personal acquaintance, in one of my first letters to you[75]. I made a drawing there, which will soon be published in almost the same form.

I think you got the It (in a literary, not an associative way) from Nietzsche. May I say that in my paper?

Hattingberg[76] does not deserve so much affect. He merely practices the behaviour of the uninformed when he is showing a tendency to create theories like Jung who built a theory on the first analysis he understood. A pity that it is so difficult to teach analysis, the more pity that there are so many people who do not want to be taught. They discover anew all the mistakes the older men have managed to bypass. I am sorry about Hattingberg, yet I am afraid there is nothing one can do for him.

I wittingly undertake to plead the cause of your It book vis-à-vis Rank. But you do not know how difficult it is to work at the moment. The publishing house is in a critical position because of the depressed conditions of the market.

Best wishes for the coming year to you and my charming translator[77].

Sincerely yours FREUD

Baden Baden, Werderstr. 14, 11.3.1923

Dear Professor,

One of my patients has been at work for a number of years on an analysis of Aristotle in the original language. The provisional result of this difficult digging is the enclosed paper[78] which he begs me to send to you for inspection. Perhaps you will find an hour for it. The writing got more and more obscure, however, the more he worked on it. I have the impression that the core is still intelligible; in other words this is proof for the Aristotelian philosophy that it is rooted in the impotence complex. I personally believe that it is the root of every conceptual philosophy, in decided contrast to the mythologically based *Weltanschauung* philosophy. A narcissism based on a sense of guilt with a castration complex behind the desire to masturbate which is defending itself with words.

I shall start work again in a few days' time. Apart from a little botany and zoology I have done nothing since Christmas, but this has not been without consequences for my analytic activities.

With best wishes
Your grateful disciple GRODDECK

Vienna, March 25, 1923

Dear Doctor,

To begin with congratulations on the publication of the It[79]. I like the little book very much. I consider it a matter of merit to put people's noses up against the fundamentals of analysis from which they constantly try to withdraw. The work, moreover, argues the theoretically important point of view which I have dealt with in my own forthcoming work *The Ego and the Id*[80].

The public will of course react to it with even more aversion and indignation than it did to *The Seeker of Souls* which could be taken as an artistic treatment of the undesirable. Your self-esteem will hardly be affected by this.

The discourse on Aristotle you sent me I find rather unpalatable. A sentence like: 'the *an sich* lives in the what, in so far as this lives in it' is sufficient for my miserable philosophical sense to paralyse understanding and judgment for good. I have to rely on your opinion that the paper of your disciple has produced certain results. I find his own presentation obscure enough.

I will wait for you to let me know what to do with the essay in question.

Warmest regards to you and my translator
Yours FREUD

Baden Baden, April 1923

Dear Professor,

Many thanks for your kind words regarding *The Book of the It.* I am prepared for it to be received with indignation. I will be helped in this not by my self-esteem, but by the inertia which does not allow me to linger over pleasant or unpleasant impressions too long. But I am sensitive to praise or criticism.

77

I beg you to return Herr von Roeder's manuscript on Aristotle to me because I no longer hope that you will accept it for publication in *Imago*. You honour me too much when you use the expression 'my disciple'. I have never had disciples, am rather convinced that my talent is essentially one for treating patients. I also consider my writing apart from *The Seeker of Souls* as not very important.

With best wishes for Easter
Ever your loyal disciple GRODDECK

Baden Baden, May 10, 1923

Dear Professor,

I have written the enclosed article[81] for my own instruction. If you were to consider publishing it I beg you to let it appear in the *Zeitschrift,* or otherwise return it to me. Personally I am of the opinion that some kind of admonition to use thought is necessary. The sentence that people respect what they are told by people who do not really believe what they say expresses my conviction. Your life's work will never be doubted, yet its development is hampered, no longer by external, but by internal forces. Yet it may be presumptuous of me to believe that these forces could be removed by me. The emphasis of the essay lies not on its real content but on the way it is written.

Unfortunately I have not yet received the Id and the Ego. I am looking forward to it. *The Book of the It* is beginning to have its effect in the circles of my patients.

Affectionately
Your disciple GRODDECK

Vienna, May 27, 1923

Dear Doctor,

I hope you have now received *The Ego and the Id* which was sent off before your reminder.

Your little work put me into some embarrassment. I willingly accept *Nachlust* (after-pleasure) but what shall I do with *Nachbewusst* (after-conscious)? Quite incomprehensible. Couldn't you separate the two *Nachzügler* (stragglers)? Some louse must have crawled over your liver. Where is it now?

Yours most sincerely FREUD

Baden Baden, May 27, 1923

Dear Professor,

Many thanks for sending me *The Ego and the Id*. As the god-father of this term I am now expected to say something about it. Yet the only thing I can think of is a comparison which throws light on our relationship and our attitude to the world, but does not say anything about the book. In this comparison I appear to myself as a plough, and you as the peasant who uses the plough – or perhaps another one – for his purposes. The one thing we have in common is that we dig up the ground. Yet you intend to sow and perhaps, if God and the weather allow it, to harvest a crop. The plough only wants to dig up and, by the way, reduce the stones which might blunt it. And since the plough has no eyes, but is afraid of stones, it occasionally sticks in order to make the farmer watch out and prevent the plough from getting blunt. For the plough this is a vital question, for the farmer ultimately a question of money since he can replace the unusable plough with a new one. Nevertheless it is not pleasant for the farmer if his tool becomes unusable.

My work 'Vorbewusst und Vorlust' (Pre-conscious and fore-pleasure) was such a case of 'sticking'. This is no stone yet, but it marks the plough's anxiety since it does not know what the farmer's intentions are, is at the mercy of the soil and cautious as to the soil's condition. You can survey the whole field, I merely have the dim impression of stony ground. Take, for instance, your derivation of sadism from the destructive drives. There I stick and do not want to go on, for I am afraid that the soil will destroy the seeds and cause weeds to grow. I may be wrong, but I believe that I know the effect you have on the soil, e.g. on your pupils, better than the farmer. For him a crop failure in this or that spot is not so important. The present-day generation of your disciples is of importance only to us, not to you.

Then there is a real stone, or at least something that I

consider a stone: the psychological factor; the farmer knows: here the soil is stony, and this is sensed by the plough from the cautious movements of the hand that guides it. It also notices that the farmer keeps an eye on the fertile ground of the It which is next to it. Yet it does not understand why the farmer insists on ploughing the stony ground first, the plough does not like going into the ground of the Ego where the distinction between psychological and physical is too pronounced for it. And the sentence 'It is to this ego that consciousness is attached; the ego controls the approaches to motility – that is, to the discharge of excitations into the external world'[82] makes a real dent. The plough, which has finally through hard experience come to the conclusion that it is not an Ego, tends to consider the concept of It as an illusion produced by the It. At least it cannot decide to do without the assumption that every cell has its own consciousness and thus possesses independent discharge. The Ego, in its opinion, is apparently not even able to control the motility of voluntary muscles, much less that of the intestines, kidneys, heart, or brain. In doing this it does not deny the Ego or the Super-Ego. Yet they are merely tools for it, not existing entities. I have the impression that for some reason the farmer remains in the region of the so-called psyche, at least for the time being, and can perhaps ruin a number of ploughs without producing a big harvest. In other words, the plough considers the farmer a little obstinate. But then it only has the brains of a plough.

Now I have started to ramble, after all, and must ask you to forgive me. A gleaming light was for me the explanation of unconscious guilt by way of the Oedipus complex and identification. On the father question I am aware of my own complexes, but I cannot so far prevent myself from getting on better with the mother rather than the father. This may improve when my homosexuality is more liberated. Yet the investigation of castration can hardly bypass the act of birth, or of sucking and weaning, and I believe for the time being that this anxiety is centred as much in the mother as in the father, and that a third root can be found in discharge. Separation of semen and ovum, and – related to your destructive drive – the elimination of material which the cell's It does not want to use.

Finally – I could go on for much longer but the essential

points are contained in the comparison, I am by nature simply an unreasonable creature, a tool – finally a secret laugh about displaceable energy, about libido which is taken into service by the pleasure principle in order to prevent blockages and to relieve the flow, and which is to a certain extent indifferent to how the discharge comes about. And we can put aside the forever unanswered question of whom it belongs to, since we possess the tool of this displaceable energy and at most lend it to other creatures who make the tool displaceable.

Most sincerely

Your anxious GRODDECK

Baden Baden, May 31, 1923

Dear Professor,

I am not astonished that you do not know what to think of *Nachbewusst*. Only now do I understand what you mean by *Vorbewusst*. Up to now I imagined that the pre-conscious was close in front of the conscious (spatially) and this is why I fantasised about something that is close behind the conscious (spatially) and moreover lies after the conscious (chronologically). Leave it at that, it is only of value as a sign of evil intent and the same may apply to *Nachlust* and disappear forgotten and forgiven.

This brings me to the little louse which is really a huge louse. On my part the anger started when you compared me to Stekel. That is now a year and a half ago. Apart from the fact that I had heard what you think about Stekel, I felt guilty that I had appropriated a number of ideas from Stekel's book in my dreams without really digesting them. I do not feel guilty about thefts when they conform to my nature. Yet I sometimes steal things which are not me and then there are evil consequences. The anger was increased by Rank's correspondence[83] about *The Book of the It* and by a few words you wrote on it. And finally there was the Berlin congress that finished me off. I fell violently ill afterwards and the whole time is an unpleasant memory for me. Particularly the farewell party and the meal at Eitingon's. Hattingberg's performance caused a fit of rage which is rare with me these days. I know roughly what led up to all these things. In September 1921 Ferenczi had his first treatment with me and I know that I felt proud and thought to myself: 'What stupid people analysts are.' I also told him a number of times; 'You do things like this or like that, but I . . .' And I made no exception of Freud. This was also connected with the treatment of Veneziani which I was proud of in those days, though it became apparent later on that it was a mistake. In short, there was a lot of bad blood, and it started in September, at the time of the anniversary of my father's death. Next year, Ferenczi came to me again, I treated him again and was analysed by him about six or seven times. He talked to me very seriously about my father complex. I listened to all this and the result was that a few weeks later I said to his sister-in-law and stepdaughter: 'The other paralytics' (instead of analysts), and the unconscious self-mockery of this still makes me laugh. This too happened around the anniversary of my father's death[84]. Now this afternoon something strange occurred. I had had a cold for a few days, had gone to bed, taking advantage of the holiday, and in my waking sleep I saw my father's face, very angry, with raging eyes. Gradually it changed into the face he had on his death bed. I am not sure whether today is really my parents' wedding anniversary[85], but the fact that I have had the thought is sufficient. Now you do not in the least resemble my father but both you and your daughter Anna whom I did not want to recognise have my mother's eyes. And your name has lost the end bit, it should have an –e [*Freude* = joy]. The death and castration wish is obvious. I cannot say any more at present, only beg you, but it is unnecessary, to allow mitigating circumstances for my poor soul while you are reading these ramblings(!).

Yours most sincerely GRODDECK

Vienna, June 21, 1923

Dear Doctor,

Thank you for your letters which have smoothed everything out. Do not be astonished about my belated and short answer. I have been ill myself and had an operation inside the mouth[86] and now I have lost a dear grandchild after three weeks of suffering from miliar tuberculosis. That hurts and silences one.

Sincerely yours FREUD

Baden Baden, November 8, 1923

Dear Professor,

It is a long time since I last wrote to you. I have thought of you rather more often. Indeed, the thought of Freud never leaves me.

In spite of all the strange happenings in Germany we are still living our old lives. Work goes on, sometimes successfully, sometimes unsuccessfully. Twice in the course of this summer I had the opportunity of watching pregnancy, birth and a baby's first week of life. The hunch that in the field of obstetrics psychoanalysis will prove to be particularly useful has been confirmed by this. The complications of pregnancy – both women were having their first babies, one of them was 33 years old – disappeared very quickly, in both cases birth was easy and quick, the older woman even cried, when the head broke through the vaginal exit: 'Oh, how beautiful, how beautiful.' I was strangely touched by the course of confinement. The common aversion among women to feeding their baby themselves was traced to its roots and eliminated, and with one of them, when lactation stopped for 24 hours, the secretion of milk started up again after it emerged that she harboured an old carefully concealed hostility towards her own mother. Yet above all I learnt to understand that quite a number of baby complaints are produced by the mother, consciously or unconsciously, and disappear after an analysis of the mother. It was all so very instructive that I began to wish for more technical ability in obstetrics. Then I would add a maternity hospital to my sanatorium without fail. There is still a lot to be learnt about the mother's and the baby's psyche as well as about the practice of obstetrics.

I have had a number of other experiences in my field of interest. The longer one is active, unfortunately, the less confidently one deceives oneself about one's own discoveries and the more difficult it becomes not to lose one's way in the labyrinth of the unconscious because of the multiplicity of routes. There is hardly anything that is communicable. More and more I am content to observe attentively, without giving in to the ambition of understanding what's happening. In mid-December we shall close the sanatorium. Then we will go away – Emmy and I, by the way, have at last got married at the registry office[87] – to Holland, Denmark, and Sweden, where I am to give some talks. But this is not yet confirmed.

Every now and then I have news of you, I have also been told about your operation. My thoughts and best wishes are with you whom I love so much.

Yours most sincerely GRODDECK

Vienna, November 25, 1923

Dear Doctor,

First of all my congratulations, at bottom I'm all for doing things the proper way. Now I am of course also interested to know whether you will allow your wife the freedom of pressing on with my translations.

Your professional writings are, as always, interesting, new and promising. Yet I shall willingly refrain from any attempt at influencing you, something you do not always receive well.

About myself I can say that I am ill. You seem to know the details. I know of course that it is the beginning of the end. However, one cannot know whether it will develop steadily or at intervals. But there has to be an end, and that does not mean that there will not be further developments. One of them will be found with you.

With warm regards to you both
Yours FREUD

Baden Baden, Werderstr. 14, 5.12.1923

Dear Professor,

Your letter confirmed what I had heard by way of rumour. I am sad, I cannot say more about it.

You ask about the Swedish translation[88]. The fact that this letter is typed[89] shows you how far it has progressed. I am about to type out a clean copy. As far as I manage to be impartial I feel that this first attempt has been very successful. We shall travel to Sweden at the end of January and shall talk to the publisher in person. The lectures will be translated next. Then, if you are agreeable, *The Interpretation of Dreams*.

I have been asked to give talks in Harlem and Stockholm, also perhaps in Copenhagen. Typing the Swedish text helps me polish up my knowledge of the language.

The sanatorium is closed until the middle of March, thus I have time for work. But so far I have not been in the mood. The second part of *The Seeker of Souls* has not yet surfaced enough for me to write it down. I want it to be good. *The Book of the It* I had already distanced myself from before I wrote it.

Now I must come back to your illness once more. I have become so enamoured with my views that I cannot believe in incurable diseases. Failure is due to the doctor, it is not inherent in the illness. Yet the doctor has to be willing and the patient, too. Since you are both in one person, only one of them will have to be persuaded to be willing. It is not fitting that the egg wants to be cleverer than the hen. But I love you and cannot do without you.

This is the first letter I have written on the typewriter. Maybe the mistakes show you what has got repressed. I am, as ever,

your grateful disciple GRODDECK

Vienna, December 18, 1923

Dear Frau Doktor,

The story of your working block and how it was overcome amused me very much. Of course I am much milder in my opinion of the people you met in Berlin in 1922 and allow them their human weaknesses.

Your repeated kind invitation to come to Baden Baden with my daughter cannot be rejected out of hand. For the time being, however, you are going back to Sweden, I am not fit for travelling; when I have recovered in the Spring I shall have to work, and what will happen in summer nobody can predict. Yet one should not be too sure of anything. By the way, isn't there a meeting before that, at Easter in Salzburg?

If you should ask in Stockholm about my chances of getting

the Nobel prize you will hear that I have been a candidate for a number of years and always failed thoroughly. Perhaps the application, which was not of course initiated by me, is thus null and void already.

With warmest regards for both of you and best wishes for your coming journey.

Yours FREUD

Baden Baden, Werderstr. 14, 4.1.1924

Dear Professor,

My reply to your kind letter to my wife is the news that the translation of *Everyday Life* into Swedish is ready for printing. We are taking the manuscript with us on our trip to Sweden, where my wife will ask a Swedish expert to look at it, and will then hand it over to the publisher. Then he will start immediately on the translation of the lectures and wants to ask the publisher to send her a copy of the latest edition for the purpose. As far as I can judge the translation is good, i.e. it follows strictly the words of the original.

We are going to Sweden to visit our relations there, at the same time I am to give some talks in Stockholm and Gothenburg. I have also put myself down today for a paper for the congress: 'On the future development of psychoanalysis', which I shall prepare myself for this time since it is to deal with fundamental questions. If I were to rely on the inspiration of the moment for it, it wouldn't be what it should be.

Herr von Roeder, whose essay on Aristotle is in the latest number of *Imago*, would like to take part in the congress. I have written to Berlin for a ticket, but I wanted to let you know about it at the same time.

My wife will accompany me to Salzburg. Perhaps she will get a different impression there from the one she got in Berlin. In fact for some years now I can hardly bear to be in Berlin.

While translating, my wife made a discovery which may be of value to you, if you haven't thought of it already. The observations of a completely impartial person are always of value. The matter in question is the number 2467^{90}. Since you have communicated this numerical example my wife concludes that everything connected with it has a special importance for your unconscious. As far as she knows you are 67 this year, exactly the age at which the master of ordnance was retired. My wife believes, and I share her view, that there might be an access to the deeper layers of your unconscious which might perhaps lead to the curative layers of your being. We send our best wishes, with hopes for a meeting in Salzburg and ultimately in Baden, too.

I remain your loyal disciple GRODDECK

I have looked again briefly at the passage with 2467 in it and consider it necessary to go into it also because I myself changed the 2467 to 4267. The explanation for my error is interesting, but I leave it out in order to discuss your numerical example. Shortly before it there is the story of the reversal of names and the nursery maid. Her sister, Rosa, Dora (which probably has a special meaning), *the poor people who cannot even remember their names* (marriage? name forced on one by the state), Erna, Lucerna (Luzern?). There must be some sense in your publishing the hysteria fragment of all things.

Immediately after the story there is Adler. Perhaps the word Adler has more meaning than the man for you. I believe that in the case of an illness as persistent as this one should be suspicious of the early suggestions because they are used by the It in a cunning way, though correct in themselves. In the sentences in between you talk of some cases with very intimate content which defy communication, and continue by saying 'therefore I want to'. This 'therefore' has no rational basis and is bound to strike one since you are otherwise so very precise in your sentence constructions. Afterwards, by the way, the expression 'discretion' is used in connection with 'unfortunately'. The word and concept 'discretion' play too great a part in your works to explain this away as the discretion of the doctor or of the decent human being. Here, somehow, the ideal Ego is speaking, and the It stands behind it and laughs. It struck me, moreover, that in the Adler example there is the number 17, that is exactly the same as the number in your example where a displacement from 19 to 17 takes place. That I was struck by UB [*Unterbewusstsein* = unconscious] must be due to my own circumstances, but I must tell you that before my wife came along with her 67 I had thought of the abbreviation UBW, accompanied by the often felt and often examined sensation of aversion for the sign UBW. – The next story has the numbers 17 and 19, and when you take the word yourself again, we get 426718, that is almost 2467. 'The youngest child in a long row of children and a father lost early on.'

Now to the story itself. The friend, the letter, *corrections*, dream interpretation, 'no longer meaning to change', *mistakes*. The sentence: 'It would be best to quote (why best?). . . . caught redhanded.' The letter is certain to be very meaningful. You put next to the general, a rare exception in the book, the initials E. M. Does that mean something? The explanation why you followed the career of this man is so strange that you can direct your attention to it. And now your wife appears with a question, and in this passage you are again uncustomarily ambiguous or you leave something out. For why does your wife ask in a way as if she were identical with the general? The reader cannot follow. Something is missing. I protest. A firm point in my memory. You decide to retire at 67. Finally there is a sentence which starts with the word 'evidently' and draws the conclusion. The word 'evidently' is suspect, like the words 'probably, certainly, etc.'.

I did not deceive myself that my words – now I am about to write something quite different from what I wanted to write. Instead of distortion the truth. I want you to be prompted by this digression to investigate your illness again closely and – come to Baden.

With best wishes to you and your family
the two GRODDECKS

Vienna, January 15, 1924

Dear Doctor,

So you and/or your wife noticed it, too! I have been cross all the time that it might possibly have given the forces of the occult a confirmation. Now fortunately it seems to have been avoided, I have started a new working year.

Best wishes for your trip!
Yours FREUD

Baden Baden, December 18, 1924

Dear Professor,

You are right, I have not written to you for a long time[91]. Ferenczi told me a few things about you and I hope he did the same to you about me. There is not much to report. When I heard that you were not coming to Salzburg I lost interest in the congress and rewrote the talk I wanted to give and put it in my files, a clear sign that I had written it with you in mind as audience. I also understand better and better that I love you but not the curious atmosphere of many congressional lions striving against one another. I am only friendly with Ferenczi, and he is nice enough to come and see me here. Otherwise I continue in my quiet course of practising medicine and admiring Freud from a distance. An interruption was a trip to Berlin with my wife where I much enjoyed giving a few quite successful lectures[92].

My opinion of Count Keyserling[93] is very subjective. Personally I like him very much. I do not know anything about his philosophy, but I was pleased that he did not at all mind my ignorance, not even after he had given me a few of his works and realised that I did not read them. His article on psychoanalysis[94] I can also only judge subjectively. He talks so much about me[95] that I have to assume that somehow he has played Judas in his conscience towards himself and towards me. But that would only prove the fact that he has a sensitive conscience, something I already know from the short time I treated him, and that I have made a mistake in the course of his treatment. I liked him because he is a happy enjoyable mixture of man and child in which the harmless and the kind, a small, boastful, intuitively reacting child predominates. This is the reason, I believe, for the astonishing influence he exerts on individuals and crowds. He knows how to create a contented equable mood at least for the time that one is with him, and if he ascribes this effect to his wisdom he indulges in his tendency to boast, I believe. The nice thing is that he knows of this tendency and laughs about it. He has an overwhelming laugh, when he talks about himself honestly. He is very vain, but not at all conceited. The interpretation of a dream, in which a butterfly called Kohlweissling figured, seems to me to be characteristic of his nature. '*Weissling, Weiseling* (= wise one), that's me', he said, and 'I am talking *Kohl, Kohl* (rubbish)'. This is about all I have to say about Count Keyserling. I only want to add that you haven't seen him alone. I know from my personal experience that one is only honest with you when nobody is listening. This is something that can be explained from your nature, something that may become the fate of other analysts after 30 years of confessional work and can be felt with you particularly, because you are the king.

A polemical attack on Keyserling I believe would be pointless. Your work lives, grows, and flourishes of its own accord and will outlast many Keyserlings.

My wife sends her warmest regards and many thanks for your kind words.

I remain, as ever, your loyal disciple GRODDECK

Vienna, December 21, 1924

Dear Doctor,

I am really rather pleased that you have a sympathetic view of Keyserling. I could not make him out when I met him. Of course I never contemplated a polemical battle with him. My remarks in this direction arose from the fear that you might suspect such intentions behind my questions. But then his remarks on psychoanalysis[96] in his most recent essay were particularly naive.

I am, of course, disturbed by a trait of yours which I would like to influence, even though I know that I shall not make much headway. I am sorry that you want to erect a wall between yourself and the other lions in the congress menagerie. It is difficult to practice analysis in isolation. It is an exquisitely sociable undertaking. It would be much better if we roared and cried together in unison and in the same boat, instead of grumbling in our different corners. You know how much I value your personal affection, but it is time for you to transfer some of it on to the others. The cause would be helped by this.

Your mention of Ferenczi makes me sense the reproach that I have not yet visited you in your beautiful home town. I would like to, but you must realise my present situation and how difficult it is for me now, perhaps for ever, to travel.

With warm regards to both of you
Yours FREUD

Baden Baden, March 16, 1925

Dear Professor,

I feel like writing and would like to tell you that I am thinking of you. It may gradually emerge why the urge is so vivid at the moment to actually make me write. The last few years have not been quiet for me, now it seems to be better again. Above all there is a growing urge to sum up my experiences since 1920. In what form this should be done I don't yet know. I am drawn neither to the irony of *The Seeker of Souls* nor to the curiously mixed mood of *The Book of the It*. Something autobiographical is stirring in me; at least I am busy reading all sorts of memoirs and dreaming vaguely about how something like this could be done analytically. Presumably one should stick to the actual course of one's life. Yet I can imagine an associative form as well.

And this is the reason why I am longing for you so much. In an analytical biography of that kind you would play an important part. The pater peccavi comes into my mind. And everything that should go into the book will, before I accept it, have to wait until I have told you of my plan. This does not mean officially that it will be carried out.

Greetings to everybody who is interested in me and warmest regards

Your grateful disciple GRODDECK

Baden Baden, April 15, 1925

Dear Professor,

I have read your autobiography[97] and enjoyed it very much.

In the final sentence there is so much simple force that I am convinced of your recovery. Everything is certainly leading uphill and the observer and investigator knows that this wanderer will continue to climb for a long time and with firm steps, full of vitality and the ability to take in and digest impressions.

Landauer[98] told me that he will visit you in Vienna. I am looking forward to hearing more from him. He is a pleasant person whose nature and words I trust and whom I like listening to.

We experience all sorts of things here, some things I believed I had known for a long time assume new and stimulating forms. I am curious to know where it will all lead to. So far I can only tell by my fattening belly that I am pregnant again. I am keen to write an analytical biography. My wife is trying to persuade me to write a methodical work on the It. Maybe it will all evaporate into a few small articles.

Best regards from us two.
Your loyal disciple GRODDECK

Personally I am flattered that you have again expressed your view on the qualification of non-medical practitioners to practice psychoanalysis[99].

Vienna, April 26, 1925

Dear Doctor,

Thank you for your two latest letters. I am glad that you like the autobiography. I wrote it without inner urgency merely on the insistence of the editor.

That you are gestating and that there may be an eruption soon I am glad to hear. You know I like originality even if it is linked with a little obstinacy. The latter on its own, as it manifests itself in Hattingberg, I cannot stomach, it seems to me a poor substitute for the former. I am not very well locally. My masochism as object of treatment is almost used up, it is time for me to be independent of the doctor.

With warmest regards to you and your wife
Yours FREUD

Baden Baden, June 13, 1925

Dear Professor,

Do not get frightened about the content of this letter, it does not demand to be read. But you have a right to know what I am doing. The meetings[100] which are mentioned in the enclosed seem to go well. There are almost only laymen here, only occasionally a doctor turns up. The discussion is about God and the world, and people are learning gradually to express themselves freely.

I saw Keyserling recently and he told me about you. He was deeply impressed by you. And what he said about you made me happy. I have reason to think that he doesn't wish me any harm.

Will you come to Homburg? I have put myself down for a talk[101] and hope that I shall be more successful this time in putting over my ideas. Yet for me everything depends on the moment and very much on the audience.

I wish you all the best, more than you believe possible. My wife sends her best regards.

Ever your loyal disciple GRODDECK

Vienna, June 18, 1925

Dear Doctor,

Thank you for your reports and enclosures. Everything from you is interesting to me, even if I may not follow you in detail. I do not, of course, recognise my civilised, bourgeois, demystified Id in your It. Yet you know that mine derived from yours.

Keyserling made a better impression on me this time. We spent a very interesting evening together. He talked very well of you while declaring H. – probably in a complimentary fashion – the biggest ass he had ever known.

I shall not come to Homburg. I have to get used to all kinds of renunciation. But of course if what you wish for me comes true, better things than I think possible, then I shall come.

Warmest regards to you and your wife
Yours FREUD

Budapest, Hotel Szent Gellert, 13.11.1925

Dear Professor,

On the 24th and 25th my wife and I shall be in Vienna on our way back to Baden Baden. If you have time and inclination to receive your most loyal admirer you would please him very much.

With all best wishes
Your disciple GRODDECK

Vienna, 17.11.1925

My dear friends,

If I do not happen to be ill again around the 24th of this month I shall be very pleased to see you both in my house.

Yours most sincerely FREUD

Vienna IX, Berggasse 19, 23.11.1925

My dear friends, as expected I was ill again, this time with a non-specific tooth trouble, have not quite recovered from an operation, and now dare invite you to a conversation tomorrow Tuesday 24th of the month, at 12 o'clock.

Yours most sincerely FREUD

Wiener Psychoanalytische Vereinigung
Vienna, 11 October 1926

On your 60th birthday our association sends you its warmest congratulations. Even your enemies in the scientific field are admirers and friends of your person. We are all grateful to you for the idosyncratic views with which you opened up barely explored areas. Then we all want to thank you for the happy laugh into which you transformed our normally so serious investigation of the psyche, in your *Seeker of Souls*. May your very own It continue to live for a long time for your own sake and that of your friends and patients.

On behalf of the Wiener Psychoanalytische Vereinigung,

Chairman
signed FREUD
Secretary DR. R. H. JOKL

October 13, 1926

My Ego and my Id congratulate your It on its fait accompli, hoping that it may please its inscrutable decree to allow itself a long happy lease of life.

FREUD

Baden Baden, Hütte, October 17, 1926

Dear Professor,

Many thanks for the charming wire. As far as I can tell considering the enigmatic nature of my It it seems to be willing to allow itself a long happy lease of life. In any case it is pleased with the sympathies of your Ego and Id and proud.

We have gone on holiday again after an eventful year, at first into our beloved hut, but soon we want to go to Berlin where I am to give some talks[102] again and after that probably to London.

Ferenczi and Frau Andreas-Salomé[103] were here and told me about you and your state of health. I receive all the news which is related to the object of my last passion greedily and remember it.

My wife sends her warmest regards and wishes.

Ever your grateful and devoted disciple GRODDECK

Baden Baden, October 17, 1926

To the Wiener Psychoanalytische Vereinigung

Many thanks for its honour-conferring congratulations on my 60th birthday.

The interest which the association and the entire international psychoanalytical movement have shown in my views is

95

an effective stimulus to me to push on into areas ahead of us and barely explored and to make them accessible in such a way that they become susceptible to the investigations of methodical science.

The Seeker of Souls, which I consider the expression of my best efforts, I hope to revive in the not too distant future so that laughter will not be forgotten in the midst of so much seriousness.

With heartfelt thanks DR. GEORG GRODDECK

Vienna, September 7, 1927

Dear Doctor,

To follow up your news that the publishers have not yet answered your question[104] concerning the continuation of *The Seeker of Souls* I shall protest energetically to Storfer[105], when I send him the drawings. I can only influence the matter by sympathetic words, the objective situation is known only to him. The drawings caused me a certain embarrassment. I would like to judge them as you do. (The page with the urinating lion seems to be anatomically wrong.) Yet I have repeatedly had the experience that cartoons like these neither give pleasure in themselves nor increase the pleasure in the text. I had it with the illustrations by Benikshank – I believe he is written like this – to Dickens, with the illustrations to the big Balzac edition which I possess, and most recently with the woodcuts for the posthumous edition of Anatole France which I receive from the French group since I turned 70. I would therefore prefer to declare myself quite incompetent.

In the story of the second Seeker of Souls I miss the continuation of a thread which sticks out of the first part: the relations of T. W.[106] to his niece. Otherwise I am glad to see your creative vein flowing again, after having got yourself into a position of cancelling all distinctions and into an unsatisfactory monotony with regard to the It mythology. I cannot hide the fact that P. T.[107], even though I borrowed something from him, seemed much less sympathetic to me than T. W.

I think you were missed at the congress[108]. Your warning about overestimating professional medical interests would have had a welcome effect. At all events it ended with a rejection of the narrow-minded claim by the Americans and a recommendation at least for lay analysis. The new president, Dr. Eitingon, is above all cautious and conciliatory, probably the right helmsman in a stormy sea. I am very pleased to have our friend Ferenczi close by. So far I have had no opportunity to talk to him alone, so much do the visitors after the congress claim priority.

Greetings to you and your wife FREUD

Baden Baden, September 9, 1927

Dear Professor,

A letter from you produces high spirits which I shall use to answer you straight away. This is not meant to be taken as begging for a further letter though I cannot deny that it would please me.

I share your view about the unfitness of illustrations for books like these but the public occasionally has curious wishes. It is possible that it might like an illustrated edition. The publishers will know best whether the attempt would be rewarding.

I know that you do not like *The Book of the It*. But I have never understood why you put it in the same class as Stekel's books. The expression It mythology does not help me, it might be taken as a compliment as well as a reproach.

The value of a book is decided by the reader, and there is no point in an author's defending his book; one knows anyway that he likes it, otherwise he would not publish it. But you are not really a teacher who is responsible for his pupils' achievements, you are not even a reader in the normal sense of the word, but you are Freud and as such you better judge the follies of your admirers with leniency. In the same way in which your praise invigorates your criticism kills.

When I look at the achievements of psychoanalytic literature in the last years I find the same monotony which you found in the It mythology, only in a different key. Why do you not allow me the mitigating circumstances you allow others? In spite of your rejection I believe that this book possesses some merits that should not be underrated. First, all the facts in it are true;

97

they are true not only to my own gullible person, I receive more and more confirmation of the reality and spiritual truth of my arguments from licensed and unlicensed doctors. Secondly the book is not boring. Thirdly it discusses frankly a number of issues which urgently needed discussing; and fourthly, it deals with a subject I know better than other people.

The fact that not one of the members of the society dared follow my suggestions – Deutsch[109] and the American[110], whose name I now forget, do not count seriously – is not due to the wrongness of my case; there are enough people outside the society who are trying with difficulty to learn from the *corpus vile* of the patient what Freud has been saying and what cannot any longer be ascribed to the field of neurosis. I cannot help thinking that this striking behaviour of unity is due to fear of your disapproval. One knows your opinion of *The Book of the It*, yet one does not know or at least one pretends as if one did not know what your view is on the use of psychoanalysis in cases of organic disease. I am conceited enough to draw a conclusion from your years of silence on my activities which goes as follows: Groddeck has a useful idea, but I – Freud – cannot approve of the way in which he puts it; he must and will have to help himself alone. This is an honour for me, but it was very painful for very long.

Please recommend us both to your family and accept the most respectful regards from myself and my wife

Your loyal disciple GRODDECK

Vienna, September 7, 1929

Dear Doctor,

When I meet Dr. Runge I shall be pleased to help him as far as is in my power. Now I shall go to Berlin with my father for a while, but in October I shall be back with the Vienna Society and Dr. Federn is sure to introduce him there.

My father is very well here as you are certain to be told by Dr. Ferenczi, too.

Kind regards
Yours ANNA FREUD

Baden Baden, September 1, 1930

My most respected teacher and dearly beloved human being,

Since I have reason to distrust the legibility of my handwriting you must excuse my writing to you by typewriter instead of by hand, though I have not yet learnt to dictate, I manage quite a reasonable speed this way.

Your picture gives me great pleasure and was a surprise such as I rarely have. I did not realise that you knew what you meant to me personally.

Unfortunately I heard too late that you were awarded the Goethe Prize. As far as I have heard, all kinds of people consider it necessary to comment on this. If I may be allowed to judge by my experience then there is no one in the whole wide world who would deserve it more than you do. I was brought up in Goethe worship, but I did not understand him very well until I learnt about psychoanalysis. On the assumption that psychoanalysis, which for me is not a medical affair but something totally different, has enabled me better to ask the right questions I am turning to you, the new careful disguiser, in the hope that you will be allowed to tell the boy something at least of the best things you know.

When Faust is carried to heaven by the angels after his death a few words accompany this event which your disciple has pondered until his head was spinning round like a mill-stone. What bothers me, are the inverted commas round the expression 'Whoever strives and toils can be saved by us'[111] – they are in the Weimar edition even, in which the colon after 'evil' is left out. According to Eckermann Goethe told him that the enigma of Faust is solved in this riddle. Though I do not trust Eckermann very much – a family tradition – I cannot assume that he has misunderstood, particularly since he tells us at length in what follows the other remarks that Goethe made about it; this sound like genuine Eckermann, it only confirms that a mention may have been made of the importance of this passage. The inverted commas prove that the famous words about striving and toiling are a quotation, and do not necessarily tell us the angel's opinion. If it is true, as I assume, that this sentence is the evil itself, that to believe one could be saved by striving and toiling is evil, I would be helped a lot.

I do not intend to coax an answer out of you with this question, I would much rather you refuted me. Much as I would like Goethe to be a star witness of my perverse ideas, my godlikeness makes me afraid.

The best thing is perhaps not to answer, but the best is not always the pleasantest for your disciple, now grown old,

GRODDECK

Would you please tell Miss Anna how sorry I am not to have greeted her in Frankfurt. I trust her to have a forgiving heart.

Grundlsee, September 5, 1930

Dear Doctor,

As you know one is not obliged to express one's thanks for congratulations, particularly if they are related to a public recognition.

Fortunately your letter contains other things, too, about which I can be pleased.

When I am back in Vienna and near my bookshelves I shall try and puzzle out the passage you singled out, shall consult Eckermann, whom I find as unsympathetic as you do, and shall write to you about it.

Meanwhile I do not understand Goethe any better than Groddeck. Will I be lucky as a Goethe critic? It seems to me hard-earned bread.

The celebration in Frankfurt is said to have been very nice. My daughter would certainly have liked to see you in the Goethehaus.

Yours most sincerely FREUD

Baden Baden, February 7, 1932

Dear Professor,

To go straight to the point: I do not expect you yourself to read the enclosed manuscripts but maybe Miss Anna has still got a soft spot for me in memory of our meeting in The Hague which I recall often. I beg her to sacrifice a leisure hour and to report to you briefly.

I am in roughly the same situation as I was at the time of *The Seeker of Souls*, yet I do not know whether you can help me this time. It is possible that you are of the same opinion as I am that the material I deal with would be better published as the opinion of the slightly morbid Thomas Weltlein. But at the moment and probably for the rest of my life I lack the strength to tell stories and invent structures. This is why I have chosen the serious approach.

It is a book in which the idiosyncrasies of language and fine art[112] are used to prove how close the connections between symbol and life have always been. Medicine, particularly in the first part, will only be loosely linked to it, yet at the same time I want to discuss the influence of the symbol on the whole of the organism and its individual parts[113] – either in a volume on its own or in individual pamphlets. I enclose a sample of both projects, which might be sufficient to decide whether the psychoanalytic publishing house can consider the matter or not. The first chapter was accepted by Storfer[114] for the psychoanalytic movement and will probably appear in the next number; I enclose the two following chapters. The fragments on vision give an impression of the second part. It is all very unfinished still and needs revision. I hope by autumn to finish the first part and a considerable chunk of the second.

The fact that I submit the work in the form of a monster and do not wait until the baby is presentable is due to the uncertainty of whether the publishers will decide in principle to publish the work. This should not turn into an obligation, it is merely a request. Since I know from experience how long it takes when one has to go from publisher to publisher selling a finished work, I shall try to start the whole business off at least.

Storfer told me that he is leaving the publishers on the 1st of April. If I understood him rightly your son is taking his place. I told him at the same time of the step I have taken vis-à-vis you. Will he be kind enough to send me the manuscripts some time, no matter whether I get a yes or a no for an answer.

I remain with best regards and wishes your now unfortunately a little senile and fragile, but always grateful disciple.

GRODDECK

Vienna, March 25, 1932

Dear Doctor,

In spite of your kind letter to me my father insisted on reading your manuscript himself. He wants me to tell you that even before it he had not believed in your 'spiritual senility', but all the less so after the reading. But I am to tell you that the pleasure he found in it unfortunately does not have any practical consequences. This is not the manuscript's fault, it is the situation the publishing house is in at the moment. My brother[115] has taken it over in order to steer it slowly and cautiously out of the dangerous financial situation. This caution unfortunately implies a big reduction of production which for a while has to be confined to the journals and – to books for which the authors themselves will pay the printing costs. I hope this won't last long, but apparently it is the only way to keep the publishing firm alive.

You will understand this. For there are so many similar stories about these days. I am sorry that your letter does not sound as if you were in high spirits and that I am not doing anything now to improve these.

I am to give you my father's regards. He is well, again and again he overcomes the physical difficulties he encounters with wonderful energy and vitality.

Most sincerely yours ANNA FREUD

Vienna, March 4, 1934

Dear Doctor,

To read one or two articles by you remains a pleasure even if one cannot bring oneself to take your side, as happened to me this time. As for the Melancholia print[116] I cannot think myself into the intensity of that particular age's thought. Cancer is unfortunately much nearer to my mind, but what you say about it[117] seems too indistinct to me and probably to you, too. However, I shall certainly present the two essays to the editors of *Imago*.

You are important to us if only as somebody who takes a continuing interest.

Most sincerely yours FREUD

Baden Baden, March 6, 1934

Dear Professor,

Many thanks for your kind letter. The two essays were deliberately kept indistinct. Otherwise I would have started with Amor in the Melancholia print. I consider the print an illustration of the consequences which ensue when the erotic principle of life is denied. To write more explicitly about the cancer question than I have done does not seem advisable to me yet. I sent you the things because you have so often proved your interest to me in my activities and because I wanted to send you a sign of life. I did not count on publication, but if *Imago* wants to print them, it can have them.

Ever your grateful disciple GRODDECK

NOTES

1. First published in Georg Groddeck, *Der Mensch und sein Es*, Wiesbaden, 1970.

2. *Nasamecu. Der gesunde und der kranke Mensch,* Leipzig, 1913.

3. *Zur Psychopathologie des Alltagsleben,* Berlin, 1904. Trans.: *The Psychopathology of Everyday Life,* Standard Edition, Vol. VI.

4. *Die Traumdeutung,* Leipzig and Vienna, 1900. Trans.: *The Interpretation of Dreams,* Standard Edition, Vols. IV and V.

5. Alfred Adler (1870–1937), Austrian psychoanalyst, later founded individual psychology. See his fundamental *Study of Organ-Inferiority,* Vienna and Berlin, 1907.

6. Carl Gustav Jung (1875–1961), Swiss psychologist and psychiatrist.

7. 'Das Unbewusste', Vienna, 1915. Trans.: 'The Unconscious', Standard Edition, Vol. XIV, p. 187.

8. Sandor F. Ferenczi (1873–1933), Hungarian psychoanalyst. The paper referred to was published under the title 'Von Krankheits-oder Patho-neurosen' (1916), and is translated as 'Disease- or Patho-Neuroses' in *Further Contributions to the Theory and Technique of Psycho-Analysis* (London: The Hogarth Press).

9. J. B. Antoine de Lamarck (1744–1829), French scientist.

10. Ivan Petr. Pavlov (1849–1936), Russian physiologist.

11. Emil Abderhalden (1877–1950), Swiss physiologist.

12. Groddeck, 'Psychic Conditioning and the Psychoanalytic Treatment of Organic Disorders'. See Chapter 2 below, pp. 109–31.

13. *Imago*. Zeitschrift für Anwendung der Psychoanalyse auf die Natur und Geisteswissenschaften. (A journal for the application of psychoanalysis in Science and the Humanities.) Vienna, 1912–1937.

14. Ludwig Levy, 'Sexualsymbolik in der biblischen Paradiesgeschichte', *Imago*, V, 1917. See Groddeck's discussion of this paper in Chapter 4 below, 'The Compulsion to Use Symbols', p. 158.

15. See note 12 above.

16. The letter containing this remark could not be found among Groddeck's papers.

17. *Rosmersholm*, play by Henrik Ibsen.

18. Dr. Hanns Sachs (1881–1947), psychoanalyst.

19. Rebecca West. Groddeck, 'Tragödie oder Komödie. Eine Frage an die Ibsenleser' (Tragedy or Comedy. A question put to readers of Ibsen), Leipzig, 1910. Reprinted in *Psychoanalytische Schriften zur Literatur und Kunst*, Wiesbaden, 1964.

20. *A Doll's House*, play by Henrik Ibsen. See Groddeck, 'Tragödie oder Komödie', *op. cit.*

21. *The Master Builder*, play by Henrik Ibsen. See Groddeck, 'Tragödie oder Komödie', *op. cit.*

22. *The Wild Duck*, play by Henrik Ibsen. See Groddeck, 'Tragödie und Komödie', *op. cit.*

23. 'Der Wanzentöter oder die entschleierte Seele Thomas Weltleins' (The bug killer or the unveiled soul of Thomas Weltlein). A psychoanalytic novel, published later under the title *Der Seelensucher* (The Seeker of Souls), Vienna, 1921.

24. *Op. cit.* See note 12 above.

25. Hunderfünfzehn psychoanalytische Vorträge, gehalten im Sanatorium Groddeck Baden Baden 1916–1919 (115 psychoanalytic lectures held at the Groddeck Clinic, Baden Baden). Manuscript.

26. Paper read November 8, 1916.

27. Paper read August 24, 1918. Printed in *Psychoanalytische Schriften zur Literatur und Kunst*.

28. Paper read May 22, 1918. Max Klinger (1857–1920).

29. 'Der Wanzentöter', see note 23 above.

30. 'Wunscherfüllungen der indischen und göttlichen Strafen' Wish fulfilments by secular and heavenly punishments), *Intern. Zeitschrift für Psychoanalyse*, VI, 1920. Reprinted in *Psychoanalytische Schriften zur Psychosomatik*.

31. Reference to article on wish fulfilments.

32. 'Über das Es' (manuscript dated 1920). Trans.: 'On the It', Chapter 3 below, pp. 132–57.

33. 'Eine Symptomanalyse' (A symptom analysis). *Intern. Zeitschrift für Psy-*

choanalyse, VI, 1920. Reprinted in *Psychoanalytische Schriften zur Psychosomatik*.

34. The hero of Groddeck's novel, *Der Seelensucher* (see note 23 above).

35. Félicien Rops (1833–1898), Belgian painter and etcher.

36. 'Über die Psychoanalyse des Organischen im Menschen' (On psychoanalysing the organic in human beings). Paper read to the Sixth International Psycho-Analytic Congress in The Hague, Sept. 1920. *Intern. Zeitschrift für Psychoanalyse*, VII, 1921. Reprinted in *Psychoanalytische Schriften zur Psychosomatik*.

37. *Op. cit.* See note 36 above.

38. Otto Rank (1886–1939), Austrian psychoanalyst. At the time Managing Director of the Internationaler Psychoanalytischer Verlag.

39. Anna Freud (1895), daughter of Sigmund Freud.

40. *Op. cit.* See note 36 above.

41. *Op. cit.* See note 36 above.

42. *Beyond the Pleasure Principle* (1920), Standard Edition, Vol. XVIII.

43. 'Der Symbolisierungszwang' (The Compulsion to Use Symbols), *Imago*, VIII, 1922. See Chapter 4 below, pp. 158–71.

44. *Op. cit.* See note 43 above.

45. *Der Seelensucher*.

46. Review of *Der Seelensucher* by Sandor Ferenczi. *Imago*, VII, 1921.

47. The first five letters of *Das Buch vom Es*, Vienna, 1923. Trans.: *The Book of the It*, Vision Press, London, 1950; Vintage Books, New York, 1961.

48. *Group Psychology and the Analysis of the Ego* (1921), Standard Edition, Vol. XVIII.

49. Hippolyte Bernheim (1837–1919). Physician and psychiatrist. Freud studied the effects of hypnotic suggestion with Bernheim in 1889.

50. *Das Buch vom Es. Psychoanalytische Briefe an eine Freundin* (The Book of the It. Psychoanalytic letters to a lady friend). See note 47 above.

51. *The Book of the It*, 1961, p. 102.

52. *Ibid.*, p. 109.

53. Wilhelm Stekel (1868–1940), Viennese neurologist, psychoanalyst.

54. Wilhelm Stekel, *Die Sprache des Traumes* (The language of dreams), Wiesbaden, 1911.

55. The brother, Hans Groddeck (1860–1914), journalist.

56. 1915 first encounter with Emmy von Voigt, née Larssen (1874–1961), who became his wife and assistant.

57. Sister Caroline, 1865–1903.

58. Mother: Caroline Groddeck, née Koberstein, 1825–1892.

59. Dr. Karl Abraham (1877–1925), psychoanalyst.

60. Ernest Jones (1879–1958), psychoanalyst.

61. Eitingon, Max E. (1881–1943), psychoanalyst.

62. Emmy Groddeck.

63. *The Book of the It, op. cit.*

64. Gisella Ferenczi.

65. Alfred Polgar, *Berliner Tageblatt*, 20.12.1921.

66. Eugenie Marlitt (1825–1887), romantic novelist.
67. Sigmund Freud, 'Fragment of an Analysis of a Case of Hysteria' (1905), Standard Edition, Vol. VII.
68. *The Book of the It,* 1961, p. 222.
69. Gustav Schwab (1792–1850), editor and writer of German legends and folk tales.
70. The second volume of the novel *Der Seelensucher.*
71. Von allen Geistern, die bejahen
Ist mir der Schalk am wenigsten zur Last.
(Modified quote from Goethe, *Faust* I, Prolog im Himmel:
Von allen Geistern, die verneinen,
Ist mir der Schalk am wenigsten zur Last.)
72. *Introductory Lectures on Psycho-Analysis* (1916–17), Standard Edition, Vols. XV and XVI.
73. Arthur Kielholz, Jakob Böhme (1575–1624), Ein pathographischer Beitrag zur Psychologie der Mystik. Schriften zur Angewandten Seelenkunde, 1919. (A pathographic contribution to the psychology of mysticism. Essays on applied psychology.)
74. Groddeck's lecture on the It at the International Psycho-Analytic Congress in Berlin (25 to 27 September 1922). The manuscript does not exist.
75. 17.4.1921.
76. Dr. Hans von Hattingberg, German psychoanalyst. His lecture to the Congress was entitled: 'An analysis of the psychoanalytic situation.'
77. Emmy Groddeck translated Freud's *The Psychopathology of Everyday Life* into Swedish.
78. 'Das Ding an sich. Analytische Versuche an Aristoteles' Analytik (The thing in itself. Analytical essays on Aristotle's analytics), by Egenolf Roeder von Diersburg (1890–1968), Doctor of Philosophy. *Imago,* IX, 1923, no. 3.
79. *Das Buch vom Es* (*The Book of the It*). Dr. Oskar Pfister mentions the following remarks made by Freud, in *Schweizerische Zeitschrift für Psychologie,* Vol. IX, No. 2, p. 153: 'Freud told me soon after the publication of *Das Buch vom Es* (1923) in conversation: "Groddeck is quite certainly four fifths right in his belief that organic illnesses can be traced to the It and perhaps in the remaining fifth he is also right."'
80. *The Ego and the Id* (1923), Standard Edition, Vol. XIX.
81. 'Nachlust und Nachbewusst' (After-pleasure and after-conscious).
82. *The Ego and the Id,* Standard Edition, Vol. XIX, p. 17.
83. Rank had suggested modifications and cuts in *The Book of the It.*
84. 22.9. (1885).
85. 14.9. (1852).
86. Jaw operation for cancer.
87. The difficult financial situation during the war and inflation had delayed the divorce from his first wife.
88. See note 77 above.
89. This letter was not among the letters sent by Anna Freud to Emmy Groddeck in 1934. A copy was found among Groddeck's papers.

90. *The Psychopathology of Everyday Life*. Standard Edition, Vol. VI, pp. 242–3.

91. The Freud letter mentioned by Groddeck was not among his posthumous papers.

92. Lectures at the Lessing Hochschule, Berlin, October-November 1924, title: 'Das Es. Einführung in die Psychoanalyse' (The It. Introduction to Psychoanalysis).

93. Hermann Graf Keyserling (1880–1946), philosopher and social psychologist. See the Introduction, p. 21.

94. 'Heilkunst und Tiefenschau. Der Weg zur Vollendung' (Therapy and Understanding. The Way to Perfection). Gesellschaft für freie Philosophie (Society of Free Philosophy) Nos. 8/9, Darmstadt, 1924.

95. In the above-mentioned paper Keyserling writes: 'Groddeck is the least prejudiced among the psychoanalysts and moreover the doctor most aware of the implications of his trade I have met.'

96. 'Heilkunst und Tiefenschau'. See note 94 above.

97. *An Autobiographical Study* (1925), Standard Edition, Vol. XX.

98. Karl Landauer, psychiatrist and psychoanalyst.

99. Sigmund Freud, *The Question of Lay Analysis* (1926), Standard Edition, Vol. XX.

100. Saturday evening meetings at the Groddeck clinic with discussions on psychoanalysis and other subjects.

101. Groddeck read a paper to the Hamburg congress (September 1925) on 'The It and Psychoanalysis' ('Das Es und die Psychoanalyse'). *Die Arche*, I 10 (20.9.1925) Reprinted in *Psychoanalytische Schriften zur Psychosomatik*.

102. Lecture series 'Das Es' (The It) Lessing Hochschule, Berlin, Autumn 1926. *Die Arche*, II, 1926, 15, 16, 17, 18. See Chapter 9 below, p. 222.

103. Lou Andreas-Salomé (1861–1937), writer, friend of Nietzsche and Rilke, came into contact with the Vienna Psychoanalytic Society and with Freud in 1911.

104. Groddeck's letter to the publisher is not in the posthumous papers.

105. Albert Josef Storfer (1888–1944), director of the Internationaler Psychoanalytischer Verlag in Vienna, 1921–1932.

106. Thomas Weltlein, hero of the novel, *The Seeker of Souls*.

107. Patrick Troll. The letters in *The Book of the It* were signed Patrick Troll.

108. International psychoanalytic congress, September 1927, in Innsbruck.

109. Dr. Felix Deutsch (1884–1964), psychoanalyst.

110. Smith Ely Jelliffe (1866–1945), psychoanalyst.

111. 'Wer immer strebend sich bemüht, den können wir erlösen' (*Faust* II, V). See Groddeck, 'Ein Faustzitat'. Reprinted in *Psychoanalytische Schriften zur Literatur und Kunst*.

112. *Der Mensch als Symbol*. Vienna, Internationaler Psychoanalytischer Verlag, 1933.

113. See, for example, Groddeck's article 'Vision, the World of the Eye, and Seeing without the Eye', Chapter 5 below, pp. 172–96. Two other such articles are 'Vom Menschenbauch und dessen Seele' (The body's middleman) and 'Vom Mund und dessen Seele' (The mouth and its soul), both included in *Psychoanalytische Schriften zur Psychosomatik*.

114. See *Psychoanalytische Bewegung*, IV, 2 (March/April 1932).

115. Martin Freud (1889–1967).

116. Dürer's 'Melancholia'. See *Psychoanalytische Schriften zur Literatur und Kunst*.

117. 'Von der psychischen Bedingtheit der Krebserkrankung' (The psychical conditioning of cancer), fragment 1934. Included in *Psychoanalytische Schriften zur Psychosomatik*.

Psychic Conditioning and the Psychoanalytic Treatment of Organic Disorders*

On June 5, between noon and 1 o'clock, I suddenly felt very tired during work. Yet after a while the tiredness disappeared again. In the afternoon between 4 and 5 o'clock, I felt ill and had difficulty in swallowing. The back of the palate, the velum, and the uvula were very red. That night I had a vivid dream, a rare experience for me. On June 6, a very busy day, the pain increased, the red areas expanded, and both tonsils were considerably swollen.

June 7 was a holiday. In the morning I began to analyse my dream and the symptom of swallowing difficulties and came to the conclusion that my unconscious, my It, refused to swallow a piece of knowledge it found unpleasant. It was the knowledge that certain ideas concerning the interaction between an individual's unconscious and his life were not my own, as I had been telling myself for years, but Sigmund Freud's. My rational mind had drawn these conclusions already, as can be seen from my correspondence with Freud. Yet in the course of analysis it became apparent that deeper layers of my being resisted my conscious thoughts.

On June 5, between noon and 1 o'clock, during the hour when I felt temporarily tired, I had a short meeting with a lady called Dora. The word Dora, a name that appears in Freud's fragment of an analysis of a case of hysteria, was the instrument by which my conscious recognition of Freud's priority tried to penetrate into my inner unconscious mind. The resistance my unconscious put up took the form of tiredness which effectively counteracted the name Dora and all its associations. In the afternoon between 4 and 5 o'clock there was another attempt at

* 'Psychische Bedingtheit und psychoanalytische Behandlung organischer Leiden', Leipzig, 1917. Reprinted in *Psychoanalytische Schriften zur Psychosomatik*, Wiesbaden, 1970.

getting the unconscious to recognise the priorities. This happened in connection with a conversation on mortgages and
debts. In the analysis mortages led to hysteria, debts to guilt
and thieves. The unconscious resisted this second and more violent attack by closing off my inner self by means of a painful inflammation. It took hold of the word *Gauner* (thieves) and chose
the defensive line of the *Gaumen* (palate), continued to fortify its
position by implicating the uvula and the tonsils, and finally
expressed its anger in dreams.

The result of my analysis of dreams and symptoms on the
morning of the 7th which I have given in its conclusions only
was the disappearance, in the course of 30 minutes spent in
analysis, of the entire tonsil swelling and of most of the redness
on the palate. To my astonishment, however, some time later
the inflammation started up again in a virulent form until in the
afternoon the illness had reached the same intensity. This time
I conducted the analysis while my assistant watched the symptoms of the inflammation. Before starting, the tonsils, the
palate etc. were carefully examined and felt. I then followed this
up with an experiment in association. Now the inflammation
receded quickly and after a quarter of an hour of analysis had
disappeared, apart from a sharp and thin red line across the
palate. This went away, too, in the course of the evening.

What had I learned from this analysis? I discovered that the
struggle of the conscious against the unconscious mind was not
centred on the word Dora-Freud, but on the word Char-
lotte-*Scharlach* (scarlet fever). Just before I talked to Dora I had
been shown a child with an exanthema which on first sight I
took to be a scarlatina exanthema. There was evidence that the
sudden tiredness had not started when I was with Dora, as I
originally assumed, but in the interval between Lotte and her.

Scarlet fever has played a fateful role both in my own life and
in that of a number of my nearest relatives, and I am haunted by
the fear that I might perish one day from the after-effects which
I never quite overcame. The resistance of my unconscious was
mainly directed against the death association Char-
lotte-*Scharlach* which was closely connected with the vanity and
inability complex Dora-Freud. The focal point was the word
Schuld (debt and guilt) which occurred frequently in the conversation on mortgages and bills of exchange on the afternoon of

June 5. At the time when I had scarlet fever. I suffered from a strong sense of guilt which was due mainly to the sexual experiences of my adolescence, clearly revealed by the analysis. Apparently I still retain some remnants of this, although rationally I have long since come to understand that my experiences were harmless. In a way that is very familiar to me and may be compared to chemical processes in statu nascendi, these remnants which were surfacing got mixed up with the psychic poisons from the Dora-Freud complex and thus caused the outbreak and the curious remission of the illness after the first attempt at analytical treatment.

To the simple description of this illness I would like to add some remarks which might be of general relevance. At first sight the description does not establish with certainty that the illness was psychologically conditioned or that it was cured by means of psychoanalysis. It goes without saying that the inflammation must have involved other features too. In no case is it possible to establish the complete chain of causes. We can only name the most obvious links. In talking of the cause of an illness or of casual treatment we have to bear in mind that we consciously switch off this better, purely human knowledge in favour of clinical treatment. I should also stress the objection that my interpretation is based on a play with words or ideas, while in reality other conditions which are generally recognised in science obtained. To be specific, I have not so far mentioned the fact that I had a patient at the time who complained of a sore throat, among other things. It is possible that I caught the infection from her. But it is not probable. I have known the woman a long time; every few weeks she suffers from swallowing difficulties which for her have become a weapon against the difficulties of life. These attacks are rarely accompanied by the symptoms of inflammation; and on this occasion anyway I could detect no redness or swelling.

If it is nevertheless assumed that my illness was caused by transference, then the problem has merely been shifted and enlarged. The question then is whether the individual can become infectionable through the interaction of his conscious and unconscious mind, a question which I would answer in the affirmative.

In as much as a personal It which lives man continuously

transforms the secretion of digestive juices, the blood distribution, the activity of the heart, in short, the entire organic
life of the personality under the influence of certain sensations,
impressions, or unconscious associations, in as much as this It
protects itself against the menace of chemical and mechanical
and bacterial attacks by its incalculable abundance, it may set
up conditions in which the pathogenic agent becomes effective,
if it considers that an illness will serve a purpose.

The assumption that only the hysterical personality is capable of producing an illness for certain purposes I consider to be
a fundamental and dangerous error. Every person has this ability and everybody makes extensive use of it. The hysterical
and, to a lesser extent, the neurotic personality forces the
observer more often than other patients to assume that the illness in question is deliberate. And he himself harbours this remarkable idea, which is not at all easily explained. But in
penetrating deeper into the complex forms of mental life one
will soon discover that apparently conscious intentions are
merely offshoots of unconscious forces, and that the symptoms
of illness which the hysterical personality produces do not at all
correspond to his original intentions but, as in every other
person, to deeply hidden decisions of his unknown It. It could,
in fact, be said that it is often easier to uncover fragments of
such unconscious processes in persons who are not neurotic
than in hysterical individuals whose mask is very difficult to lift
because they are ashamed and full of suspicions against themselves.

Turning now to the question of one's capacity to fall ill, i.e.
the individual, local and temporal disposition in the given case
of the throat infection, we learn something first about the temporal disposition.

Special circumstances triggered off two complexes on one
particular day – Dora-Freud and Charlotte-*Scharlach*, both containing fears of impotence. Throughout life every human being
is accompanied by this fear of impotence. As long as the idea of
inferiority is linked with hope, it supports life and releases
mental and physical forces in the form of ambition and a desire
to learn and to compensate for talents that are lacking. If it is
accompanied by doubt or even despair, then all vitality is
sapped. The individual's It tenses up, makes him feel exhausted

and tired, and partly as an excuse for his failure, partly in order to gather new strength, it makes him ill. To bring out this point I need only mention the well-known transference mechanisms of inferiority complexes from the mind to the body which occur in daily life, physiologically and pathologically, such as the failure of muscle power or the digestive troubles accompanying depressions or the changes in breathing or circulation, or a reduction of sexual potency. In my own case the idea of being inferior to Freud was repressed for at least eight years with great effort, but the decision was looming up just at the time of my throat infection. The ghost of scarlet fever with its implications of the impotence of death or infirmity has been with me for more than three decades; it was and still is pushed back into deeper layers of consciousness but it caused all the more damage when it was aroused by the sight of a scarlatina-like exanthema.

These suggestions have certainly not explained the inner connection between the unconscious activity of my Ego and the temporal disposition, yet they may have described them sufficiently.

As an effective temporal factor I picked out from the matter constituting the It the idea of impotence, mainly in order to emphasise its universality and its significance in all processes of life. In dealing with the individual disposition I want to draw attention to a peculiarity of the human unconscious, of the It, which might be called the caution of the unconscious; I am almost tempted to use the expression the understanding of the It since its manifestations are so similar to those of conscious reasoning, except that they are far superior to the latter. For the unconscious selects from among the wealth of phenomena, opens itself up to what it wants to let in, and shuts itself off from those sensations and their consequences which it considers damaging. It may suffice to draw attention to the reflective activity of the lids, the conjunctiva, and the iris. Less often noticed, yet certainly not less remarkable, is the fact that countless times in the course of a day the It – in order to avoid visual impressions – turns the head, the eyes, the body away from the object, or that it diminishes the intensity of perception temporarily or permanently, or even that it immediately represses perceived impressions into deep or superficial layers of the unconscious. Only a very small fraction of our visual input reaches our consciousness. Nor should it be otherwise, else there would be great confusion.

Experiments which have so far had to be rather cursory but which make up in quantity what they lack in quality have convinced me that the unconscious rejects those impressions, among others, which recall uncomfortable memories and would thus stir up conflicts that are not completely solved. The It's sensitivity varies from person to person, a fact which has not proved explicable so far even though it is reasonable to assume that some kind of shock, usually at an early age, often prenatal and perhaps even before conception, must be responsible for this. To put the matter in another way, it is as if at some time or other a foreign body had got into the unconscious and caused infections all around it. As a consequence it is painful not only when the splinter is touched but in the surrounding area too. Likewise an initially minor complex may expand gradually and over-sensitise one or more of the sensory organs. It is certainly easy to see that a human being does not perceive or misconceives objects which are unbearable for its It, even when they are pushed in front of his nose. If the early-acquired sensitivity of an eye is too great, the It protects itself most simply by short-sightedness, in certain circumstances even by blindness. If, usually by means of psychoanalysis, there is a successful attempt at diminishing this unbearable sensitivity, mild short-sightedness can be observed to recede. It is significant in terms of this disposition to being cured that short-sighted people occasionally perceive certain objects clearly which they should not be able to see considering their degree of short-sightedness. The It's dealings with the problem of age, of imminent death, are particularly curious. It makes the eyes long-sighted, puts everything, even death, symbolically into the distance, prolongs life as it shortens the step of the old and makes their way longer with the same object of creating an illusion, reduces, moreover, the ability to sleep in order to extend the duration of life.

Just as the sensory organs are guided by the It – and this applies to hearing, to the sense of smell and above all to touch as well as to sight – so is every expression of life. It makes a person's walk steady or unsteady, makes him place his feet outwards at an angle so that he can move easily in two directions, or forwards for attack, or inwards in order not to get caught in the traps set by life. This sensitive It sends out constant warnings within the confines of daily life, and when somebody's temper, passions, fears get dangerously out of hand it weakens his foot at the ankles, makes him trip, puts brakes on to curb his haste in the form of corns, bunions, blisters; glues him – in the case of the high-flying dreamer – to the ground as a spastic and throws him atactically into the air, renders painful the protuberant, groping toes, deposits mineral salts in his joints and finally strikes him down with gout, which temporarily or permanently immobilises him.

All this is not necessarily so – life is too varied, its vital forces and their interactions are locked away in mysterious depths which no human mind can fathom; it is not necessarily so but it can be and is not infrequently like this. Every now and then we manage to catch a glimpse of man's nature and are puzzled by that thing which we call disposition, constitution. Occasionally the unconscious obliges and answers with an improvement or a cure when its inner burdens and poisons are brought to consciousness by investigation and guesswork and are rendered harmless.

This unconscious, into whose territory we are only now beginning to penetrate, again and again creates human beings with eyes, ears, legs, hands, and necks from semen and ovum; why should it be difficult or even impossible for it to shape the character of its creation in all its mental and its physical aspects? If it shapes the body, shouldn't it be able to endow it with certain dispositions for certain reasons or make these disappear again as it makes breasts grow and wither, or hair or skin? In fact, it does create these dispositions, and will make a change to the heart perhaps or the lungs. And if we listen to its voice instead of switching ourselves off through the prejudice that we are fond of calling knowledge, then we may find out quite a few secrets.

This unconscious, this It, does not always and not often enough consider health the greatest good. The ancients thought of the poet as blind; and it makes sense that his eyes have to look inwards. Hephaistos had a limp, Wayland the smith was unable to move. The It ties a person down, if necessary, it saves him by illness from dangers of a more serious nature than danger of life can ever be, it forces him to certain activities by certain disabilities, to rest through heart disease or tuberculosis.

The question, to what end?, has been neglected for too long in our medical thinking. In spite of the bad reputation which teleology enjoys now one should try and investigate for once to what end a person contracts a lung or heart disease, why the It makes him disappear or prohibits him the use of stairs, for what reason it blocks his anus and makes him unable to excrete or causes food and drink to race through his intestines so that thousands of substances which seem harmless to reason yet dangerous to the unconscious are eliminated quickly. In certain circumstances the It wants a man to stay lean, weak, or fat. Hunger and thirst, lack of appetite and inner secretions are used by the It for certain purposes which can often be discovered. The It influences fat formation, growth and character as if it were a rational being. It is the duty of the doctor to find out what meaning this uncomfortable obesity may have, with its attendant dangers of a stroke, heart trouble, or dropsy, what this leanness and tuberculosis may signify. The unconscious does not merely reveal itself in dreams, it reveals itself in every gesture, in the twitching of the forehead, the beating of the heart, yet also in the quiet warning of a uric-acid diathesis, a sensitive sympathicus, the phthisic behaviour, and finally in the insistent voice of illness too.

Occasionally this language can be understood. There is a fat man; they say he eats too much or drinks excessively. Maybe he does, maybe he doesn't. When one searches his soul one may find that his belly is fat because as a child he was worried about the facts of life, because he longs to be pregnant and have a child, because symbolically he is constantly being impregnated, because almost any kind of food, an egg, a carrot, a bean, a cherry, milk, beer must once have given his unconscious the idea that a child would grow in him. Or the idea came from a picture or a book or religion or a kiss or from having his palate medicated, and now it is constantly half awake and one imaginary pregnancy follows another. But maybe there is also an inner emptiness which needs to be filled, perhaps an easily hurt sensitive It which needs a thick skin. Doesn't the person who is

116

always lean and weak act like a baby without knowing? He is longing for the mother's breast and loses weight because this is not given to him even though he sees breasts everywhere which are withheld from him. He demands sympathy or he punishes his parents from a very early age for having hurt him or he, his unconscious, considers soft fleshiness as too feminine, etc.

The observation of the It in its individual dispositions can be made from various points of view. I stressed one characteristic of the unconscious, caution, because this procedure of our deepest mental forces can easily be traced in my own life. In the ability to fall ill the sensitive It somehow creates secure positions for itself into which it can escape. The illness, be it acute or chronic, infectious or not, makes the individual rest, protects him from being hurt by the outside world or from well-known phenomena which are unbearable. My own psyche constantly uses such long-prepared places of refuge, and it has done so ever since a certain day in my childhood when it was deeply shocked.

An apparently harmless wound on the knee which, looking back, proves to be the cause of a permanent weakness and vulnerability of my left leg, the leg on the bad side, caused a change in my physical make-up which was accompanied by a change of character, from being forthcoming to being curiously reticent. I was thus given an obstacle to guard against hastiness, a compulsion to be cautious. In the course of my later life I developed sciatica and gout troubles with deformities of the joints which for decades, temporarily and apparently never without reason and purpose, made it impossible for me to go for long walks and sometimes even prevented me from walking at all. In recent years this condition has improved decisively – I may be allowed to say only by applying self-analysis – and not only has the pain gone, but my toes, which once pointed sideways, have now reverted to the normal straight position. And yet I can still discover a curious interaction between the physical pain of gout and the cautious hesitation which makes me avoid or reduce physical danger, and I always derive a special kind of enjoyment from this, such as one only gets from the ironic observation of one's self. Among other things I remember that a year ago I treated a patient whom I did not find sympathetic. When I was on my way to her I regularly felt pain in my left leg which disappeared at once when I reminded myself of the reasons for it, namely as a warning not to show my antipathy. I was moreover able in a few cases of polyarthritis and arthritis deformans to bring about a deterioration or an improvement of the condition experimentally by stirring up and solving repressed complexes.

At a later time, at the beginning of my twelfth year of age, I suffered from an acute illness with high temperatures which was called, in old parlance, a nervous fever; this was again connected in time and probably in origin with particularly important emotional events. I had to stay in bed for a long time and was reduced to a state of stupor, which totally prevented me from thinking, by headaches such as I had never experienced before. After that I developed a tendency to headaches which became unbearable particularly in the first years of my medical practice. They, too, have now disappeared and, more importantly, the bony hard swellings on my temples and on the ends of the muscles at the back of my head which had changed the shape of my head for decades have receded too.

Using headaches to stop thinking and instinct is one of the most common and well-known of the techniques employed by the unconscious. The migraine suffered by women during their periods is a means by which their unconscious silences the sexual drive that is highly active at that time but according to custom cannot be gratified. How curiously and thoroughly the It functions is evidenced by the back pains during the period which prohibit the forward movement of the pelvis required for sexual intercourse. There would be more systematic knowledge in the confused and obscure field of female complaints if the decision were made to find out in individual cases why these complaints come about. We would then discover that over and above individually conditioned cases it is the ominous influence of the morality of our time which forces women without exception to be hypocritical and to dissimulate. The female personality is taught not to feel sexual pleasure, and this has been so strictly enforced that the modern age assumes frigidity in women to be a natural endowment, while people in the past never had any doubt that women are more in need of sex than men. The problem of the falling birthrate does not need complicated investigations for its causes to be seen clearly since everybody can see daily how pregnant women are expected to be ashamed of their condition, that they hide it from view, that people, particularly children, giggle behind their backs, and that the neighbours' comments in the beer cellars are about 'breeding like rabbits'. To relieve the senseless torture inflicted by this hypocritical environment woman is helped by her unconscious. It gives her dizziness, fainting, heartburn, deformation of the body, unpleasant smell, white discharge, infection of the ovaries and the womb, unpredictable bleeding, and finally cancer; all this keeps temptation away and repels everything that might excite her desires. The menopause with its temporary increase in sexual desire in both male and female is particularly instructive in this connection, puberty perhaps even more so.

The emergence, during the teens, of unpleasant character traits, the reduction of intellectual achievement and concentration are not the only signs of resistance put up by the It to relieve the pressures that exist during this age of one's life when custom forbids desire while nature provides it at its most intense. The deformation of the body is apparent even without the usual paleness and spinal distortion, without consumption, and it is truly astonishing that nobody seems to understand the reason for this, particularly when comparison is made with the boyish and girlish personality of a more innocent age. The cold sweaty hands of the developing adolescent are not without reason, they are to ward off the tender touch of other hands; the chapped lips are clearly a kiss-repellent, and acne, so characteristic of puberty, keeps the courting admirer at arm's length. All these teenage phenomena combined with the senseless admonitions of parents, teachers, books are also a warning against the inescapable and harmless auto-eroticism and self-gratification.

Can all these processes be explained mechanically and chemically, in purely material terms? In material terms, of course, but not in purely material terms. Is it a shortcoming of our discipline that it has persisted in the materialist position which elsewhere has receded into the background again. Doctor and patient rival each other in their resistance to the idea that the body is dependent on the soul. The patient still considers it shameful if the doctor seeks out psychological reasons for his physical complaints. The body is so much more powerful and apparently almost nobler than the soul as well. If only somebody could do away with this narrow single-mindedness of research and thinking!

The success of psychoanalytic treatment speaks for the dependence of health and ill-health, of body and soul, on unconscious forces, and the legitimacy of its use in cases of physical illness forced itself on me against my own will. I did not come to psychoanalysis through treating nervous diseases like most of Freud's pupils but was forced to practise psychotherapy and psychoanalysis because of my physico-therapeutic activity with chronic physical complaints. The success of *post hoc ergo propter hoc* taught me that it is as justifiable to consider the body dependent on the soul and to act on this assumption as vice versa.

Post hoc ergo propter hoc; I have no hesitation in assuming that this notorious conclusion is verifiable – under certain circumstances, because I would not know how one could ever have arrived, or how it could ever be humanly possible to arrive, at a different conclusion than by equating post and propter. Indignation is not justified when it is directed against the equation per se, only when the equation is performed rashly. I have waited long enough before applying it to the interaction of soul and body, to the influence of the unconscious It. And even when I came out with it for the first time, in a book on the healthy and the sick personality* in 1912, I still considered it necessary to take a stand against psychoanalysis. I regret that I wrote and published sentences there which are wrong, and I am sorry that I only learnt very late, from his works, about Freud's doctrine when I had already been practising it unconsciously for a long time, a doctrine whose validity is only disputed by people who do not know it or do not understand how to apply it.

The fact that man blushes when he is ashamed, goes pale when he is alarmed, sheds tears when he is sad, breathes hard or with difficulty, that his heart beats faster or stops in passion, that the intestinal tracts move faster when he is anxious and that there is a sweat of fear is well enough known, apparently too well known for notice to be taken of it. Should it be so impossible that an organism's temperature balance, like its system of circulation and its growth, be governed by psycho-

* *Nasamecu. Der gesunde und kranke Mensch*, Leipzig, 1913.

logical influences and that fever could have psychological causes? Of course it could be so, because the unconscious does not make a distinction between body and soul; according to its own purposes it uses the body in some cases, the soul in others. I have ample proof of this from my practice, proof which I find convincing. Occasionally, the It does not even bother about creating a definite local disturbance when it produces a fever. Suddenly there is a high temperature, as sudden as the dizziness caused by the repression of an idea. I remember a patient who suffered from such inexplicable bouts of fever. He was treated by many doctors, including myself, unsuccessfully; one could not find any trace of a diagnostically useful symptom. Only years later, after I had become more familiar with the technique of analysis, did I discover by chance the characteristics of this fever. One thing was constant in its apparent irregularity, namely the fact that occasionally a bout started when the patient went to visit his mother or returned from a visit to her. It took a long time to progress from this discovery to the complete solution of the complex illness behind which the unconscious had hidden a passion, but eventually a successful cure was achieved.

Hysterical fever. – As far as I know nobody has ever diagnosed it as hysteria. But words are always available and I cannot prevent people from using the term hysteria. To counter the objection, however, I want to mention another case history which is remarkable for the fact that fever could be produced experimentally, so to speak, by uttering certain names or words. This illness, too, had been treated by many doctors. For two years we tried to find something and thought of tuberculosis as well as syphilis as explanations. The tuberculin reaction was negative, however, but at least the Wassermann was positive, and a blistering rash, ulcers on the penis, sore throats left little doubt as to what the diagnosis should be. And yet one doctor after the other dropped the original assumption of a syphilitic disease. The ever-changing patterns of the case did not seem to fit any category, and the symptoms did not respond to any therapy. They came and went as they pleased. Finally I tried psychoanalysis and the attempt was successful beyond my expectations, as far as the therapeutic results and the enrichment of my own experience were concerned. It was interesting in this context that the syphilitic symptoms could be produced at will by deliberately stirring up still un-analysed parts of the syphilitophobic unconscious.

The above-mentioned illness which occurred when I was twelve supplied my unconscious with another weapon – sleep. From that time until I was in my mid-thirties I slept 12 to 14 hours a day. I could sleep at any time and in any situation, apparently without dreaming or at least without remembering on waking what I had dreamt. During my time at boarding school I was often punished for this addiction to sleep; finally, since punishment proved of no avail, I was sent to a doctor. He interpreted my excessive sleeping correctly and gave the advice to let me be. In this way I avoided many things which might have destroyed my soul. Later, like every doctor, I met patients with a similar need for sleep. The sudden tiredness and the ability to go to sleep at once probably lead to fainting and spasmodic fits, hysterical or otherwise.

Two other strange characteristics appeared then which might be seen as protective measures taken by the sensitive It: periods of half-awake states of vegetating, and an ability to forget details or whole periods of my life. Generally this unconscious procedure of rendering uncomfortable impressions harmless should be considered a fortunate gift; it makes life easier, concentrates energy on special achievements and keeps us alert for a few hours. Yet it is possible that too much material is added to the original kernel of the complex; the It becomes more and more sensitive; the need to stop thinking and to forget is applied to more and more areas of life, and this prepares the ground for increasing imbecility of a senile or different kind.

In its desire to avoid disturbing impressions, the unconscious quite often tries to obstruct the proper functioning of certain systems in the organism, by a slowing down or an acceleration of the circulation, of breathing or of food intake in the widest sense of the word. This has the most varied consequences starting with mild degrees of constitutional weakness and going on to grave cachexias on a local or a general basis.

During my feverish illness I also developed a phenomenon, the significance of which I mentioned earlier on. My face was covered with a rather extensive impetigenous rash which was followed, after cure, by loss of head hair in the celsi-form area.

It seems to me significant that this same summer I received my first conscious explanation about the relations of the sexes. I was never troubled by adolescent acne. Yet I have constantly observed a phenomenon in myself, the occasional appearance of small eczema on the hairline of my head, on the eyebrows or lips, which goes away sooner or later. By and by I have had to convince myself that this constitutes an attempt at resistance on the part of my unconscious. These hardly noticeable skin complaints only occur when I begin to get irritated by somebody present. Every time I tried to make conscious the specific nature and object of my libido and the unconscious complex hidden in it I managed to get rid of the rash in 24 hours. Yet certain phenomena make me wary of using this kind of treatment on myself unless absolutely necessary since the usefulness of the unconscious measures adopted by the It is all too clear. In the course of my practice, however, I have gained experience of eczema on the hands, psoriasis, boils etc. which considerably enlarged my knowledge of the ways in which the It expresses itself and functions. The unconscious is particularly effective in the way it uses deformations of the nose, an organ whose connections with sexuality are more numerous than is generally assumed. Having observed a few times the influence of psychoanalysis on red noses or rhinoma – which, however, does not make itself felt from one day to the next – one can hardly fail to endorse the interpretation I have just given, that it is an attempt at repulsion.

Perhaps the most astonishing event of my medical practice was the treatment of a grave case of scleroderma which led to a surprising result. For a long time I intended to use this case history as an illustration of unconscious activities in the body organism, yet finally I decided to use my own case since it would not entail considerations of discretion.

There were events in my 17th year which were of decisive importance for the whole of my later development and were closely connected with the story of my throat infection. I contracted a disguised form of scarlet fever. In retrospect I assume that in this event, too, the protective forces of my unconscious became active in order to deal with newly aroused sexual complexes which were in need of repression. In the course of the illness I suffered a grave diphtherial throat infection with abscess formation and a kidney infection that became chronic. Perhaps one could investigate the reason why the unconscious used a kidney infection to function as the policeman in my life. Yet here I have to fall back on speculation again and am unable to find cogent reasons. I can merely add that some of my earliest memories are of rainwater tubs, gutters and wells, and that I had a tendency to enuresis nocturna until puberty. Whatever that may signify, the lingering traces of scarlet fever and neph-ritis came into the open again combined with pneumonia – again in connection with sexual complexes – and led to a long drawn-out oedema. Oedema in the retina made my eyes weaker, and for a long time I was troubled by a tendency to nausea and vomiting. Temporary blindness and the wide-ranging restrictions on movement and work forced me to retreat completely into myself. I was barred from the quick route to public success which, as I understand now, would have been my undoing, considering my nature.

Rarely in my life have I met conditions which so strikingly proved the practicality of unconscious forces as this illness. It took about ten years before I had overcome the consequences of this caesura in my life, as far as I could rid myself of them at all. I shall not enter into any further discussion of what the It intends and achieves when it strikes a person down in the midst of an intensely productive period, leaves him dangling over the abyss for a long time, and gives him the spectral company of death and infirmity. The question of education by illness would lead us too far afield in the present context.

In mentioning the oedema I have jumped ahead in this account of my illnesses, and I shall now return to events which relate to an earlier phase of my life. They tell us something about the reasons why the unconscious chooses certain parts of the body as strategic points of its illness-producing activity, in other words, how a local disposition arises. Already during the scarlet fever the tendency of the unconscious to close off the en-trance to my inner life becomes evident. In general, the uncon-scious rarely uses throat infection at a mature age as a weapon of resistance, while in childhood and puberty the tonsils serve as the constantly active guards of the sensitive soul. In contrast to this the mucous membrane of the respiratory tract remains sensitive throughout the whole of life with many people; often the It finds it so useful as a control point that more or less chronic catarrhs develop. During my 20th year my unconscious fell back on this weapon which we find so frequently used by children, and it has continued to do so ever since.

At the time I was doing active service as a one-year volunteer. By nature, for reasons unknown to me, I do not respond well to compulsion and silent obedience, and that is why I still consider this period as a soldier a particularly hard time of my life. It was only bearable because I coughed away insufferable impressions, a kind of defence mechanism which my It never gave up and which is very common among human beings. Almost everybody coughs occasionally, and there is a wide range from the barely noticeable clearing of one's throat to the heavy attacks resembling fits of suffocating. It is well known that many people start the day by coughing. This way they cast out the impressions of their dreams and blow away the minor and major anxiety fantasies and embarrassments of the day which are associated with these. Whatever manages to penetrate in spite of this and appears poisonous to the It is dissolved and wrapped up in mucus, brought out and finally even spat on. The curious thing about this process is that the unconscious equates physical and psychological intruders and treats them the same. If one is at all attentive it is easy to discover in daily life that a single word which stirs up a poisonous psychological complex releases the same cough as the breathing-in of chlorine. There is no reason to be surprised about a reaction like this. Every child knows that a repulsive sight may cause vomiting as if it were a genuine case of poisoning. And since the sight or smell of delicious food or even the rattle of plates causes the saliva and stomach glands to secrete their juices, it is understandable that the mucous membrane of the respiratory tract can behave in a similar way.

The usefulness of the larynx entrance as a control station for psychological impressions was considerably increased later by my unconscious in that the nasal tracts acquired the ability to swell up when certain associations were activated. Even this seems not to have been enough for the unconscious, and in the past few years it has put the secretion of mucus into the service of these easily-recognisable purposes, and the comparison with former times is striking. Every now and then I have met people in my practice who have reacted even more intensely than I do to the evil smell of a word or a thought. Almost at once they start a cold in the nose which often disappears within half an hour. These remarks reveal plainly that I assume a psychological cause for hay fever and act on this assumption – not unsuccessfully. I also feel compelled to draw the conclusion that the disposition to any kind of bronchial illness and lung complaint can be created by the unconscious.

We cannot presume to understand the purposes and reasons of unconscious life. It is necessary to bear in mind that every observation is one-sided, and it is advisable occasionally to look deliberately at one side of a question only, as I did when I considered the purposiveness of action. Yet I want to stress the point that I am aware how this rigid stance distorts the perspective of all objects. Nevertheless I beg acceptance of the idea that the It considers the throat to be the entrance into the inner human being. This idea is fertile and practical even if it may be wrong or crude.

The complexity of the unconscious operations when a particular spot is chosen to be a local disposition and a guardian of human survival can be shown by another event in the chain of my illnesses. About 1904 the It built itself another barrier on my neck in the shape of a goiterous growth which originally kept to the left-hand side, the sin side of the thyroid, and later extended to the right-hand side, the relation side, as well. In both these cases there was a fibroid growth with a hard core surrounded by areas of loose tissue. Gradually the core and the loose new tissue got bigger and so did the neck triangles as the face became swollen. Within a few years the circumference of my neck increased from 39 to 45 centimetres. The consequences were breathing difficulties and restriction of movement and activity, which proves the meaning of the illness if one considers its aim. Other connexions are less obvious, yet they make more sense if the close interaction of thyroid and sexual function is remembered. In particular the almost normal thyroid enlargement that occurs during the adolescence of girls should be taken into account here. Freud proved in his work on the sexuality of children that we all believe in the intestinal pregnancy for a time and from this it follows naturally that impregnation occurs when the seed is swallowed. This idea disappears from the conscious mind later, yet it seems to remain in the unconscious. During puberty the problem of making and having children returns with more urgency, not only into consciousness but also into the unconscious, the repressed complexes of which are associated with the conscious thought processes and with all kinds of fantasies of spiritual and godlike impregnation and illegitimacy. The enlargement of the thyroid coincides in time and, as it appears to me, in origin with these curious processes which have so far been unexplored. On the one hand there is the wishful thinking of having a child in one's throat, on the other purposive preventive measures are taken by the It against oral fertilisation. This ambivalence will only astonish those people who have never studied psychoanalysis in depth. Those who know how to use it know that the It fulfils not only two, but various and inexplicable functions simultaneously. There are analogous processes at work when a grown-up develops an enlarged thyroid, and that these must have been very active in my case is proved by the result of my self-analysis, in the course of which the goiter disappeared almost completely, including the fibroid core.

The objection that a man cannot have the wish or fantasy of pregnancy is invalid. Apart from the fact that every human being is and has to be man and woman at the same time, which should not be forgotten when the question of unconscious and conscious fantasies regarding self-gratification and self-fertilisation comes up, apart from this fact theories of oral fertilisation are held at an age when a child has not yet grasped the impossibility of a male pregnancy. By means of these childhood ideas about conception the understanding of throat infections, particularly those of an early age, can be grasped in one detail of the poisoning complex. The interrelation of poisoning and pregnancy complexes recurs again and again.

The investigation of the local disposition is a source of enjoyment for the psychoanalyst as long as his chief pleasure lies in surprising discoveries and sudden results. Often the subjective, localised experience of an illness can be eliminated or greatly improved when the question of the symptom's purpose arises. The unconscious gives astonishingly precise answers, for example, that hoarseness makes us whisper when we communicate a secret, or that a pain in the arm warns us of a tendency to brutality or stealing, that bad breath helps us hide an intense emotion, blushing to disguise the face behind a veil etc. Many of the sudden cures which we attribute to the suggestive power and the personal influence of the doctor can in fact be traced back to the It's sudden decision that an individual is no longer in need of this or that protective measure. By looking at those forces of the organism which dispose us to contract illnesses I was led deeply into the problem of the unconscious. Has the problem been solved? No. It has not even been grasped, only hinted at. A conclusive statement about what the unconscious really is cannot be gleaned from my argument. The statement that an It, a God, dominates our body and our soul means as little as the idea that bodily and mental life are nothing but external changing forms and embodiments of an It. The saying that life consists in the interaction between body and soul is no more than another way of stating the problem, not an explanation. In the last resort one is again made to understand that all knowledge is fragmentary, that the 'X' of life cannot be fathomed, that no more can be said about the words body and soul than that they are words which cannot express the idea.

I have thus come to the point of admission that there is no psychological cause for physical illness. The unconscious is neither psyche nor physis. Personally I doubt whether the question can ever be put properly or that there will ever be an answer to it. This would mean that we could survey and judge the unconscious without conscious thought, the unconscious to which consciousness is either a partial or a complete adjunct.

The fact that the question is not answered and that it cannot even be posed is of little relevance to us doctors. Our profession is one of practical achievement. It does not matter that we should say how the patient is helped but that we should give him help. Our task is less that of thinking up valid theories than of finding working hypotheses that are of use in treatment. With the help of working hypotheses that have been proved false, astonishing discoveries have been made in all fields, in chemistry, physics, and particularly in medicine. So far practical medicine does not have any exact theories, but its history demonstrates that those doctors are most successful who have the courage to be singleminded without troubling themselves about the anathema of logic and who listen to one of the many voices with which the It talks.

Thus the question is not whether we can say with certainty: this or that unconscious idea has produced the illness, but whether we have a right to maintain that the illness disappears when this or that context has been revealed; in other words, if there is any prospect of affecting organic illnesses positively by using psychoanalysis.

Nobody has ever doubted that we can influence the It in its psychological and physical functions by material intervention of a chemical, physical, or surgical nature. The idea that by psychological intervention the matter of the It, or, if one may use the expression, the human body can be changed, that it can be brought from illness back to health or vice versa merely sounds strange, yet it has been known for a long time and as long as the world exists it will be put into action all the time and at every moment. Both procedures have ultimately the same result, they both have the same point of departure, namely the unconscious of the human being. The amputation of a member is not a healing process, the reaction of the unconscious to the amputation is rather to revitalise the wounded stump and the organism that is impaired by the specific illness and the operation. Whoever has had the idea that it is not the operation which helps the leg and consequently the patient to recover – an insight that seems to be easy and yet it is very difficult –, that our medical practices can never effect a direct cure but merely set some healing factors in motion that are completely unknown to us, that the aim of treatment is not to cure by means of our art as if by magic but to set free unconscious forces, will also understand that it might make sense under certain conditions to stimulate these healing factors of the It by using psychoanalysis.

One might picture the process of recovery as if it were a restructuring of the organism. In the unconscious the personal organism possesses all its labour force, and usually all its materials too, with which to set about this restructuring. If it does not go about the restructuring work out of its own free will as it does more or less successfully in most cases, then there must be some obstacle that paralyses the unconscious forces. Maybe there is a wall which has to be demolished from outside, or debris which has to be removed; every now and then some building materials are lacking, then the surgical operation, the physical or chemical treatment is necessary. Perhaps the It's labour force is lazy, has got too used to the familiar conditions and has become too comfortable, or it underestimates its own abilities and does not dare to do the work. Then suggestion, persuasion, orders are needed. Yet it is also possible that a strange prohibition, a prohibition issued by former masters or present tenants who are under contract inhibits the It which feels in honour bound, or that its characteristic gifts have been developed into wrong techniques by education. If this is the case then the best approach is to lift this apparent prohibition and the wrong techniques from the depths of a former or more recent past, and force the It to make a new decision. This is the psychoanalytic technique, an approach which has the advantage that it recognises the aspect in charge of the restructuring, namely the It, and negotiates with it as if it were the expert.

At times all these approaches are possible, at others only one of them is, occasionally they have to be changed. Yet it would be negligent, since Freud has shown us the way, to leave out one of them, namely the psychoanalytic one, because it was forgotten for a long time and has not yet become fashionable, or merely to use it in cases of neurosis because it is assumed that the body can only be treated physically – a statement the untruth of which is testified daily by every doctor, even against his will, by his actions.

In the comparison with restructuring I spoke of a prohibition which can inhibit the unconscious forces. This is a different way of expressing the concept of repression which plays an important part in psychoanalysis. In the practice of psychoanalysis and the treatment of repressions of this kind, one sooner or later has the surprising experience that during analysis certain phenomena appear and disappear with a regularity that cannot be accidental and is apparently connected with the analysed complexes. One can observe psychological and physical changes of objects which existed long before the individual's memory threshold sets in, i.e. before the fourth year of age. It is necessary therefore to assume repressions of a kind which cannot be brought back into the patient's consciousness. Finally, the significance of prenatal events has to be resorted to, and with success. Yet here we are very much in the dark and we would be in trouble if the beneficial influence of analysis was dependent on completeness. It has never been possible nor will it ever be possible to be exhaustive in any single analysis. Yet in reality the matter takes quite a different course. Treatment does not have to go as far as that, it cannot go as far as that and confront the Ego consciously with all the complexes of the past. What is necessary is to prod the It into activity.

This too can only be discussed metaphorically. The It possesses fermenting forces which might be latent in certain conditions. When they are awakened by intervention – be it physical or psychological – they start working independently and penetrate one or the other part of the unconscious according to the kind and force of the ferment activated and they put it into action. Yet the unconscious is timeless, it lives and lets live from the moment of conception. The same forces which are at work in the 20-year old are already at work from the beginning. Fermenting forces might have been switched off in the earliest stage of life and come into action later. That they come into action is only due in a small degree to our treatment; the real decision for health or illness is not made by us doctors, it is up to the It, the unconscious. I have no doubt that the It is able to influence deep layers which are not accessible to human consciousness by the fermentation activities of higher strata.

I am prepared for my views to be received with surprise – even among some psychoanalysts, though not all of them, not to mention physicians who are misinformed about Freud's doctrines as I myself used to be. I have tried to be one-sided and am therefore aware of the mistakes which have crept into the argument. My only intention was to state as clearly as possible that the restriction of psychoanalytic treatment to the area of neurosis does not correspond to our knowledge of the effect of analysis. This restriction is too narrow.

Psychoanalysis must not and shall not stop at organic illness. The whole extent of its range will reveal itself.

3

On the It*

This is a study of the It. The sentence 'I live' is replaced by the idea 'I am being lived by the It'.

I have no answer to the question of what the It is. Yet I can give some clues as to how the following statements should be read.

(1) The three-year old child talks of himself in the third person, stands away from himself, acts as if there is a different personality clothed in his skin who is being lived by something else. The concept and word I is learned rather late by the child, at a time when he is capable of thinking and acting reasonably. This fundamental fact should never be forgotten. It leads to the idea that the I is merely an outward appearance, an expression of the It.

(2) At the moment of birth the child starts to breathe. He acts with a purpose by adjusting to the new conditions of life and the new atmosphere, an action which, looked at without prejudice, seems to be as well reasoned as a man's escape from a burning house or the opening-up of an umbrella when it starts to rain. There are similarities between our reflex actions and conscious actions. This raises the question whether there is a difference between conscious and unconscious life, and the possibility has to be considered that everything which we call the conscious expression of a personality is really the disguised working of the unconscious, the It, one of whose measures is the compulsion towards self-deception.

(3) From the human semen and the human ovum a human being is made, not a dog or a bird; there exists an It which enforces the making of a human being and builds up the human body and the human soul. This It supplies its creature, the personality and ego of a human being, with nose, mouth, muscles,

* 'Über das Es', 1920. First printed in *Psychoanalytische Schriften zur Psychosomatik*.

bones, brains, makes these organisms functional, activates them even before birth and causes the developing human being to act purposefully before his brains are fully ready. The question is whether this It which can do so much may not be able to build churches, compose tragedies, or invent medicines, or even whether perhaps every human expression of life, be it physical or mental, of health or ill-health, thought, action, or vegetative function, can be traced back to the It – which would mean that body and soul and conscious life are an illusion, a self-deception.

Everyday life as well as philosophy and religion prove that every human being and the whole of mankind have from the earliest times been preoccupied with the idea and examination of the It. Sigmund Freud gave us a tool in psychoanalysis with which we can perceive and describe the mystery. If my attempt to make his ideas more familiar by means of this study does not succeed, let me remind the reader that it was not Freud who wrote this book, and that psychoanalysis must not be held responsible for the incoherent stammering of one individual.

I purposely use the expression stammering, not out of modesty, but because it is not possible to *talk* about the It, merely to stammer. One difficulty in making oneself understood lies in the fact that words like body, soul, I, personality have to be eliminated from these investigations, or at least would have to be used in a different sense from the normal, which is not possible. On closer inspection one finds that all concepts and names are inadequate and imprecise when applied to the It because they contain symbols, and as a result of the compulsion to associate they overlap with other conceptual areas and thus expand into more or less sharply defined complexes.

In order not to frighten off the reader with too much scientific matter I want to illustrate with an example what I call the compulsion to associate and to symbolise. The symbol of marriage is a ring, yet most people do not really know why the ring expresses the concept of marital union. To define the ring as a shackle or as eternal love without beginning or end allows us to draw conclusions as to the mood and experience of the person who makes this definition, yet it does not throw any light on the phenomenon why some unknown force chooses a ring of all things in order to symbolise the state of marriage. Yet if one assumes that the meaning of marriage is sexual fidelity, then it is easy to find the interpretation: the ring stands for the female sexual organ while the finger represents the male sexual organ. The ring must not be put onto any other finger except on that of the wedded husband; it is thus the vow never to receive another sexual organ in the wife's ring except for the husband's.

This equation of ring and female organ, finger and male organ is no arbitrary idea, but is enforced by man's It, and anybody can find daily proof of this if he observes people playing with the rings on their fingers. This kind of playing, consisting of moving the ring up and down, of turning and twisting it, happens under the influence of certain emotions which are easy to guess. Certain points of the conversation, the sight of images, people, objects or all kinds of sensual stimuli trigger off actions which reveal to us hidden emotional processes and are more than sufficient proof of the fact that man does not know what he is doing, that an unconscious forces him to reveal himself symbolically, that this symbolising activity is not due to deliberate thought processes but to the unknown activities of the It. For which human being would deliberately make certain movements in the presence of other people that reveal his sexual excitement, that publicly exhibit the secret, always hidden act of self-gratification? And yet even people who can interpret the symbolism continue to play with their rings; they have to play. Symbols are not invented, they are there; they are part of man's inalienable make-up, and it is even possible to say that all conscious thinking and acting is an inescapable consequence of unconscious symbolising and that man is lived by the symbol.

As inescapable for man as this symbolising is the compulsion to associate, which in reality is one and the same thing since association consists in the stringing together of symbols. The above-mentioned playing with the ring reveals the unconscious symbolism of ring and finger as female and male as an obvious image of sexual intercourse. If one traces, in an individual case, the dark course which leads from the half-conscious perception of an impression to the action of moving the ring up and down, it can be found that certain ideas flash through the mind which are repeated with other individuals in other cases. There are compulsive associations. The symbolic use of the ring as a sign-

post of marriage originated in unconscious compulsive associations. Deepseated connections between this primitive playing
with the ring and ancient religious ideas and customs as well as
important complexes of personal life emerge in the course of
such investigations and force us to follow the mysteriously
entangled paths of association by giving up the illusion of self-
imposed regularity. We will then soon recognise that the interpretation of the ring as shackle or as union without beginning or end originates in resentments or in romantic emotions
which use and have to use the store of symbols and associations
common to all mankind.

In drawing the reader's attention – after all these remarks –
to the fact that I personally claim the universal human right of
imprecise expression I believe I have given an idea of what I
consider the insuperable difficulties in talking about the It. The
only way of reaching an understanding seems to me to jump
straight into the centre of things.

The assumption that we are being lived by an It annihilates a
number of concepts with which we are accustomed to do our
thinking; thus I have already mentioned that the It knows
neither body nor soul since they are both manifestations of the
same unknown entity; that the Ego, individuality, becomes a
doubtful concept since the It can be traced right back to the
moment of fertilisation and even beyond this to the chain of
parents and ancestors. Thus the temporal limits are eliminated
since the beginning and the end are lost in obscurity. Life and
death, from being genuine opposites, are turned into arbitrary,
artificial concepts as nobody can know when the It makes death
or life. There is no spatial separateness of the It either; it is fused
with the environment; it is not possible to mark the point when
a piece of bread, a sip of water, a breath of air, an object of sight,
hearing, smell, taste becomes the property of the It. The differences of sex are blurred; male and female are one in the human
It from time immemorial and are mixed anew in the act of fertilisation. Age cannot be determined because the It contains
parts of every lived phase of life, counted not only from fertilisation but from ancestral times. Finally, and most importantly for the purpose of my argument, the consciousness of man
loses its central position and yields it up to the unconscious, yet
there is no definite dividing line between the two.

The route that I have taken leads clearly to the sentence: All things are one. Yet since this would not serve the purpose of this study, I have to assume temporarily an artificial It-individual with temporal and spatial limitations subject to life and death, a man's It. I reserve the right to remind the reader every now and then of the separation from the universe that is an artificial construction undertaken for certain purposes. On the other hand I shall make ample use of the fact that the individual is neither male nor female but both, that he is of no particular age but simultaneously one, ten, thirty years old, that everything which enters his consciousness depends on permission being given by the unconscious. Whoever doubts that my statements about sex, age, and mind are true should ask the next woman he comes across whether she has ever known a man who was wholly man; or the next man whether he ever found a creature that was wholly woman. He should look closely at a grown-up and will notice that he will suddenly be like a child in posture, movement, facial expression, action, and thought. He should listen to the voice of his partner in a conversation and will notice that in the middle of a sentence it goes up to a higher pitch like that of a child's. He should remember, too, that we allow only a small fraction of all that we see and hear into our consciousness; that we hardly ever know at a particular moment what our hands are doing and almost never whether our chest is expanded or not; that our thought, action, and talk is based on foundations which were laid in earliest infancy.

It follows from all this that it is useful to choose the child as the object of It investigation. Sex distinction does not yet play a role, the apparent differences of age are irrelevant, and as a rule there is no mention of a conscious life when the mindless child is referred to. The result of an investigation of the child's It may teach us that the saying 'unless you be as children, you will not enter into the kingdom of heaven' is legitimate, that the aim in life is to become a child again and that we have only one choice – that of becoming childlike or childish.

Looking closely at childhood one is struck first by the fact that the first three or four years contain the most important experiences and events of the human life: birth, the growth and development of the organism and its parts, the learning of vital functions like breathing, eating, seeing, thinking, walking, talking, getting to know one's environment and certain re-lationships with it etc. – These achievements which the child manages in such a short time are big; they are so big that every-thing else achieved in later life dwindles by comparison. In this light the patronising smile of the grown-up at the child's activi-ties seems to be like the foolish boasting of a brutal butcher's apprentice with regard to the frail body of a scientist or artist whose activity is of genuine value. The curious thing is that we have no memory of this time although it is then that the foun-dations of later life are laid, down to the smallest details and without the participation of the self-conscious Ego. These events remain active, right into the future, even without being remembered consciously, in fact without ever having been impressed on our consciousness. The conclusion is this, that apart from conscious memory there is a much more powerful unconscious memory and that memory is no yardstick for the importance of an event, and even that the human brain has the tendency to forget events more thoroughly the more deeply they have influenced its existence. Therefore we cannot merely rely on somebody's memories when we want to trace his develop-ment, and we would be well advised to bear in mind that in all probability we won't be told the things which are important. For the same reason accounts of relatives and friends should be treated with caution in evaluating events and influences, quite apart from the fact that for other reasons they are unreliable guides. The study of involuntary emotional expressions during the telling of events, the way in which this is done, the pauses in mid-sentence, the softness or loudness, high or low pitch of the voice, the facial expression and posture, offer many more clues. Even more important is the observation of results, manifesting themselves in the individual's psychological and physical ap-pearance which can be considered the final links in the chain of events. Of decisive importance however – and I say this in full awareness of the significance of this assertion which seems to contradict our inductive method of investigation – are the arti-ficially arrived-at final conclusions drawn from the universally valid premises on which a child's life rests. I am thinking above all of the fact that the infant cannot exist on his own but is de-pendent on the support of other people, particularly his mother.

In the mother's womb the child is made for nine months; it lives, grows, and develops in the womb. Never again in his life does the human being have relations as intimate as those that he entertains with his mother during pregnancy. The extent to which we harbour the wish to love and be loved is conditioned by this period of most intimate togetherness. The idea 'mother' dominates our emotional life with regard to our relations to other people; the longing for the kind of togetherness we once had continues and determines the choice of friends and work colleagues, makes us desire women, helps us choose a partner to marry and gives us a union with another person for a few seconds in the embrace. The It in us retains the memory of a state of perfect togetherness and urges and seeks a repetition, breaks up the unified love of the child into a thousand ever-changing parts which are being transferred to people, animals, plants, dead and living objects, ideas and creations, and now and then they produce larger emotional complexes.

We know little about human life before birth, yet we can draw some conclusions which deserve notice and are drawn from later phenomena. The state of rest in which the child lies dozing in his mother's womb seems to mean a lot to man's unconscious processes. Again and again this need for peace and quiet asserts itself, be it in the form of regular sleep which comes about under the influence of nocturnal darkness and is thus analogous to the dozing in the womb, be it in the indefinable but no less urgent need for security in some kind of enclosed space. There are needs which more often than not seem mere moods and may turn into torture because they cannot be gratified. The boy who puts his hot head into his mother's lap to make her stroke his hair and forehead, the man who rests exhausted in a woman's lap, the old man in his armchair by the fire – they all embody this human longing for rest which increases and decreases and yet gradually builds up in to the ultimate longing for the grave. That birth and grave are one, is an old truth which finds its expression in language and thought. All ages, traditions, and languages have known the concept of 'mother earth', and it is no accident that in German, we talk of a woman's lap and of the 'lap of earth'. We entrust the seed to the soil and to woman; both make it germinate and bear fruit. The ploughed field is the symbol of woman; from there a bridge of peace leads to the grave-yard where man is laid to rest in peace in the hope of some kind of reawakening.

The relationship between grave and mother, death and love, will be touched on often and will enable us occasionally to glimpse into the depths of the It. Yet now I have to investigate the mysterious connection between the ploughed field and the woman.

I have called the ploughed field a symbol of woman, but I do not mean this in the sense that a visionary poet found the analogy between woman and field in an obscure emotion, or even that a clever brain brought the two concepts together. To me this and similar kinds of symbol indicate that in the long period of his existence man has constantly been driven to possess woman; he has been forced by his It to open up the furrow of this living earth and sow his human seed into its depth, and this led inevitably to the moment when he had to turn into a peasant. For me there is no superficial, rationally derived similarity between a woman and a ploughed field, between sex and the tilling of a field, but the symbol itself existed and created agriculture as well as all the other kinds of culture on earth.

Certain inventions of man's show a surprising similarity to the structure of his body and were, in fact, made before the organ in question was properly understood in its functioning. This applies for instance to the camera and the human eye, or to steel construction and bone structure. To state this fact may be enough. Yet as soon as this is seen to be more than an accidental phenomenon and assumed to have an inner connection by which the human brain is made to project organic forms into creative works, then it has to be admitted, too, that in the same way the drives and functions of man are somehow turned into manifestations of life and that the development of culture follows the same forces as the development of the individual.

Analogous to the rest which the child has in his mother's womb is another existential condition of foetal life that is the basis of a chain of developments, namely the protection which the growing foetus enjoys in the womb. 'As safe as in his mother's womb' goes the saying that expresses this condition. From this fact of protecting and being protected developed man's habitat as with other animal species; all hypothesis which omit the fundamental fact of living inside mother while attempting to explain the structure of the house and the course of architectural history will lead to the wrong conclusions. It was not man's reason that looked for protection against weather and enemy and invented the house or developed its manifold forms. Architecture originated from the mother's womb, and the unconscious urges gave it tools, materials, and forms. The house plan of antiquity with its impluvium, vestibulum and atrium proves this; the urethra and the entrance to the vagina are symbolised in it even in the naming of its parts. And just as in woman's nature the warmth of love is the vital and guiding force, so the fire on the hearth is the focal point of the house which gathered around it all love and respect from time immemorial. A confirmation of the idea that blind eros is at work here are our dreams, the language of the unconscious, which use house and room as symbols for woman, and there its workings can be traced in detail.

Many of the phenomena which make up our daily life can be seen to emanate from this single conclusion. Everything that contains something or stores something, from cupboard and suitcase to parcel and letter or bag and clothing, was given to us by the dark forces of the mother, and daily and hourly these close relations can be observed in the small, mostly unnoticed expressions of thought and conversation, in physiological and pathological manifestations of life, as for instance in the fainting fits, the nausea, the headaches women experience when they pack suitcases, or in the difficulty of writing a letter, of wrapping up a parcel, of getting dressed etc. Once one's eyes have been opened to the workings of the unconscious one finds ever new proof of this way of looking at things.

Curious in this context is the use of the vault, which clearly symbolises the womb and gives the impression of particular firmness, of special protection. Let me mention the treasure chamber which enhances the value of the objects stored in its vaults, stored in the woman in the form of child or lover. The concept vault, however, leads on to the church and opens up the way to the understanding of how certain beliefs and ritual expressions of these beliefs developed from the It of Motherhood. The church receives children as the Lord's bride and holds the believers in her lap. This mystical connection of temporality and eternity, religion and eros, which exists in the Catholic faith in particular, is revealed to the eye in the building of a church which symbolises the union of the sexes. The maternal vaulting of the nave with its vestibule, the water font at the entrance, the altar where Christ's body is sacrificed, are followed by the steep rise of the tower which was always a male symbol, and inside hangs the bell duplicating the symbolism since bell-tower means woman and clapper man. On top of the tower the gleam of the golden cock which represents in all languages the male who turns towards the tempting and coquettish woman. This architectural game is further reinforced by the dome, the sanctuary's breast and pregnant body. The temple of antiquity already demonstrated these erotic associations since it cannot be a mistake to see the pillar, its dominating formal element, as a phallic symbol with or without the detour via the tree stump. Yet the force of the symbol is particularly conspicuous in the structure of the Jewish temple; its vestibule is often separated from the sanctuary by a curtain which opens up for the high priest.

The truth is that what we are accustomed to call the achievement of human thought and human reason is in reality a product of the unconscious, of the It, whose activities are revealed to us in the symbol and are perhaps productive through the symbol. It is as well to remember that the symbol is active in all human beings, even in those who cannot recognise it. Everybody is subject to the symbol, is born with it; his hands are guided by it at work, and his legs when he walks and his tongue when he talks, yet few people are conscious of this dependence and nobody, no matter how theoretically convinced he may be of the complete purposefulness of life, is able really to apply this determinism in his daily life. The idea of man's free will is a condition of life which is forced on him by the It and which he cannot really escape.

The protective relationship between mother and child directs the organisation of private and public life. To make this clearer I want to point out that the state of being protected is the first experience felt by the incipient human being, that this experience lasts for nine months and is later, during childhood, supplemented in different ways, and that in the course of these nine months all the organs are being formed with which human life is lived. Since all the essential features of man, every cell and every organ, every primitive emotion and every action, are from the first given the security of somebody else's support and help, the need to be protected and supported becomes an inseparable part of every human being. Man cannot but lean on other men, on objects, on God, ideas, look out for the other and others, escape solitariness and separateness. From this love of other human beings came the family in whose lap the individual lives; from it grew man's capacity for building and furthering society. And its driving force imposes on us a godhead of some form, which is a necessity even for the atheist, and makes everything work out for the best and is responsible for past, present and future.

In contrast to this desire for the other there is the love of solitude which is a necessity of the soul and originates in the same conditions of pregnancy. Just as the experience of loneliness can at times be frightening, so man tires of intimacy with his dearest companion and retreats into himself in order to forget everything else. The experience of separateness in the womb teaches man to retreat from the world into his deepest feelings, thoughts and creative activities, to become a world in himself and to find everything in himself, to be creator and creation at the same time. Everything we admire in an individual's achievement originates in profound solitude, love of self and intercourse with one's self. From the interaction of these two contradictory tendencies, which hinder, mix with, accelerate, slow down and further each other and drive the individual to reveal himself and to retreat into himself, comes life that grows away from the mother's womb and strives in unconscious longing to get back to the mother's womb again.

In the stillness of foetal life we have an experience – that of rhythm – which is no less important for the formation of mankind than the features mentioned so far. For many months the child is exposed at regular intervals to the beat of a heart; one is tempted to call this the one and only, certainly one of the most powerful sensory impressions of this period. We do not know whether and how far the child in the womb is capable of perceiving auditory stimuli, and we shall probably not know for a while. Yet the constantly alternating shaking of the whole organism which is brought about by the heart does not cease to influence our development because we think later on that we cannot perceive it any more. A fallacy, by the way, which is refuted by every silent night and every excitement that makes us sense our heart beat. Rhythm dominates not merely music and poetry, speech, and movement; even thought follows certain rhythmic laws; a sense of rhythm is a precondition of creativity as well as of the perception and recognition of certain phenomena in nature. It is the indispensable precondition of human development. I do not believe that the heart beat is the only or the most refined means used by the It to steep human consciousness and the unconscious in the sensation of rhythm; yet to make this connection is a reasonable assumption. After birth the regular rhythm of breathing is perhaps just as important. In this context I want to point out the significance of the child's floating in the amnion fluid. The result of this curious contraption by the It which serves to reinforce the protective mechanisms since it enables the foetus to avoid external shocks, is a gentle rhythmic rocking when the mother moves, particularly when she walks. This early habituation to a rocking movement plays a part not only when the mother rocks her baby to sleep in her arms or in the cradle but also in eroticism; in fact, it apparently has a dominating influence there since the sexual act has to be seen as a rocking and swinging movement and in a certain sense as a longing and striving to get back into the womb. The erotic significance of a swinging movement is easily seen in every child's face; it is also known in the unconscious of the artist, as testified, particularly, by rococo imagery. Another factor apart from the swinging and rocking is apparently the sensation of flying through the air; at least in gliding sexual pleasure leading to ejaculation is a frequent occurrence. I also believe that man's ancient longing for the ability to fly is largely due to the rocking movement in the womb. Yet it should not be forgotten that after birth the baby experiences daily journeys through the air from the bed or from the floor on to the mother's arm and that it is of the utmost pleasure to be whirled about by the father or even thrown up into the air. Here, again, one can see the significance of the dream in which flying symbolises the sexual act. The fact that Cupid has wings confirms this erotic connection. The strange fact that the angel of Christian faith is given wings in iconographic representation, too, further reinforces the curious connection between religion and eroticism

143

which finds its explanation in the powerful and often repeated impressions of childhood. The importance of the rhythmic structuring of human life, which is based in essential points on habits and their rhythmical consequences, can be demonstrated by a number of physiological and pathological phenomena of which I want to mention only the feeling of discomfort when our usual routine is disturbed due to unforeseen circumstances, particularly at bedtime or when seasick.

Closely connected with the time in the womb is the enjoyment of warmth in both a literal and a figurative sense. The need to dress warmly and to heat our living rooms, the enjoyment of a warm bath, of a warm handshake, or of the warm feelings of dear friends, are due to this prolonged experience of the mother's womb temperature, which, as I must repeat again and again, is important because of its influence on growth. Significant in many ways, too, is the enjoyment of a warm bath which is nothing but a repetition of prenatal life, a return to the womb. The soothing, soporific effect of the bath can largely be explained by this, and many other events to which we attribute simple chemical or mechanical causes are strongly reinforced by unconscious processes. A proof of this mysterious identification of bath and womb are idiosyncratic aversions to warm baths which can always be traced more or less easily to grave conflicts with the mother. Accidents in the bath, too, can often be traced back to a mother conflict, yet it should be noted that the hot water heater is often used by the It to symbolise danger of pregnancy when desire is aroused, and the tap (shower) as an image of a man passing water.

The child's growth in the womb has curious consequences. For both mother and child the lack of space and increase in size gradually becomes unbearable. The wish to get out of the narrow container into which he is crammed is as great with the child – once he has learnt to enjoy movement and knows the pleasure of stretching arms and legs – as the mother's longing to get rid of the big belly and its burden and be able to live like other people again. The child's increase in weight and size automatically destroys the pleasure of close proximity and awakens the wish for separation. In my view birth happens only when the wish to separate turns for both parties into a decision. Birth is thus not a mechanical process, but a mutual agreement between two unconscious individualities that somehow play an active part in it. When this common activity does not exist, the child remains in the mother's womb and petrifies there. Cases of over-prolonged pregnancy can be explained by the fact that there is some reason why the child cannot appear. It is of course difficult, but not always impossible, to get to the bottom of the child's objections to being born. As for the mother, it is quite often possible to make conscious her unconscious processes. It emerges that fear is the most important factor, fear of the grave consequences of giving birth, of the possibility of the child's physical deformation, etc. Birth is often delayed when there are important reasons for wanting a son, and the birth of a girl might cause a quarrel or permanent rift between the parents. Complex emotions and obscure feelings of guilt seem to be involved here. For miscarriages and premature births one can easily trace an unconscious wish to abort or murder the child, and for this reason there is no justification in making a distinction between miscarriage and the abortion of a child. The apparent difference is due to the over-importance given to deliberate intention and to an underestimation of the It.

The womb gradually turns into a prison for the growing child. I think it is probable that incarceration, the chaining up of body and limbs, the locking up of children in dark rooms or cellars, derive from unconscious memories of prenatal life. One root of man's strongest drive, the urge to be free, certainly goes right back to this period. Man strives to get away from cramped space into the wide open, away from being tied down to conditions of unfettered movement. The identification of womb and prison which occurs frequently in dreams, for instance, represents the strange mixture of hatred and love that is characteristic of human beings. The strongest negative and positive effects are always directed against the mother, and the fear of being buried alive, like the fear of darkness at night and of hell, go back to prenatal conditions. Here, too, one can see that the fundamental direction of man's and mankind's life is already given in the womb.

The same applies to the two deepest and most powerful passions, love and hatred. It is hardly rewarding to talk about the mother's love which has been praised in thousands of different ways and which has become a strong weapon, one is almost tempted to say a danger, in the mouth of women. Even though the mother's dictum that she feeds the child with her blood is too presumptuous, used unconsciously, to gain her the gratitude and curtail the freedom of the child, the fact remains that the mother protects the child and makes it possible for him to exist and develop, and she can thus consider and ought with apparent justification to love the fruit of her body as her creation. I want to draw attention to a different source of mother love which is usually forgotten because it goes totally against the beautiful legend of the pain of pregnancy and the resulting maternal sacrifice; the appearance and mood and the astonishing health of pregnant women contradicts this view. Yet it is worth mentioning that the essence of woman is an unfilled emptiness, a hunger for content, and that the child represents such content and satisfies her. The growth of a creature in her body, however slowly it may happen, is a great, a supreme enjoyment for woman, the length of which makes up for all her suffering and produces a longing for repetition, and the stirring and moving of the new life in the womb momentarily produces sexual pleasure.

It is just as easy to understand that the child's love for the mother starts in the embryonic stage; everything I said above could be repeated here.

But in contrast to this there is the fact, which goes unnoticed, that nature fosters hatred between mother and child during this period too, and I am convinced that most of my readers consider the idea that a hatred of this kind exists and is even a necessity of nature as totally nonsensical. And yet this hatred is there, and it is of such intensity that one is almost tempted to consider its consequences just as important in the course of human life as those of a mutual love. I mentioned earlier on that the act of birth is made possible only because there is an increasing aversion. On the part of the child, where analytical investigations are difficult, there is the angry kick which any sensible mother distinguishes easily from the embryo's contented and joyful movements. The wish to take revenge for the long and uncomfortable imprisonment expresses itself with elementary force when the child performs the perineal rupture, which is often a tearing because of the hard push of skull or shoulder. In later life examples of the child's hostility towards his mother are so numerous that it is legitimate to draw such conclusions, particularly since I maintain that these deliberate acts of vengeance on the part of the child are attributable to the unconscious, the It, which operates beyond the realm of deliberate intention. I want to mention here that ordinary people are well aware of this apparently blasphemous conception of the mother-child relationship. The fourth commandment, 'honour thy father and thy mother', is the only one for the observance of which the legislator felt he had to offer a special reward, which is a sure sign that he considered it hardly observable. It is a strange irony of fate that the promise of the fourth commandment gradually assumes the nature of a curse. For since man takes it for granted that long life and prosperity are the precondition of his future, he cannot help but turn the rider of this commandment round to read, if you do not honour your parents you will fare badly in life and die young. Yet since the commandment cannot be kept, for nobody is capable of exclusively honouring his parents (we shall see later with what infinite cleverness nature prevents this honouring of parents, what kind of forced measures it employs and has to employ in order to separate the child from the mother), the promise has no other function but to arouse man's sense of guilt; thus it assumes a significance similar to the curse in the first commandment by the strong and jealous God who is seen in the image of the father and who punishes man's misdeeds into the third and fourth generation. Yet we shall see that anxiety and guilt, like contentment and pride of achievement, are used by the It as vital forces, too. This does not exclude the fact that in certain conditions the fourth commandment can be particularly harmful because it is at its most intense during the age of puberty when there are dangers all around. I object on principle to the argument that the Old Testament law is irrelevant for our time by referring to our educational customs. But the fourth commandment in particular has retained its influence and will continue to keep it as long as our family structure exists, because it expresses the basic idea of this structure and is inseparably linked with the parents' determination to remain masters over their children.

More pronounced even than the child's is the mother's growing aversion to the embryo in the course of pregnancy. It finds its strongest expression in miscarriage and premature birth, in processes which I referred to above as the consequences of unconscious intentions. The conflict between Ego and It, between consciousness and the unconscious, is particularly pronounced here. There are numerous attempts at aborting the child, yet often the mother's It defends itself so effectively that pregnancy continues undisturbed until a normal birth occurs, against the intention of the Ego and in spite of all efforts at a violent interruption such as riding, carrying heavy loads, falling, etc. The widely used custom of attempting abortion by taking a hot bath is almost comical. I have a wide experience in the field of hot baths during pregnancy since I have prescribed daily hot baths to every pregnant woman for thirty years. These further the healthy development of the child and make birth easier as a consequence of speeded-up circulation, which is not surprising. The It suggests an evil intention to the Ego which, when put into practice, keeps the child alive in total opposition to the conscious aim. There are a number of similar ruses employed by the It in order to make use of the Ego's evil intentions; they are often so astonishing that one cannot help – in Nietzsche's words – but take life's laughter seriously and be entertained by its tears.

One feature of pregnancy which is closely connected with the mother's aversion to having a child is vomiting. From a primitive psychological point of view nausea and vomiting can be seen as a desire on the part of the It to get rid of something inside it, something poisonous. The successful cures of the so-called unavoidable vomiting of pregnant women which I achieved by revealing psychological conflicts through analysis entitle me to the assertion that conception is often seen as a poisoning and is treated as such by the unconscious. Poisoning, by the way, is a well-known symbol of pregnancy in dreams. It can probably be explained mainly by the fact that a woman's beauty is destroyed by pregnancy and giving birth, the effects of which are thus equated with the effects of poisoning. In addition to this the minds of young girls are constantly being fed with horror stories about the dangers and horrible consequences of having babies, by experts and non-experts alike. This complex is further reinforced by the young girl's habitual fantasies about the feelings and the situation of the unmarried mother, a kind of mental masturbation practiced by every female, in my opinion, which reaches its climax in the fantasy of child murder; curiously, but explicably, it is associated with the idea of burning on the stake, an idea which is based on the secret concept that excess of passionate love is punished by death through fire for which the popular mind has found powerful expression in the image of hell. Curious as it may sound, this identification of hell fire and passionate love also underlies the wish which many people have of being cremated after death. It is partly a revival of the idea of purgatory, partly the unconscious wish to make punishment impossible for God by totally destroying the flesh in the fear of resurrection or, if this should not succeed, to persuade him to be less severe by this hint at a physical destruction by fire. Yet ultimately it expresses the instinct to enjoy the heat of passion even in death. A similarly contradictory view of the punishment of sins is contained in the concept of migration of souls which is now so fashionable among both women and men, but it is a sweet punishment to be transformed into an animal since this would allow the indulgence of all animal desires.

I know that my way of presenting things is not pleasing to the reader and might seem to confuse him utterly when he seriously tries to understand. Yet I cannot help the fact that human affairs cannot be tidied up like the content of a drawer; they are inextricably entangled. At the risk of causing even my most patient readers to give up reading this chapter in amusement or irritation, I shall mention certain implications here of nausea and vomiting in a person's life which will not reveal their true meaning until later. It is useful in my view to keep in mind the association pregnancy-poisoning-nausea-vomiting. There are mental pregnancies and poisonings too, and once this is admitted it soon becomes evident that these are very numerous, that they are constantly at work within us without regard to age or sex, and that the It's answer to them is the so-called stomach upset which is ultimately a symbol of pregnancy.

The well-known phenomenon of toothache at the beginning of pregnancy is another attempt by the mother's It at damaging the child. The teeth are the symbol of children, a fact the importance of which in human life cannot easily be over-emphasised; they grow in the cavity of the mouth, which is seen as the womb by the symbolising It and finds its expression in the parallelism between the lips and the labium of the vulva, the mouth and the orifice of the uterus, as well as in many popular customs and sayings. The association shared by every human being, no matter how superior he may feel to the superstitious beliefs of the uneducated, between the shape of the mouth and the shape of the female genitals, its size, narrowness, softness, fullness, is forced on us by the unconscious and is very meaningful in relation to the choice of the sexual object. Teeth symbolise small children; the language of dreams is a proof of this too. Birth appears in a double symbol, once when the new teeth are emerging and again when they fall out, and that also symbolises the death of the child. In terms of this, the It sees toothache as an illness of the child, a messenger of birth, and a menace to life. In other words, the It makes the tooth rot under certain conditions because it wants to get rid of one of its spiritual or real children. The tooth troubles of pregnant women are a representation of the wish, cast in the form of illness by the It, to remove quickly and thoroughly the hated state, to reject and kill the child. Possibly there is a connection between the decay of our masticatory apparatus and the more and more pronounced tendency towards a two-child system, but a further investigation of this idea is not possible until an answer has been found to the question of whether the progress of civilisation is responsible for tooth decay or not.

When the facts of embryonic life are searched for their affects, one reaches the remarkable conclusion, which contradicts our habitual thinking, that we are capable of experiencing love and hatred for one and the same person, that we like or dislike the same objects or people according to whether we look at them from the right or from the left and, furthermore, that our aversions and affections are as changeable as the weather. This discovery is important, because it throws a clear enough light on our concepts of eternal love and absolute fidelity to see them for what they really are, namely unconscious agreements for certain reasons to keep family and society alive. It is obvious that this coexistence of love and hatred produces conflicts which decisively determine an individual's character and actions as well as his health and illnesses. I beg the reader always to remember this characteristic of man's emotional life which can be grasped in the concept of parallelism, otherwise the whole argument cannot be understood.

From the parallelism of love and hatred which wrongly appear to be in opposition, and from the ensuing conflicts during pregnancy, the unconscious psychological conditions of birth are shaped. It clearly marks a stage in the process of the child's separation from the mother which will continue throughout life from this moment. The interaction of the two notions causes the child to emerge from the womb, gets him down from the mother's arms, and makes him stand on his own feet, chases him from the lap on which he is sitting into the room, from the room into the open and to school, makes him turn away from the mother to the father, to siblings, friends, teachers, to work and enjoyment, it produces moments when the hatred comes into the open, when the boy is ashamed of his mother in front of his schoolmates, the girl engages in open and hidden rebellion. Yet secretly in the unconscious mind the ties remain, and while the bond between mother and child is apparently completely broken by the establishment of a family of one's own, it is ultimately the mother, the image of the mother, the innermost experience of a prenatal age which drives the man to penetrate the woman, which moves him to love her who resembles the mother in some essential feature, essential to him, which makes him turn the mistress into the mother even though he knows that thereby she will lose her physical attraction, which makes the girl turn into wife and mother, and chases all human beings through their lives towards their one and only goal, the earth mother.

Man is the child of his childhood, and everything he lives is the long drawn-out fruitless attempt at growing up, at breaking away from his mother which ends with the child in him surviving and becoming more noticeable again the older he gets. His vitality decreases again, he loses his hair and his teeth, his movements and actions become childlike, the mind is freed of disguise and he lives for the moment. The meaning of personal life is to turn into a child again or rather to revive the never-lost child, and this remains after the Ego's long battle, lost before it begins, to become independent, to grow up, escape from the mother; nothing remains for the individual himself, but everything for the community of man and for the process we call the development, the progress, the history of mankind.

The mother, the love of the mother and the hatred of the mother, gives man everything, even his God. For God is in us, we are God, the It is God, an omnipotent It. The idea of the existence of God springs from the depth of the It; we are forced to believe in God because we are ourselves God. The idea of God is an imperative consequence of a kind of self-knowledge which nobody can escape. A person who calls himself an atheist or persuades others to call him that is merely trying to avoid a name because he wants to deny his childhood, because hatred and love of the mother are directly and incompatibly confronted in his mind. Because he wants to get away from the authority of his mother complex he covers up that part of the godhead with words so that he believes he cannot see it any more. This has made him partially blind, and the It uses him in his partial blindness for certain recognisable ends. The last few decades in particular, with their materialism which already seems strange to us, show us in their results, their technology, science, and art that the It with a smile makes its obstinate children, who turn their boyish fantasies of high aristocratic birth, of prince turned beggar child, which spring from their hatred of the mother image into a novel for grown-ups, do useful work. For every individual who passionately or calmly rejects God it can be proved with the help of psychoanalysis that he conducts a very personal battle against his mother which has nothing to do with a thirst for knowledge but is based on the feeling of omnipotence that is innate in every human being, of not being a mother's child but separate from her, independent, grown-up. I shall come back to the meaning of the last three words behind which the problem is hiding. First I shall try and show the way which leads to the recognition that the idea of God is a human necessity by dint of the foetal experience. I start from the assumption that the child in the womb feels and has to feel omnipotent not merely because it follows chronologically and thus understands more fully the It's activity from the development of the fertilised egg to the fully developed human being, but also because every moment gives it the feeling of its omnipotence from outside.

The needs of the new-born child are satisfied in some way which is almost totally unknown to us, yet they are being satisfied, and one can assume on the basis of this fact that the child's

It harbours wishes which it fulfils by its own efforts. In the small world where he lives, the child is his own absolute master. As in the fairy tale, the wish and its gratification are as one, without the wish having to be uttered at all. The certain result of this situation is the feeling of omnipotence which, modified in various ways by the events of individual life, squeezed in and almost made to disappear, accompanies man through his whole life and never leaves him. Yet the urge implanted in us, for whatever reasons, to overestimate consciousness and reason and to suppress the knowledge of how powerful the unconscious is into the depths of our vanity-motivated nature succeeds in making us misunderstand the omnipotence which in fact persists right until the end of our life, and attribute it to our Ego. Since the Ego has no power at all and since that becomes obvious again and again in the course of life – for everything that is conscious is deception, the foolishness of vanity – the belief in our omnipotence becomes more and more eroded over the years, a process we call the loss of illusions. Yet instead of making us look at ourselves and try and understand the It – a task which becomes the more difficult the more intelligent (in the ordinary sense of the word) somebody is, while the simple-minded and the mad solve it automatically – we project our omnipotence outwards and make a God for ourselves. Here we find the root of every religion and all religious feeling that will come into being wherever the It's love for the mother complex predominates, while the philosophies and pseudo-philosophies which grow from the same soil owe their shapes to the It's hatred of the mother. This can often be seen on first sight and in the detail of myths, articles of faith, and systems, and in the attempts at making literary use of the flashes of insight which are so numerous in legend and fairytale. I want to emphasise that the notions of God, miracles, spells, magic, telepathy, mechanics, power, centres of energy etc. are merely a consequence of the curious dichotomy between consciousness and the unconscious, between Ego vanity and It humility.

There is no doubt that omnipotence exists in the foetal phase since the foetus develops by its own efforts alone. In order to clarify the assertion that this omnipotence continues into later life too, I want to direct attention to the digestive processes. While the human individual in the womb cannot consciously supply itself with food, we assume in a curiously presumptuous manner that some time after his birth man starts to find his food himself by means of conscious thought. The falseness of this assumption reveals itself in the fact that the moment in time cannot be determined when such intentions of finding food and other necessities of life first manifest themselves. Neither is it permissible to equate this moment with the beginning of man's money-making activities, or with the first articulate request for bread. In principle there is no difference between the crying of the newborn baby and the advertisement for a job by a worker in the newspaper. The advertisement, in other words, is as much an expression of the It's power as is the baby's cry or the silent wish of the unborn foetus. We invent differences because we are not aware of the fact that the conscious intention is merely one form of expression used by the It, and that this relates to the unconscious forms of physiological attraction which we assume for the embryo's feeding processes in roughly the same way as the verbal order relates to the gesture. This will probably become clear if we look at the feeding of one human organ, the brain, rather than that of the whole organism. The brain chooses quite independently from among the substances circulating in the human body what it needs, just as an individual buys butter, bread, eggs in the shop because he needs them. And like the person who tells the grocer what he wants and shows his dissatisfaction when this or that article is of inferior quality or not available, the brain orders from its suppliers this or that substance and makes its needs known in an occasionally very emphatic manner. The only difference between the two processes is this, that the person assumes when he shops that he is acting by the force of reason, without attributing reason to the unconscious shopping done by the brain cells. In both cases, in reality, the acting is done by the omnipotent It; it only changes its tools like the gardener who sometimes uses the spade and sometimes the hoe.

I hope that by now the reader has an idea of what I meant by the statement that omnipotence continues until the end of life. That life destroys our belief in this omnipotence is one of its cruel jokes, a punishment for man's arrogance which, however, life itself has taught us.

Curiously, the crumbling of our sense of omnipotence runs

parallel with the apparent expansion of our conscious powers. While the child in the womb has no other instrument except unconscious wishes, the newborn baby learns to use his voice, then gestures, words, and finally actions, and with every new acquisition he loses some of his omnipotence and his sense of omnipotence. In its stead life makes him a rather ambivalent present which sometimes lifts him up and sometimes casts him down almost to annihilation as the It chooses: the feeling of responsibility which is closely connected with the feeling of guilt. We shall see later how this feeling of guilt will be used in the process of separation from the mother, and how on the other hand it feeds on this process and thus contributes to the curious curve which characterises the relations between parents and child and thus all phenomena of life.

This curve reaches its first apex in the hour of birth. The process of giving birth is surrounded by so many legends that it is difficult to look at it with a fresh eye. Otherwise a curious fact would be given more attention, namely the fact that the expression and the behaviour of the woman in labour does not at all correspond to the normal idea of her suffering. Apart from the labour pains the woman's spirits are usually high, her face is very red and her eyes are shining brightly, an appearance otherwise found at the moment of sexual excitement. The natural conclusion is that giving birth is not a horrible experience but somehow a climax of physical pleasure, and women who combine the very rare qualities of honesty and attentiveness will confirm the observation that labour pains are pleasure pains, and that the passage of the child's head through the vagina is more pleasurable than any other erotic sensation.

I can well understand that my view of labour pains as a kind of sexual excitement may be considered paradoxical, yet I have often been told that this is so. But the reader might be readier to re-examine the matter after considering that it would be much more conducive to human reproduction if nature invested the process of birth with the most powerful vital stimuli rather than put women off it by disagreeable pain. Nature is far too sceptical to rely in matters of such importance merely on the ethical advantages of the female sex, though I readily admit that it knows how to use these too. It is, however, in the nature of the vaginal walls to demand extension, and this is the more pleasurable the fatter the object which fills their emptiness. The objection that because the woman screams she must be suffering does not hold water. The woman in labour is in pain, but she does not suffer, a distinction of great significance for human life. The stories mothers tell about their sufferings are immaterial; they only confirm that they are also prone to the rather comical human characteristic of boasting about their pains and illnesses and are no different from the hen which tries to draw attention to its own importance by cackling. The unconscious tendency of deceiving the world is reinforced by the shock to the mother's It caused by the child's breaking away. This first experience shows her the menacing rift which opens up between her and her child, and it is understandable that she tries to bridge it by every means, even by lying and particularly by the lie 'I suffered and bled for you'. The exaggeration of the pains and dangers of birth has the same power-seeking roots as, for instance, the expression 'you are my flesh and blood' – which is not true – or 'I live only for my children' – which is even less true, for when did man live for somebody else but himself? He may perhaps die for another man, even though that too is still rather doubtful. But how should a human being, even a mother, live for another person, breathe for him, eat, drink, sleep, go to the toilet or use the pot for him? All this and more everybody does for himself and couldn't possibly do for anyone else. If we are honest we have to admit that everything we do we do for ourselves, only for ourselves, and it was not without reason that Christ described the highest of human aspirations as: love thy neighbour as thyself, and not more than thyself. A lot is gained by being honest once in one's life.

I beg not to be misunderstood, as if I were accusing mankind or even mothers. It is not my duty to accuse; I merely try to find out what things are like and I cannot overlook the existence of lies, that to lie is part of man's nature, that he has to lie just as he has two legs and two hands, that his lie has a meaning and a purpose. People who condemn lying out of hand and call it the greatest of vices I can only warn to be cautious, for psychoanalysis has taught us that those who eagerly condemn a vice usually possess a high degree of the vice themselves. In one of the apocryphal gospels we find Christ's answer to Pilate's question, What is truth? It runs like this: Truth is neither on earth nor in heaven, nor between earth and heaven. Whoever remembers this saying will be aware that truth is contingent, that what is false today will be true tomorrow and false again the day after tomorrow; he will not believe easily and least of all those who boast of being truthful, yet he will not condemn liars since he knows about the inescapable lie in himself.

To know oneself is a great happiness, perhaps the highest happiness man can ever achieve. That the mother tries to escape from the knowledge of her inner dishonesty makes her by nature and by experience a tragic figure before whom we all bow. However loudly she may talk about her child and her love for her child, she cannot drown the voice in herself which says: 'You are lying, only for short moments are you your child's mother.' Mother love is compounded with vanity which likes to call merit what is made in a moment of ecstasy, with hatred which again and again blames the child for the physical deformation and pain, with the pleasure of hurting which uses the child as a valve for all its irritability and enjoys the sight of suffering; it is a pleasure to watch the spreading pain in a child's face, and in order not to become aware of our own cruelty we call it harmless teasing or even education. Education is nothing but enjoying the sufferings of others or, in other words, if nature hadn't endowed us with the pleasure of hurting we would not have the strength or the stimulus to bring up a child. For this reason and in order not to be too much disturbed in our own comforts, and ultimately because we want to be convinced of our own greatness, we bring up and educate the little creatures who are incapable of resistance, and this is as it should be. Because nobody, not even the mother, would move a finger if it were a matter of the child's interests alone.

The act of giving birth itself shows up the mother's cruelty most sharply. For what could be more painful than to squeeze a human head through an opening that is too narrow. It only needs a look at the face of a new-born child, the observation of a child's behaviour during a long drawn-out birth and an awareness of the fact that man comes into life screaming to know that the real sufferer at birth is the child and not the mother.

4

The Compulsion to Use Symbols*

In this journal another writer[1] interpreted the myth of the Fall of Man with the help of symbols. The snake which seduced Eve and every woman who came after her is seen as the phallus; the gay tree which is a joy to eat from and lovely to look at means the same, while its fruit are the male testicles and penis and, when proffered by a woman, the breasts and vagina. The validity of this explanation is confirmed by what follows in the story of the human couple who feel ashamed about their nakedness as soon as they have eaten from the tree of knowledge. Only those people who suffer from a sexual guilt complex are ashamed of nakedness and can be ashamed of it.[2] The fall of man is really the sex act between man and woman, and the expression *Erkenntnis* (knowledge) has the meaning it often has in the Bible of knowing, mating, cohabiting with the woman.

Considering the facts of the matter, it would be silly to say that analysis arbitrarily superimposed the symbolism of snake, tree, and apple on the story. It was there already, and whoever has eyes to see can see it. Even more difficult is the assumption that there is an artistic intention when the story is continued. God utters a curse on snake, woman, and man which is curiously interlaced with symbols. 'Upon thy belly shalt thou go', he says to the snake, 'and dust shalt thou eat all the days of your life'; with every step a man takes the penis swings to and fro from the belly and its mouth is turned towards earth. Further, 'I will put enmity between thee and the woman, and between thy seed and her seed; it shall bruise thy head, and thou shalt bruise his heel.' This is the symbolism of the sexual struggle, the bruising of the head is the slackening of the penis after erection and ejaculation, and the bruising of the heel, which lives on in nursery tales as the stork bite, is the act of giv-

* 'Der Symbolisierungszwang', *Imago*, VIII, 1922. Reprinted in *Psychoanalytische Schriften zur Psychosomatik*.

ing birth: the curse against woman supplies the explanation for this; the field which Adam is to till in the sweat of his brow, that bears thorns and thistles; this field from which he has been taken away is the woman whose voice he obeyed.

A cluster of symbols like this can hardly be the result of an artistic plan. I believe I should say here that symbols are not arbitrarily imposed by the poet, or at least not always. Yet where do they come from, what are they, and, if they have not been thought up by man, how do they get into his work at all? An answer – if there is one at all – can only be found by investigating the use of symbols in literature. As an example I shall choose the fairytale of Snow White and shall try simply to enumerate the naked symbols in it.

A woman dies while giving birth to a daughter. The daughter is the symbol of the female genitals, and the description of Snow White's appearance fits this; the body is as white as snow, the organ itself is as red as blood, and the pubic hair is as black as ebony. White, moreover, emphasises the organ's untouchability. Birth is the birth of sexuality, the attainment of marriageable age, the blood in the snow is the first period, the cut in the finger is a hint that the period is seen from the child's perspective as castration. Marriageability causes a change in the affectionate relationship between mother and daughter, woman and sexual organ; since it is a punishment by castration the mother is transformed into the stepmother who is hostile towards Snow White, her sexual organ, and wants her to be killed, in her innocence and beauty for two reasons: out of a desire to be deflowered and out of shame because of this desire. Gazing into the mirror should probably be taken literally; to look at oneself in the mirror and to look at the sexual organs is a universal habit among girls. Yet looking at oneself in the mirror is also a symbol of masturbation which in its turn is the wish to have proper intercourse with the man. In order that she should be killed Snow White is sent to the wood – the pubic hair – with the hunter, who represents the man, while his knife is the phallus – the desire for the wedding night is there. Yet no intercourse takes place. The child remains untouched and instead the hunter kills a young boar which suggests a slackening of the penis. Snow White now lives in hiding behind the mountains – that could mean the posterior – with the dwarfs. The dwarf is a

159

well-known symbol of the limp penis. The number seven stands for head, trunk, limbs, and penis; the male is the sacred seven while the woman is the evil castrated seven.*

The passage in the story when the seventh dwarf has to sleep with the sixth because Snow White needs his bed and is thus eliminated, is another castration symbol. The stepmother now tries another attempt at murder; she strangles the desire of the sexual organ, suffocates it. The same dwarfs – the thought of the male – revive sexual excitement again. The poisoned comb is an act of masturbation; the comb represents the hand and the fingers. The last murder attempt is particularly characteristic. Snow White is poisoned by the apple – with which we are familiar from the Fall of Man as a symbol for the male – the stepmother eats the white part of the apple, i.e. she plays the part of the frigid woman during the sexual act, Snow White gets the red part, the genital is aroused by love play. Yet the hymen is not torn. The apple gets stuck in the throat, love play is restricted to the vestibule. The glass coffin is the danger which virginity runs during this play, the prince is the male, the stumbling servant who makes the decisive jerk is the penis. The phrase that the apple jumps out of the throat with its obvious inversion of out and in means the end of indulgence in love play in favour of the sexual act itself. The evil stepmother dies while dancing in burning slippers, i.e. the prudish, hypocritical, frigid woman is sexually stimulated, a burning desire is being fulfilled for her by her punishment.

After reading this accumulation of symbols surely nobody will continue to maintain that the fairytale author put the symbols together arbitrarily to make up the story. Only a force which is his own and yet not controlled by him could have done that. And this force is the unconscious. The unconscious expresses itself in symbols, sends them up to consciousness and gives the poet the material from which he builds his structures. He is not completely free while creating; he has to go the way the unconscious prescribes to him by sending up symbols. By way of the compulsion to associate, which is also a characteristic of the unconscious, the first symbol is joined by others

* Though the word *Hexe* (witch) does not derive from *sechs* (six), it is often related with six in analysis, and six is the seven without the one, the castrated man, the sixth commandment is a reinforcement. The equating of witch-woman-mother occurs frequently.

which determine the course of the story to a certain degree.

The idea that popular literature like legends and fairytales originates in mysterious creative forces is not strange, and to call these forces unconscious will not meet with too many objections. Yet the assumption that the poem is also largely determined by the unconscious, that the symbols are inside the poet and that they force him to create something very specific to which he ultimately adds nothing but the form, will not be accepted so easily, particularly when the poem is Goethe's 'Fischer'. '*Das Wasser rauscht, das Wasser schwoll . . .*' (the water rushed, the water gushed) – rushing water is the symbol of passing water, a strong and, one could say, a physically effective symbol which everybody can easily test by walking along a rushing stream; the urge to pass water will not be long in coming. *Der Angel* (the fishing rod – interestingly Goethe uses the masculine version of the word *Angel*) is immediately recognisable as a phallic symbol, and the fisherman's cool restfulness shows how far from excitement he is. Only the expression *lauschen* (to listen attentively) suggests that there is a longing for sexual desire. Now a wet woman emerges from the moving waters. The erotic symbol that is contained in the phrase '*feuchtes Weib*' (wet woman) has been grasped by popular humour. We know anyway that the woman is one of many symbols for the female organ. The wetness indicates the excitement which takes hold of the woman on seeing the rod and which forces the glands and mucous membrane to secrete. The phrase '*herauflocken in Todesglut*' (lure up in deathly burning) is based on the relationship between death and love, while the expression *Brut* (brood) is both a male and a female symbol. The relations of the sexes are the same as in the Fall of Man. At the sight of man, of his snake, his rod, the woman's desire is aroused; it makes her wet, and only by the luring up of her female organs, her female brood, to full desire is she forced into the position of having to lure the man who is of her brood, too, and cause his penis to erect. In blaming the man for her desire she does exactly what Adam did when he answered the Lord 'The woman whom thou gavest to be with me she gave me of the tree,' or Eve when she puts the blame on Adam's snake. In place of the rod there is now the little fish which is comfortable in the deep waters, in the woman's lap. In dreams

161

and neuroses, in daily life and Primitive Christianity fish is known to be a symbol of the phallus; at the same time it is the child; the phallus fish dies in the woman in order to convalesce and be reborn as the child fish, as a new phallus fish. The next two symbols, sun and moon, lead into the deepest layers of the child's unconscious, to the love relationship with father and mother; once they have been perceived by the child, given a symbolic explanation and cast into a new symbol, they have remained active deep down and are then used as unconscious complexes by every human being to excite desire. The word '*wellenatmend*' (wave breathing) which is used in the next line corresponds to the childish observation which relates the wave movement with the loud breathing of desire. The deep sky is again the female organ which – should I say strangely or naturally – simultaneously represents heaven and hell and in whose mystery religion and myth are rooted. The word '*feucht verklärt*' (wet and illuminated) suggests the sky's excitement again, while blue as the colour of hope promises the child. The thought of the child, of the image and mirror image which the child represents, is repeated in the phrase '*eigenes Angesicht*' (own countenance) which is at the same time a symbol of masturbation, while '*der ewige Tau*' (the eternal dew) concentrates the sea, the mother symbol of all human beings, into one phrase. In the following lines symbol again follows symbol; the naked foot that is wetted is the phallus, the growth of the heart is the growing swelling of erection which finally ends in death, in no longer being seen. The ambivalence of all symbols is specially emphasised by the unconscious element of the poem's ending '*halb zog sie ihn, halb sank er hin*' (he was half pulled by her, half sinking down by himself).

I have deliberately used the expression unconscious element of the poem rather than of the poet because I wanted to suggest that the work of art – like every action perhaps – has its own life, its own soul, and that, in other words, the symbol, as soon as it has emerged, throws up new symbols by means of the compulsion to associate which make up the body of the poem. The artist's conscious activity consists merely in the shaping of the form. There, at least, he seems to be free. Yet further investigation of conscious and unconscious forces reveals that there is no such thing as the free activity and free

choice of consciousness. The two systems of conscious and unconscious activity are not opposites of equal force – consciousness is dominated by the unconscious, which does not
mean to say that the unconscious is not influenced by consciousness. To say that consciousness is contingent – to say
more is not possible, in these matters which are beyond all
understanding – is the task of this compressed study which does
not, by searching out symbols, explain anything, but wants to
remind the reader that all transitory things are nothing but
images.

The adult does not understand symbolism easily, and only
occasionally does he succeed in grasping the symbolic connections that some piece of human undertaking has with the unconscious. The child possesses this understanding intuitively, a
fact which should be borne in mind in theoretical or practical
studies of children. This intuition of the first years of life is
quickly lost and replaced by what is usually called common
sense, but which in reality is merely stupidity based on repression. I have tried just now to prove that the poet possesses the
gift of working with symbols. The way in which he is related to
the child is best illustrated by the book *Struwwelpeter* (Shock-
headed Peter) which is doubly interesting in that it says something about doctors and that its illustrations lead us into the
field of painting. I choose the story of naughty Frederick, yet I
have noticed that the same kind of symbol-searching can be
done equally well with other parts of the book. Every rhyme
and every picture convinces one that some human trait demands symbolic thought and lines up one symbol after another
through the strange power of association, and thus the poem
and its illustrations come about.

Looking at the pictures one is first struck by the prevalence of
the colour brown, which is the colour of excrement, of course;
the close connection of cruelty with anal sexual tendencies is
thus emphasised, unconsciously one should add. The anal
complex is also expressed in the chair with the high curved
back, which is the main feature of the first picture. Next to
brown in importance comes yellow the colour of urine. The
broadlegged posture in the first picture reminds one of the act of
passing water, so does the well from which the dog is drinking
and the chamber pot in front of the half-opened bedside table in

Frederick's sick-room. In accordance with this excremental eroticism, the poem deals with the child's sadistic tendencies. The accompanying pictures are full of symbols of impotence: an empty bird cage, a dead cock and a dead canary, a murdered cat which is covered by a stone. The plucking of the fly's wings introduces the castration complex which is suggested by the canary that lies between Frederick's legs, as if it had dropped off him. The tongue stuck out during the plucking of wings is characteristic of the desire for flagellation. Analysis proves again and again that every time the tongue appears between the lips either during conversation or in some other performance, it is accompanied by sexual arousal with flagellation wishes. The sexual character of the poem is enforced by another symbol: the staircase. It figures in every picture in a variety of forms and without any motivation. Another notable example of the influence of the unconscious is the emphasis given to the fly buttons here on Frederick's trousers which are not shown in any of the other pictures. Then there is the whip, a dominating symbol of the male organ, directed at the nursemaid, the representative of mother and of the female organ. In consistency with all this the female skirt is red like the menstrual blood that is thus unsuccessfully concealed behind the innocent white of the apron. Apart from the coxcomb which, like the dog's red tongue, represents the penis, the colour red here – in contrast to other illustrations of the book – is used only for the chair cover and the wine, both of which are female and menstruation symbols. From this attack on the female love object the symbolic presentation moves to the interest in the male. Between two railings, i.e. the legs, Frederick climbs up the stairs into the well, i.e. the penis, whip in hand and eyes directed on a little church, the symbol of cohabitation. The masturbation wish is stirring. He sneaks up on the dog at the well, which can be equated with spying on father while the latter passes water. Thus infantile sexual theories indistinctly come to the surface, imagining the parents' sexual intercourse as if the father urinated into the mother, and are suggested by the yellow well-head symbolising the man and the water trough symbolising the woman. Now the hatred against the father is expressed in the beating of the dog. The picture represents the son's inmost wish to castrate the father, in that the tail of the father-dog is wedged in and hardly visible while Frederick's whip is held up high and one of his legs is stretched out. The castration is then illustrated in many symbols at once. The dog bites the leg, the cap falls off the head and the whip from the hand and is then carried off by the dog with ears flying and tail proudly raised. The symbols in the doctor picture show how effective the castration was. The doctor himself is a father substitute, sitting majestically on the red of the chair, of the woman, as the dog did in the previous illustration. He holds Frederick's bottle in his hand and gives him the spoon, the cavity, the embodiment of the female principle. The naughty boy shows only one of his hands; the other one is invisible, and so is the shock of hair which in the previous picture stands on end between the two testicle symbols. Another cavity is the upturned doctor's hat, also the half-opened door of the bedside cupboard, the chamber pot, and the hollow staircase. Furthermore there is a stick next to the little cupboard, while the fathers potency is emphasised by the doctor's big nose. The little trees next to the staircase in rows of three represent the father's potency and Frederick's castrated sexuality. The last illustration depicts the dog's delicious meal at the family dining table. He is enjoying his cake and sausage and has poured wine into his glass. His tail is fully erect.

In the most famous picture on earth, Michelangelo's creation of Adam, I can see the same phenomenon at work as in the *Struwwelpeter* illustrations, namely that there are symbols in pictorial composition which correspond to the subject matter and can hardly have been deliberately thought out by the artist. God the Father is flying suspended in space. The coat behind him is inflated into a sack in which a multitude of children huddle while uncovered God stretches himself out to his full length, his arm and stiffly crooked index finger sticking out above his robe. On the opposite side, still weakly recumbent, Adam on infertile soil; yet from the limp body, which is painted as if it were hanging on a verge, one leg is stretched out gathering its strength, the other, completely crooked, is just about to be injected with life; head and back tense away from the hill, and the arm is half lifted into the air. Instinct, awakening the idea of the creation of man and awakened by it, has asserted itself, quite independently of the artist's personal achievement, in universal human symbols of the fully erect phallus as against the slowly lifting penis.

I hope that these examples have made the reader understand how I was forced, through my symbol-searching examination of objects, to the assumption that the symbol is a means by which the unconscious guides consciousness. The following observations of some other phenomena of life, which claim to be neither exhaustive nor absolutely correct in their interpretation, are intended to arouse further interest in these problems which I find most remarkable.

Greek sculpture tried to set up a canon of the male body, and one of its ideals antiquity called the *doryphoros*, a naked man carrying a spear, a well-known phallic symbol. Again the symbol asserts itself against his will in the work of the greatest sculptor of the modern age, Michelangelo, when in his *Pieta* he put the corpse of Christ on the lap of Maria, the mother who is as young as the son, the phallus, who rests in her limp and dead.

Everybody knows that the house is a symbol of the human being, particularly of woman. Yet it must be specially emphasised that it can only have been due to compulsion, the compulsion to symbolise, that man arrived at the idea of the house, that he symbolised the fertilised womb as a house. In this man does not differ from the bird building its nest, the badger its earth. This can be proved by primitive buildings, proved in their smallest details as much as by the most beautiful temples and palaces or complicated fortifications. The symbols of door or window were not superimposed on, or retrospectively derived from, the form of the house, but the facts of copulation and of birth enforced the invention of room, door, window, lock, and key, created niches and put statues into them, dug ditches and built walls and towers. Whoever moves about a house meets a symbol at every step, sees clearly how one symbol generates another and creates new images of humanness by means of association. The fire, hot passion, builds itself the hearth, the mother goddess who contains the fire within herself, and lets the child grow through the symbol of cooking. The hearth is associated with the pot, the spoon, the cup, ever new pictures of the containing space in woman. The stove that heats the room derives from this, while the light of the fire gave rise to the oil-lamp, candle, and torch, prompted by the phallus image which can still be recognised in the electric light bulb. The knife, related to dagger, spear, and every other weapon, symbolises the man's thrust, and, accompanied by scissors and fork, the thigh-opening woman, and the hand playing during masturbation, grows out of the castration complex; the table is made in the image of the nursing mother, the cupboard is the subconscious imitation of the pregnant woman, the mirror an outcome of the pleasure of masturbation, curtains are vulvae and hymen, carpets the soft mucous membrane, the bed love play itself, the couch and man the blanket, fused into one and containing the child. Foetal life created the bathroom with tub, taps, shower, and water, and – let it not be forgotten – the anal complex needed the commode and the toilet as much as the phallus needed the stick, the sceptre, and the pen.

The same applies to the taming and choice of our domestic animals. It was not reason which gave man the idea of riding, but because he rode the woman and because the child rode on the father, and in the mother man looked out for a symbol and found it in riding the horse, the camel, the donkey. He tethered the draught animal to the cart in order to represent pregnancy symbolically and invented the ship, driven by an inner necessity, in the image of the mother, with the mast as phallus.

It is particularly plausible that agriculture derives from man's compulsion to use symbols, in which case the field is the woman's lap, the plough the man who, according to infantile sexual theory, tears open the furrow in the woman in order to pour in his seed from which will grow the fruit. From there we move on to the grafting and inoculating of trees, to planting into the earth and into flower pots and to horticulture. The formal garden, which painting imagines paradise to have been, is full of symbols, from the shady tree in its centre to the water-spouting fountain, the garden path hedged in by privet, the hedge which surrounds the garden, the stream which crosses it, the rose buds and the bower in which lovers meet. The rake is the ploughing hand, spade and watering-can are phallus symbols, while the manuring of the soil, arising from childish fantasies, originates in birth and anal complex.

From the anus originates money, too, and trade is the symbol of babyhood when the feeding and care by the mother is paid off with one's very own product, stool and urine; parallel to this runs the symbolisation of the male-female bargain where one partner pays with the strength of his loins in order to have a son born to himself.

Years ago I published in this journal the idea that human language originated in the erotic drives of the unconscious. This corresponds essentially to my view that the unconscious uses the sound of the voice symbolically in order to express certain internal processes with the help of the larynx, that speech is thus an accumulation of symbols, that every individual word is a symbolic embodiment of an unconscious process.

I shall limit myself to a few suggestions to demonstrate how man's compulsion to symbolise can be studied in the field of language. First, there is the study of the child's language, particularly baby sounds. Much that is still obscure will be elucidated by this approach. Studying grown-ups I noticed curious features of the voice. In the same person it changes from being low-pitched to being high-pitched, from being loud to being soft. When one thinks about these changes, which are important for the treatment of patients, one recognises that the unconscious expresses itself in them symbolically so that, for instance, ordinary pitch goes up because the speaker is suddenly turned into a child while a lower pitch in the midst of high-pitched talking proves the change into the strong male. In order not to be misunderstood I have to mention that for the unconscious differences in age do not exist, or at least not in the sense in which they are registered by consciousness. That a softening of the voice, particularly in the form of temporary hoarseness, symbolises mystery has been said by others before me, while loudness of speech has always been considered a method of persuasion. Just as characteristic is the symbol of getting stuck in the middle of a sentence, which the unconscious uses as an expression of insecurity and hidden reservations combined with the longing to be helped by being beaten – every school lesson and conversation offers proof of this.

The origin of words in man's compulsion to symbolise is obvious in all those words which imitate sounds, and it is understandable that the names for man's primitive sounds are the same in a number of languages, for instance *kacken* (to crap), *pissen* (to piss) *furzen* (to fart) etc. At the most recent congress of psychoanalysis Frau Spielrein offered the hypothesis that the m-sound and the p-(f-) sound of mother and father can be derived from sucking at the breast, the m a symbol of greed and the p(f) a symbol of satisfaction which abandons mother and turns to the outside world. In genital sexuality individual words carry complexes of symbols which are concentrations of whole areas of human life such as the word *vögeln* or *ficken* (to fuck). While the first (*vögeln* comes from *Vogel* bird) relates to the *eros* and angel myth and contains the origin of the flying machine and the air balloon, the second gives us the origin of package and bag, of sack and satchel, of the loading of freight waggons and trade ships.

One encounters curious surprises when one looks at the individual words of a sentence as an unbroken chain of symbols and construes a context for these symbols, an approach which, apart from its theoretical meaning, is remarkable because we all use it occasionally, and certain patients frequently, and this produces misunderstandings of a greater or lesser significance.

That singing and music have a symbolic meaning nobody has ever doubted. The remarkable correspondence between the structure of the piano and of the ear has also been noticed, and now and then the idea has been put forward that in some curious fashion this instrument was projected into the outer world in an unconscious imitation of the organ of hearing. If one looks for the symbolism one finds that the piano contains one symbol after the other, from the male bass to the female soprano and the high-pitched voice of the child; that it contains the mystery of birth, love, and grave, just as the violin symbolises the ecstasy of lust in the ups and downs of the bow, and owes its existence to the compulsion to find such a symbol. In musical notation the four spaces between the lines are also a mother symbol which characterises the four limbs of woman in contrast to man's five limbs, as does the cross. Up and into this mother the baby notes climb and crawl, from the fertilised semen to the fat-bellied ripe fruit. As with musical notation so with writing. Modern handwriting in its hasty up-and-down, its combination of pen and ink-pot and oozing liquid, betrays its symbolic erotic origin, while the individual forms of writing with their deviations from the straight line up-or-down are symbols of excitement or slackness while gaps in a word indicate a prolongation of lust, and the difference in the characters shows up the aspects of child and grown-up, of cunning and confusion in man. That the individual letter, like numbers, has a symbolic origin in history is known, yet it is legitimate to pursue this further and derive the idiosyncracies of our own letters from the human compulsion to symbolise, the hooks and curves and steep lines as well as the punctuation signs. It would not be difficult similarly to investigate the invention of printing as well as that of the steam engine, the telephone, the bicycle, or the car. When I am told that all this is nonsense, I have to accept it, yet I calmly continue to believe in it, even without proof, or perhaps even because it cannot be proved; for one gets more and more suspicious of proofs the longer one has had dealings with them. Yet when I am told that I am fantasising, I say: 'thank heaven, yes', and if anyone finds this far-fetched, my answer is: 'no, on the contrary, all these things are far too obvious to be noticed, without good will'.

We all read in our neighbour's facial expressions whether he is sad or happy, we know that his face changes symbolically, we recognise his mood in his step, his posture, his humming of a tune. Perhaps he does not want to show us how he feels, yet the unconscious forces him to symbolise this. The woman who lies down in the presence of somebody else crosses her feet, she symbolically, unconsciously expresses the idea: I know what will happen to me now; similarly we hold the thumb in the cavity of the fist to wish somebody luck, similarly the Roman woman pointed her thumb down when the gladiator did not arouse her desire with his fighting, and pointed it up for the man she liked without knowing how much desire she expressed by that gesture. Our movements are symbolic, only indirectly connected with our will, and in reality dominated by our unconscious. If this is so, why not our inventions which can be experienced as symbolic?

The symptom of neurosis – personally I believe the same to be true of the organic symptom – expresses symbolically a stirring of the unconscious. Is it so impossible for the human being to think up the telescope in the same way that he thinks up the complicated structure of a compulsion neurosis or convulsive fit or madness? Surely, no reader of this journal still doubts whether religion and science, the whole of human thought and action, are dominated by the enigmatic force which we call the unconscious and whose expressions are always symbolic? no matter how we look at them. This study is therefore superfluous. Yet occasionally it is good to take another look at what is natural and known, as if it were new. And since I consider such repetitions of old ideas useful I want to emphasise, in conclusion, something which we all know but to which we pay too little attention, in my view, namely the child's use of symbols.

For us grown-ups a chair is evidently a chair; yet for the child it is also many other things: a coach, a horse, a dog, or a child. For us a tap is evidently a tap, yet for the child it is a creature that is passing water. The grown-up tries to repress and hide symbols, but the child looks straight at them; it must be and act symbolically. And those who want to will see that the child does not superimpose the symbol on the object, but perceives it because man is symbol-minded and because he is a symbolising creature.

NOTES

1. *Imago*, V, 1917. Ludwig Levy, 'Sexualsymbolik in der biblischen Paradiesgeschichte'. (See also the reference to this paper in Groddeck's letter to Freud dated 3 October 1917, p. 42 above.)
2. It is a curious fact that tradition gradually turned the fruit into an apple which is an ancient symbol of the breast and the posterior. The fig which is mentioned in the same context was avoided even though, or perhaps because, it is a symbol of the vagina.

5

Vision, the World of the Eye, and
Seeing without the Eye*

Freud's ideas about repression have made such an impact that it is surprising to find large areas of human life almost untouched by this theory. This applies, among other fields, to sensory perception. Occasionally, to be fair, the importance of repression for abnormal processes in the field of sensory perception has been stressed, yet nobody has ever said that perception without repression is impossible. We are only able to see, hear, smell, taste, touch because we are able to repress the enormous wealth of stimuli which meet the senses in favour of certain small fractions of them. The process of seeing illustrates this well.

The tool of vision, the eye, is already structured to meet the requirements of repression. The iris restricts the picture (field of vision) on its own. Yet the movements of the eye partially cancel out this nature-given narrowing-down, though only by supplying a succession of perceptions. The structural changes of the iris, which dilates or contracts the pupil, could be seen as natural possibilities of repression. The pupils contract, when strong light falls on the eye so that everything becomes too bright, or when the axes of vision are made to converge in order to look at objects close by and cancel out distant objects. Similarly the retina can be seen as an organ for repression. Seeing essentially depends on the yellow spot; yet the anatomic distribution of vision cells and the changes in the visual purple contained in the retina prove that the range of things seen is much wider than what the yellow spot perceives. Images forming outside the yellow spot are easily repressed more or less completely. Repression during the act of seeing is best under-

* This chapter is an abbreviated translation of 'Vom Sehen, von der Welt des Auges und vom Sehen ohne Augen', 1932. First published in *Psychoanalytische Schriften zur Psychosomatik*, Wiesbaden, 1970.

stood if we consider that the images on the retina are constantly covered up by new images. The so-called after-images are still on the retina when the new image is already forming. In other words, the after-images constantly have to be repressed in order to facilitate reasonably clear vision.

One could pursue this line of thought for which the eyes are a tool for repression. But more important in this context are the repressive processes during the act of seeing because they throw some light on the secret obscurities of human life. It can be proved that man only perceives part of the objects which he sees with his yellow spot, that a number of items clearly perceived by the eye are repressed from perception because the brain is an organ of repression, too. It emerges that the material which is repressed usually remains in the superficial layers of the unconscious and can be brought back to consciousness with little effort. Often, however, it sinks so deeply that only a repeated looking can bring it back, or when somebody else points it out, or perhaps it cannot be recovered at all.

The eye is the instrument of vision but not everything which the eye sees is seen by the owner of the eye. Naturally, the reverse question may be asked, whether man can also see without eyes. Of course he can. Seeing without eyes is so commonplace that it is difficult to decide whether we see with our eyes more often than without our eyes. The most important aspect of this phenomenon is the dream, which easily leads on to hallucination and illusion. The processes described by the expression 'to have a vision' are also related. It is wrong to assume that visions occur only in ecstasy. On the contrary, having a vision, that is, projecting an image that originated internally, is an activity which man is constantly engaged in and without which seeing would be completely impossible. Our modern way of living has repressed this fact from our consciousness, yet the existence of the noun 'seer' proves that this kind of seeing can be given its full credit. In our nordic languages a person is called 'seeing' (*sehend*) who sees without using the eyes, and quite often popular imagination pictures the seer as blind.

It is well-known that some people only have to shut their eyes in order to see certain objects, landscapes, or persons, or anything else clearly. Yet the idea that all human beings have this gift and use it constantly, whether the eye is shut or open, is alien to our thinking even though we could satisfy ourselves easily enough about this phenomenon. If one looks closely at how different people see one will soon meet somebody who describes the following circumstances as if they were something quite natural: The eyes are open. The exterior world within the field of vision is thus reproduced on the retina. Yet it is not this exterior world which is seen, but an image (landscape) in its stead which is not part of the exterior world. That person is thus exposed to the influence of two images, one of which is active inwards from the outside, the other outwards from the inside. The external image cannot be verified in the organ of vision, yet it is seen.

The apparently simple process of vision is thus complicated. There are at least two ways of seeing: the outside-inwards way of seeing is the one which is normally called vision. The inside-outwards way of seeing is the dreamer's, the visionary's way. This phenomenon is also present in normal vision, and seeing is thus a mixture of external and internal images. It is necessary to note that the accessible part of nature is still further restricted by human idiosyncracies determined by the individual (time, custom, etc.). One cannot disregard the fact that the human mind changes all things to suit the image of man. The external image is always distorted by a second, internal image. The real image we eventually receive is a mixture of factual or real and humanly contingent images. Because of this a purely objective science cannot exist.

It is generally believed that the seeing of images in dreams is a consequence of an individual's visual experiences of earlier times, just as one might be inclined to consider visions and hallucinations the fantastic remodelling of former visual impressions. Yet this assumption cannot really accommodate a number of very important facts, for instance the emergence of colour and coloured patterns with closed eyes, and the symbol. These and other phenomena suggest that seeing is not a post-natal acquisition but was already possible in the womb; that vision in its fundamental aspects is not learned by the eye through perceiving light and the external world after birth, but that it exists and creates the eye for itself. A possible way of understanding this mystery better would be to study the vision of persons who are born blind, particularly their way of dreaming. There seem to be few investigations of this, and those which exist are hidden in specialist literature where one can only gain access to them with difficulty.

The question whether we can see before birth, i.e. before experiencing the direct influence of light, cannot be solved for the time being; yet to ask it is worthwhile if only because it leads on to the investigation of symbols. Everyday life proves that the symbol is innate to everybody and is an essential human characteristic.

Individuals who undergo a European education have difficulty in coming to terms with the symbol. European consciousness has lost its understanding of the symbol to an astonishing degree. This fact can be used as an example to prove the power of repression not only for the individual but for whole epochs. Hardly ever does our consciousness use the symbol; it does not even have any real knowledge of this essential human phenomenon. The importance of repression is evident when one considers that human beings think, act, and suffer almost completely symbolically. Hardly anywhere else can the rift between modern life and what is universally human be seen as clearly as in this area. One example may serve to illustrate these statements; that it is taken from life leads us to further vital questions.

In modern psychology, as it has developed through Freud's work on the unconscious, the symbol plays an important part, yet it is almost entirely used as a means to the end of interpreting a number of phenomena, particularly dreaming. Psychology has never said clearly that without an examination of the symbol there would not be any understanding of the mysteries of human life. Individual symbols are mentioned, occasionally enumerated, yet the decision to study the symbolic seriously has not been taken. For most psychologists the symbol seems to be no more than a certain similarity in form and sound or whatever between two separate objects. Often such similarities are not even sought out; it is merely stated that this or that is considered a symbol. Thus the eye is seen as a mother symbol without anyone bothering to ask why that should be so. Mankind and the science of man must at one time have known about this female symbolism of the eye, otherwise the expression pupil (*Pupille*) would not have entered the language or been preserved by it. Pupil (root: *pove, puh*; derivatives fr. *pais* = boy, *pauros* = *paulus* = small, *polos* = *pullens* = foal) is the small child, more specifically the girl, and whoever has once carefully looked into somebody else's eye will know that he can see himself there in miniature. This would already be sufficient explanation of the fact that the eye is seen as a symbol of the mother, provided that the word symbol is made to mean similarity or sameness. Since every child considers the eyes of other people something strange, unknown, and to be investigated, it will discover very early that the eye it looks into contains a small child, and then the child's mind draws the conclusion that there is in fact a pregnancy going on in the eye. It would follow that the mind of the child takes the eye not to be like a mother but to be the mother. This notion has also been found in primitive cultures (Windhuis).

We are faced with the question of how the child gets to know the world and how he learns to master his environment. The child has to start from himself, from the knowledge he has collected before and after birth about his own organism. At first he cannot but judge things subjectively, he must assume that the environment is the same as his own organism. The child thinks and lives at first in symbols, not in objects. The spoon is thus for the child not similar to the hollow hand, it *is* the hollow hand. The points of the fork are not like fingers, they are fingers. The nipple is not similar to the male genital, it is a male member. The eye is not similar to a mother, it is a mother.

This fact, that every human being experiences his environment first as an environment of symbols not as an environment of objects, that it takes him a long time to give up the symbolic in favour of the objective approach, is of particular importance for both health and illness. The memory of seeing the world with the help of symbols is repressed into the unconscious, leaving hardly a trace. This does not mean that its influence has vanished, merely that it has gone from our consciousness. To a certain degree one can become conscious again, and make

176

others conscious, of this primitive symbol life, and such a re-
vitalisation releases remarkable forces. One of the ways of getting to know the world of symbols is the observation and
treatment of patients, since in illness the symbolic element of
human life is always nearer to the threshold of consciousness.
But here, again, apart from the advantage to the patient from
attention being paid to the symbolic element it is the doctor
himself who gains a wider perspective and a greater effec-
tiveness. It looks as if, without being aware of it, European culture is slowly veering towards symbolic perception, and
medicine is no exception. The example of the eye and vision
may serve as an explanation of what I mean.

It was stated above that the eye is seen as a mother symbol,
yet this statement must be amplified, because the eye is also a
male symbol; and there may have been times when this male
aspect was more important than the female one; at least for the
Greeks and the Romans the eye was masculine in gender. The
German language, too, acknowledges the masculine side of the
eye. An expression like '*jemanden mit dem Blick durchbohren*' (pier-
cing somebody with a glance) may serve as an example. The
male character of the symbol is particularly conspicuous when
eye and nose are looked at as a unit and as contrasting with the
lower part of the face. Then the nose is the *membrum virile* and
the eyes are the two testicles, while the mouth is a symbol of the
female organ. The inability of many people to remember faces
or to draw them seems to be related to this symbolism, in which
the male is shown in the same relationship to the female as in
the sexual act.

Here we come upon the fact, which is probably generally
known, that the symbol has two genders, is bisexual, bisexual
in the sense of the ability to represent either of the two sexes,
and bisexual in the fact of the union of both sexes in one entity.

Investigating the function of the eye, vision, one arrives at the
following conclusions: the object which is seen sends its waves
into the eye, or the retina is fertilised and thus fulfils the requirements of the mother symbol. This mother symbol, at the
same time, changes into the symbol of the procreating father
which by way of the optical nerve, fertilises the brain and so it
goes on, the pregnant brain changes into an activity-generating
father symbol. Remarkable is the second activity of vision

which shows the same change in an opposite direction. In order to be able to see with the eye at all, the pregnant brain has to fertilise the eye again in its capacity of father, now the eye sends its waves into the outside world as a father symbol, and in the outside world the child is born.

In this context it is appropriate to point to the mystery which remains inexplicable in terms of our knowledge of man. Our anatomical and physiological knowledge of the eye's function is of a comparatively recent date. Yet the conclusion that a study of the symbolic nature of vision can only be made on the basis of our scientific knowledge is false, since there are elements in the germ plasm responsible for the growth of man – otherwise the fertilised egg could not develop into a human being – and they already know all the characteristics of the eye and of vision.

We must confess to the conviction that the notion of vision as a symbolic activity is as vital to man as is that of blood circulation or breathing. Then it turns out that all activities of the human organism manifest themselves in a similar way through the symbol. Symbols are not invented, they exist, and it can be said of some of them that they are as old as man himself. If this is so then primitive symbols should reveal the principles of human life, and the expressions of life by the individual should manifest the living human being in such a way that he is immediately understood. We have tried to recall the primitive symbol of male-female and female-male. It merely needs emphasising that on the basis of our scientific knowledge every individual human being is simultaneously male and female both as a whole and in all his parts and in all his expressions. – Yet this does not exhaust the symbolism of vision.

We started from the fact that the retina is fertilised from outside and stated that this makes it male and that it continues to fertilise. This change-over from the state of motherhood to the state of fatherhood is made possible only by the birth of a boy who, like Goethe's Euphorion, reaches sexual maturity at the moment he can see. Thus vision symbolises the second fundamental characteristic of man, that of being simultaneously child and adult.

In order to clarify our meaning we call attention to the fact that, in painting, this male-female, child-adult symbol is embodied in thousands of madonnas with child. It is not difficult to prove that these two primitive human symbols are contained in all works of art.

In review we state the well-known yet unrecognised fact that it is possible to see without eyes, that seeing is always a mixture of external-internal and internal-external vision, that seeing is only possible with the repression of most of what we see, that it always confirms the importance of the symbolic, and that the object is always and without exception changed by the seeing subject. In contrast to the common belief that seeing is essentially a matter that can be explained by the laws of optics, we are of the opinion that these laws are in part of limited validity only, and in part irrelevant to vision.

If our opinion were right, its recognition would have an effect first in ophthalmology. The movement started by Bates may be the important beginning of such a change. It can be assumed moreover that a scientific acceptance of the impossibility of objective vision would gradually influence our research methods in all fields and in certain directions.

The attempt to base science on objective research is doomed to failure from the start. We shall never know reality, the object. Man's world is not objective, we do not know whether there are any realities. If one insists on realities at all costs then they can only exist for that entity which Goethe called *Gottnatur* (God Nature) and which can be given any other name. One can also assume as one pleases that God Nature uses the human existence as a medium, as a kind of colouring eye-glass, like the child that uses a bit of coloured glass or looks through the reducing end of a pair of opera glasses. Yet we human beings will never be able to explore anything other than that part of the world which is human. We shall never be able to say what is real or what is added, taken away, and modified by the perceiving medium of man. For man the human element is not a medium, it is an inseparable part of the object, of the real. Science is not searching for truth, it is playing with symbols. The seriousness of research merely confirms that we are preoccupied with playing and this is a good thing. The over-pretentious seriousness which believes it will find precise, objective, real truth, or at least come close to it, is nothing but hubris. We are far from forswearing science, yet we cannot conceal the fact that for us man is more important than science, that the aim of research for us is not the real but the human. And we consider the approach of symbolic reasoning viable and advisable.

Two problems lead to this symbolic approach which have occupied mankind of old and have recently been given more attention again: the problem of kinaesthetic perception and the question of eidetic vision. Our subject 'eye and vision' demands a short discussion of both problems.

Kinaesthestics is part of our subject because it poses the question of whether and how far the world of the eye and of vision is dependent on the perception of movement. There is hardly any doubt that the world-building activity of man made earlier use of perception through movement than of seeing with the eye. The foetus in the womb is moved, it moves, and lives in a moving world long before the eye is formed as a tool of perceiving the external world. We can assume without hesitation that seeing with the eye is effectively conditioned by the perception of movement, that seeing with the eye offers us merely another possibility of building up a world, and one that does not destroy the former world of moving objects but builds on to it by a constant expansion of kinaesthetic perception. We refer in this context to the studies of S. Spielrein which we found curiously inspiring. The problem of whether man's world is at first truly built up by the perception of movement and whether seeing comes later remains unaffected by it since there is the possibility of seeing without the eyes. Furthermore, seeing with the eyes is dependent on the movements of the eye. When one stares one does not see anything. The warning remains that we should not trust our eyes too much.

The investigations by Jaensch on eidetic vision are particularly important for all problems connected with vision. He uses this concept to describe man's ability to create visual images which are neither after-images nor imaginary images. It is a question rather of visual objects caught in the retina which can be projected anywhere into space where the visual object does not happen to be. Thus the eye creates an image where there is none. From the results of his careful and laborious experiments it can be concluded that this kind of vision is the rule with the human child, gets lost with the approach of puberty or, as we assume, is repressed. It is repressed, not lost, since there are people who deliberately keep it up all their lives; and that these human beings who manifest their childlike nature are not worthless is proved by the names of Leonardo and Goethe. This childlike nature of every human being reveals itself subconsciously in dreams. Jaensch's studies seem to prove that the European in particular represses his eidetic vision, while it plays an important part in other civilisations. This prompts the question whether it might be a consequence of the destructive will which substitutes belief with reason in order to live in a world of invented reality instead of symbols. In pursuance of the purpose we set ourselves of discussing the limitations of human vision and the impossibility of objective perception, we emphasise that the phenomenon studied by Jaensch proves that, whatever reality may be, the world we know is created by man and it contains – as a whole and in all its parts – real and human-made ideal elements inseparably mixed.

The question whether seeing is subject to essential laws of physics and optics forces us to investigate the expression 'seeing'. Perhaps it is the power of this single word that succeeded in narrowing down the area of physiological and pathological research. In our thoughts, language and activities we possess quite a number of expressions for the process which we have called vision or seeing, following scientific usage. A German should understand the difference between *sehen* (to see) and *schauen* (to watch, to look) since the man who is generally considered the greatest of Germans, Goethe, emphasised the difference in his well-known poem on Lynceus, the watchman on the tower: '*Zum Sehen geboren, zum Schauen bestellt . . .*' (Born to see, employed to watch out).

Doubt whether the dictionary definition of *sehen* as 'a passive action on the visual sense', and of *schauen* as 'a deliberate act of will which directs the eyes to something specific' is sufficient becomes the certainty that it is not. It is sufficient neither with regard to *sehen* (seeing, sight), which etymologically is 'a tracking with the eyes', nor for *schauen* (to look, to watch), which is somehow connected with emphasis and choice. There are other words which are associated with *schauen*. For instance the word *schön* (beautiful) which shows up best what *schauen* means since nothing else is quite as subjective-objective as beauty.

The old High German word *scûchar*, Gothic *skuggwa*, is related to the word *schauen*. In its place German has now got *Spiegel* (mirror). Originally *scûchar* means shadow container. The logic of language saw the mirror as an object that showed something and in which an image was seen.

Here we have more confusion because of our German word *Spiegel*, which does not derive from the root *sku* but from a root *spu*. The corresponding German verb is *spähen* (to watch, to spy) which is related to *species, speculum, spectrum, speos*. When we use *spähen* we know exactly what we mean. This is rare in modern languages. When we use *sehen* or *schauen* we do not know exactly. If we did not know exactly what *spähen* means we would be confused when we consult the etymological dictionary because *spu* (*Scythian* eye) *spectare, species, speculus, spectrum* do not lead to *spähen*, but to the linguistic confusion of *sehen* and *schauen*.

A similarly deliberate intention is illustrated by the word *lugen* (English 'to look'). The derivation suggests this, too, since *lugen* is supposed to derive from *luoc* = hiding place (perhaps *Loch* = hole). The word *lugen* expresses the fact that the eye rests in a cavity, looking out from its opening.

The curiosity that is part of the intention to see is expressed by the word *gucken* (to watch), which may be the *intensivum* of Middle High German *giechen* = sticking one's head out (*gockel-hahn*, a South German dialect word for cock). In Swiss dialect young plants *gucken* (peep) out of the soil. From here one can probably find connections with the curious linguistic usage of calling that part of the plant that develops into the flowering branch *Auge* (eye). We shall try later to prove that the word eye and thus all the functions of the eye contain a whole world in the logic of language. It may suffice here to point out the sexual symbol which is contained in the words *lugen* and *gucken*; the eye is equated with the penis and the cavity of the eye with the foreskin.

There is another word belonging to the field of sight which has a reasonably clear meaning, *blicken* (gaze, look). One says *er blickt ernst* (he looks seriously), *sein Blick ist unruhig* (his gaze is unsteady), *seine Augen blicken heiter* (his eyes are looking serene). *Blicken* thus means somebody's facial expression as influenced by sight. Here it is useful to go into the derivations, for *blicken* is related to *fulgere, flagrare, phlego = brennen* (burn), *blecken* = bare one's fangs, and originally it meant to shine, to sparkle. The word contains the notion of change, of momentariness and of suddenness. It implies something unconscious, unintentional; in a sense the word is a contrast to *spähen*.

So far the results gathered from etymological dictionaries are rather scant. We shall try to get closer perhaps to the secret of the human eye by other routes. If the derivation of words does not get us any further, we could have a try with the usage of words.

The German has *etwas fällt mir ins Auge* (I am struck by something) and *ich fasse etwas ins Auge* (I focus on something). In both cases the eye is used as the instrument of sight, yet in the first expression the object wants to be seen by man, in the second man wants to see the object. There is something else that is remarkable about these expressions – on the one hand an object falls into the eye, not its image, but the object itself; on the other hand man grasps (*fassen*) the object and not its image and brings it into the eye. This linguistic usage contradicts our scientific knowledge of the sense of vision, yet it is conceivable that common usage can be as justified scientifically as can optical theory.

If the mechanical and chemical processes were the decisive factors in the act of seeing one could continue on the course which ophthalmology has taken over the past century and maintain that the idea of an object falling into the eye or of its being put into the eye is based on superstition. Yet it is man who shapes the object that is seen from the image on the retina; it is not a question of superstition, but of a remarkable prophetic ability inherent in language which deals with the problem of sight in a profound and all-embracing way. We do not see the image of the object as it appears on the retina, but from this minute image vision builds up the object externally. It can be shown again and again that sight is not merely confined to the eye and that our scientific research has chosen a path which can never lead to the goal merely by inventing the word ophthalmology.

This does not mean to say that the ophthalmological approach is wrong. It also finds expression in language, for instance in the expressions *die Augen auf etwas richten* (to direct one's eyes at something), *etwas vor die Augen bringen* (to bring something into the field of vision), *die Augen vor etwas verschliessen* (to close one's eyes to something), *die Augen werden sich ihm öffnen* (his eyes will be opened to . . .); the ophthalmological approach is particularly well expressed in the phrase *es werden ihm die Augen aufgehen* (his eyes will be opened up, he will see the light).

The intention of our argument is not, as it might appear, to minimise the importance of the eye. Rather, through the study of linguistic usage we find proof that the activity of the eye is not restricted to sight, but that it ranges over every field of life.

Ophthalmology means the scientific study of the eye. Isn't it strange that not one of the many ophthalmological textbooks takes any notice of the fact that man can devour something with his eyes (*mit den Augen verschlingen*), that he can murder with his eyes, that he can *jemanden mit den Augen durchbohren* (pierce somebody with the eyes), *messen* (measure), *liebäugeln* (give somebody the glad eye) or *angeln* (fish) with his eyes; that the eye can be thrown like a stone (*die Augen auf etwas werfen*); that it can menace (*drohen*) or frighten (*Furcht erregen*). Yet the eye can not only be used for a thousand other purposes than sight alone, it is also something very independent, something that has a separate existence, as language proves. Man can be all eye (*ganz Auge*); eyes can flash, sparkle, laugh, be drunk; they can gaze, punish; they are like animals in the grazing-ground; they can be sleepy or meditative, dry or wet; they have a soulful expression or not, they are seeing or blind, physical or spiritual; one sees with one's own or with other people's eyes; it could be said of our age of spectacles that it prefers to see with strange eyes, because the person who wears glasses does not use his own vision but a corrected one.

It follows from all this that the functional range of the eye is much wider than the range with which our scientific study of the eye concerns itself. If there really were nothing else but mechanical sight, the pointers of language could be disregarded in the theory and practice of ophthalmology. Yet since sight is certainly not merely a physical process but also a spiritual one, since it is not only concerned with perception but also with the destruction of the perceivable, we have a right to insist that ophthalmology at least should again concern itself with the real eye, with real vision.

At this point it is appropriate to fall back on the experiments we mentioned earlier. We assumed then that the repressions are determined by the symbolic character of the object which is seen, or by the personal difficulties of the observer. A third reason for the curious process of forgetting an object one has just seen – in our view there are innumerable such reasons – is this manifold and random change of the qualities and activities of the eye. A laughing eye sees the object in a different way from the crying eye, a drunk eye probably sees hardly anything at all. Yet when an eye wants to punish, when it flirts or fishes for something, one can hardly assume that it will not see much. Yet who could judge whether at a specific moment an eye wants to see or to attract? The owner of the eye probably knows sometimes, other times the observer of the eye knows, often neither the one nor the other know. It is probably characteristic of the German mentality that we call the shortest span of time we experience an *Augenblick* (a glimpse of the eye). The state of the eye and its activity do not last.

Now all people try at times to repel or to attract with the help of their eyes. The majority by far makes a habit of it, and then it is only with difficulty that they manage to see impartially or not at all. They do not know this either. The effects of habit are on the unconscious. It can be seen that the unconscious areas are as huge in the field of sight as in all other fields of life. So far the science of vision still successfully represses the knowledge of unconscious influences on the form, ability, and activity of the organic. Gradually the study of the eye will be conducted in quite a different way. The testing of eyesight will become less important, and the ability and the will to see will have to be tested, too. Science and medicine will become aware of what the unconscious force of language always knew: that sight is not only dependent on the eye, but that there is sight without eyes, that one has eyes and yet does not see. Goethe calls the eye *sonnenhaft* (sunlike). That this means something different to him than the relation of the eye to the light of the sun is implied in the statement that follows: we would not be attracted by the gods if we did not have the power of God in us. As the function of the sun is not merely to give light, so the eye is not merely an instrument for perceiving or giving out light. One of my friends who is more learned than I am told me that one of the great Greek thinkers called the eye a symbol of the world, made up of the elements of fire, water, earth, air. To him the iris was earth, the pupil air, the eyeball water, and eyesight fire. The word *ophthalmos* for eye is certainly strange. It is a compound word made up of *op* and *thalamos*. *Op* is the root for words denoting seeing; one of them is *omma* and also means eye. *Thalamos* is the chamber which is shut off from the world, the marriage chamber. This would make *ophthalmos* the marriage chamber of sight where male and female know each other and beget children. This assumption that the eye is the marriage chamber of sight revives thoughts we mentioned before on the bisexuality of the eye and of sight; sight then becomes procreating and birth giving. One of the learned dictionaries states the assumption that *zeugen* (to procreate) is *zu äugen*, and is thus derived from *äugen*. *Äugen* seems to emphasise especially the personal element of sight; it implies pointing, showing, and turns into a pointing at something in order to express the wish to take possession of it; by inserting an 'l' into the word we get *äugeln* (English 'to ogle'), *liebäugeln* (to flirt). Very curious in this connection is an expression of Swiss origin which calls the prolapse of the womb in cows *äugen*. To the theory which considers individual illnesses as wishfulfilments that resemble dreams, a dialect expression like this is welcome material and – no matter whether the theory is right or wrong – it can be used successfully, in our experience, as a medicine in medical treatment. In eye therapy this *äugen* could find a parallel in the protruding eyes of the goiterous patient, as we tried to do on earlier occasions.

With regard to the words *bezeugen* (to witness) and *erzeugen* (to procreate) we have complete freedom to dream up etymological interpretations – an English etymologist was honest enough to claim the right of dreaming for his discipline: books by the experts do not provide us with any useful information on these words. Usually *bezeugen*, *Zeuge* are derived from the root *deuk* which makes up Latin *ducere* and German *ziehen* (to pull) – both words have the same meaning: the *Zeuge* (witness) is taken to be the third person who is brought in (*herbeigezogen*) to judge a quarrel. – The words *Erzeuger*, *erzeugen*, *zeugen* (procreator, to create, to procreate) are hardly explained in the recently published comparative dictionary of Indo-European languages by Walde; ultimately this latest authority is satisfied with stating that it must relate to *ziehen* (the proof lies in *producere*).

We have tried honestly to get some sense out of these derivations; we did not succeed. One could if one wanted call a child a product; there is also sense in deriving the word *Zucht* (breed, discipline), *Zaum* (bridle), *Zügel* (rein), *züchtigen* (to punish) from *ducere*, yet none of this has any relation to *bezeugen* or to *erzeugen*. It is better to dream than to walk on this path. In Latin *Zeuge* (witness) is *testis*, and this word is often, increasingly, traced to the root *trei = drei* (three; *ter* and *stare = stehen-tersto*). This corresponds to the above-mentioned third person, the *Zeuge* (witness) who is brought in (*herangezogen*), yet here the third person stands (*steht*). *Testis* also means testicles, however. Thus *Zeuge* (witness) could be the same as *erzeugen* (to create), the three in the one, the one in the three, the male principle (the two testicles who make the member stand up). If one accepts this interpretation, then suddenly a vista opens up on the widest spectrum of life.

An innocent person who is still unfamiliar with the cunning ways in which Eros has been avoided since the start of the previous century will conclude from this derivation of *testis* (*testiculus*) that one has to be male and potent in order to be able to appear as a witness; he will understand that *erzeugen* (to procreate) and *bezeugen* (to witness) are connected concepts. He will remember from history that for thousands of years only men were allowed to witness, that – corresponding to the two testicles – two witnesses were demanded for an event.

The activity of witnessing is honourable and decent. The activity of procreating could not be mentioned in respectable society in the last century. In those days people managed to maintain that *testis* was not related at all to *testiculus*, but to *teste* = potsherd, which was used in the procedure of ostracising somebody. This is one of the ridiculous curiosities produced by the attempt to escape from the erotic.

Younger people cannot imagine how curiously everything relating to sexuality was treated forty or fifty years ago. We therefore state expressly that in those days the student of medicine was not told a thing about the human sexual act in his lectures.

Procreation was explained in terms of the penetration of the ovum by the sperm. How the sperm gets into the woman was not even mentioned by the teachers.

A confirmation of the connection between the word *bezeugen* (to testify) and the male procreative organ, with *erzeugen* (to procreate) is the old custom of touching the genitals during the swearing-in. Surely, there cannot be any doubt that the raising of the three fingers during the swearing-in (also for the blessing) derives from this custom.

The Latin word for swearing-in (German *schwören*), *iurare* (*ius* = law; *iustitia*) leads even deeper into the mysterious connection between the juridical and the sexual. Its root *ieuos* derives from *ius* = to connect, and from this comes *iugum* = yoke and *oniux* = spouse; and old Indian *yoga* = harness, draught animal, which has recently become such a pleasant diversion for the educated European, is connected with it too. With a little courage one could proceed from there to the eyes considered as *coniuges* = connected under the yoke of the forehead, particularly when adding to it: old Indian *yuga* = couple and Latin *iuvare* = help. However, the root *ieu* shows quite clearly the semantic connection of law and oath with the testicles. Another Latin word *ius* means broth, soup; its derivatives can be found in all Indo-European languages, and one of them is preserved in French *jus*. Linguistics does not want to have anything to do with the relationship to sperm, although it admits the relationship of *ieu* = united (*coniux*) and *ieu* = mixing of food. This is not surprising. Linguistics is even naive enough to point out a third *ieu*; which is supposed to be different from the other two and means young (*iuvenis* = youth, *iuvencus* = young bull). Dictionaries are full of the comic unconscious attitudes of old people. – A temptation for the lay etymologist is to draw the connection with Greek *zeugnymi* = harness, unite, *zeugma* = team of horses; in sound it leads inevitably to German *Zeuge*, *erzeugen* and *bezeugen*; but the words may have nothing to do with each other. We do not know; yet we are glad that the Greeks, too, considered marriage a team yoked together; *homozyx* and *sysix* = husband, wife are a proof of this. The German word *Joch* (yoke) has the same root, of course, and since we have the expression *Jochbein* (cheekbone) in medicine with its close proximity to the eye (Latin *iugulum*, also used for our wishbone), we are imperceptibly brought closer to the idea of vision considered as an act of procreation.

Yet before we continue, we must ask our readers' forbearance for the following argument. We brought together – not without lexical justification – the concepts of *erzeugen* and *bezeugen* with regard to the Latin language in the word *testis*, and yet it is in Latin that we do not have a straight transition from *testis* to eye and sight. We hope we shall be forgiven for making use of the word *vir* = man, and assuming that this word is connected with *videre* = to see. The reader of Groddeck's Book *Der Mensch als Symbol* (Man as a Symbol) will have been through long discussions of the word and the concept of *vir*. We take the liberty of adding *videre* and Greek *eidoton*, too. If this does not fit into the linguistic laws, it is a pity.

For the word *zeugen* can also be approached from the other aspect of the symbol, from eye and sight. The *Zeuge* (witness) has to know something, otherwise he is useless, and to know is related to *videre*, it means having seen. English 'witness' and Swedish *vittne* both imply that he who has seen testifies . . .

We want to mention at the end of these fragmentary investigations of the eye that there is a Greek word *auge* = *Glanz*, splendour. It is curious that many etymological books miss this word. It is even more curious since in English the connection between *glänzen* and the eye has been preserved in daily usage in the word to glance. The plural *hai augai* means the eyes. There is a related verb *augezo*, which means to direct rays at, and, in its medium *augozomai*, to look at something attentively. *Epaugazomei* means to light up and to look at. The characteristic ability of the eye to give out light like the sun cannot be described more clearly than this (*exauges* means the lit-up object). It is understandable that Plato used these words which fitted his theory of ideas well. In German we have a similar unconscious revelation in the word *blicken* (to look) that is related to *blitzen* = flash. The eye's real function is not merely to see but to give light. Light is created by man.

Here we encounter again the thought which was our motto: *to lampro blepomen, tois d'ommasin uden horomen*, we see the splendour, but we see nothing with the eyes.

We owe this quotation to the philologist and philosopher Egenolf von Roeder, without whose help much of this essay would not have been written. It is from the Hermetic (Hermes trismegistos) work *kore kosmu*, *kore* = virgin, in particular a name given to Proserpina (ought to be explored if the opportunity arises) also means pupil; *kore kosmu* is thus the world's pupil, the heavens. The passage runs: And anyway we are always torturing ourselves (*stenazo* from *stenos* = narrow, semantic association myopia, mystery) to see with the small and wet circle in them (the eyes) their (the eyes') ancestors, the heavens, even when we do not look. This is why Orpheus says: 'We see the splendour, but we see nothing with the eyes.'

Just as some people try with the help of short-sightedness to narrow down their field of vision, to exclude everything that is far away and also some unpleasant things which are near in space and time, so old people try to repress near and short-distance objects from their perception by presbyopia. The main reason for this is probably the wish to put off death as far as possible and to lengthen life spatially and temporally. We believe that other phenomena of old age, such as insomnia which lengthens the day, reduced mobility and rigidity, shortness and unsteadiness of step, have the same reasons. The belief that presbyopia comes essentially from subconscious layers of the It which can, however, be made conscious is confirmed by the success of treatment, particularly with the Bates method. It is not surprising that an organ becomes more efficient again through exercise, particularly when greater efficiency brings with it the hope of rejuvenation, i.e. a longer lease of life. Unfortunately, as far as we know, there are no investigations of the astonishing fact that many long-sighted people get their normal eyesight back at an advanced age. We would like to connect it up with the expression 'the mellowing of old age' and the statement that wisdom comes with old age. When man has reached the point where he is no longer afraid of the symbolism of life, when he has attained the understanding (*videre*) of how little facts in themselves mean, and how they only become active when they are symbols, then there is no longer any reason for holding on to long-sightedness.

This is perhaps the moment to go into diagnostics for a while, since it occupies a large share of modern medicine. In other

publications we discussed this decisive problem in its fundamentals, and we refer the reader back to these.* Yet the subject
may usefully be discussed in connection with the eye and with
sight. We shall repeat a few ideas that are essential for the
understanding here.

It is not possible to make an exhaustive diagnosis, and the
wish itself contains the gravest danger for the physician, pre-
sumption. We insist that the physician should always consider
his own diagnosis as doubtful, that he should never forget how
often his diagnosis is inadequate and wrong, and that by
making a diagnosis he is creating the danger of assuming a state
of illness while illness is always a process. We insist that the
physician should only tell as much in diagnosis as he is forced to
by law. The state, public opinion, and the mislead patient believe that the nature of an illness can be defined by a diagnostic
opinion. We do not stand alone when we say that this is impossible; we are merely stating what the whole of medicine is
convinced of.

By believing that it is a public disgrace if the skill of diagnosing is considered the main business of a physician, we do not
mean to say that the physician should not form an opinion of
the person he is treating and of his illness. What we reject is the
careless communication of this opinion in a few words or sentences. We consider this sort of procedure a sign of the astonishing lack of scientific care in one ostensibly scientific age.

Recent decades have better recognised the unscientific approach contained in diagnosis and tried at least to diagnose the
patient instead of the illness. That this recognition has had so
little influence in practice is due to the fact that for the purposes
of state and law the name of the illness is useful, but not the
diagnosis of persons, which cannot be used for the compilation
of statistics. Yet a short look at eye diagnostics proves that
neither the diagnosis of illness nor the diagnosis of the patient is
sufficient in itself as a basis for medical science.

It is legitimate to name a patient's illness, it is legitimate to
see the individual patient as an object of diagnosis, yet it is also
indispensable for diagnosis to have a general knowledge of
human affairs and behaviour and of the symbols which express
human life, and the application of this knowledge. In order to

* 'Massage and Psychotherapy'. See Chapter 10 below, pp. 235–239.

191

emphasise what we mean, and not at all to make it seem of special importance, we want to recall that every eye is subject to the male-female-child symbolism (fertilisation, pregnancy, birth, death), and that all illnesses of the eye are governed by these principles. Furthermore we are taught by symbolism that sight and the eye are not what science considers them to be but are very complicated reactions which have thousands of functions.

We are not attempting to cover the question of diagnostics fully, and yet there is another important question to be dealt with, the question of the meaning of illness. Medicine has always professed to the concepts of *causa externa* and *interna*, yet at least up to the beginning of this century has almost exclusively concentrated on the *causa externa*, and even today there is not enough awareness of the fact that *causa* has the double meaning of reason and purpose; people who emphasise the purpose out of necessity and without therefore denying the reason because it has been neglected so far are called unscientific. Even though we are running the risk of being mocked we maintain that a diagnosis without consideration of the purpose of the illness is not a diagnosis at all.

Judging by their meaning and purpose the majority of eye complaints could be considered attempts by the It to obstruct the visual perception of the outside world. There is some justification in treating every illness of the eye as a method of facilitating the repression of disturbing impressions from the external world on to the internal world. Where the turning away of the eyes, the head, and the body, or the closing of the eyelids does not suffice we get an illness, be it a mere sty or complete blindness. Diagnosis and therapy may involve the examination and illumination of the dark unconscious; one could even say that this is the most important part of the treatment by the eye doctor. It should not be forgotten that this attempt at facilitating repression by illness could originate in decades of inner struggle or in momentary causes. Again, we want to recall the fact that in the popular mind the seer, i.e. the man who can see more than others, is blind, and that two of the most powerful godheads are represented with bandaged eyes – justice and love.

From all this it is apparent that diagnostics is certainly an art, yet one in which nobody can be perfect, as in any other art, and that it is only justified when the parts are seen as the whole and the whole as the parts. We consider this matter of such importance that we have to present it once more in different words. It is important for the medical and, we must add, for the human verdict whether it is the cornea which is diseased or the lens, the retina, the optical nerve, etc. The specific treatment will also depend on it. We do not doubt that many visual disturbances can only be understood by applying this anatomical and physiological diagnosis. Also it should not be forgotten that the majority of eye complaints do not need treatment and are not treated. It is important for the medical and the human verdict to know whether the visual disturbance affects a man or a woman, a child or an old man, what the patient's circumstances of life are, what his wishes and needs, how, in terms of his character, his nature and constitution, he should be treated, and in consideration of everything that is personal about him, his consciousness and his unconscious and his human It. Some of the patients who resist a treatment based on anatomical diagnosis will improve when the diagnosis is extended in this way. – It is important for the medical and human verdict to know whether the visual disturbances and eye complaints relate to sight, vision, observation, or to the repressive qualities of sight and eyes, and we must repeat again that sight contains the will to perceive or not to perceive, and that the eye radiates goodness as well as taking in light, that it closes itself to the world of objects as well as opening itself to them.

This kind of diagnosis leads us to the above-mentioned purposive diagnosis. For us, our intention being to stimulate thought in the full conviction that our knowledge is fragmentary, the most important aspect of diagnosis is the symbolism of sight and eye. We believe that in this field particularly it is possible to rediscover ancient knowledge which has been forgotten. The use of this symbolism is the next goal that we are striving for, and we believe that a certain number of patients will be able to free themselves from their sufferings if the doctor acts as a signpost on this possible route. Whether this will reduce the suffering in the world is a different question. We confess to the opinion that occasionally illness means happiness and health suffering. The best proof of this is that often blind people do not experience blindness as a suffering and lead particularly serene lives.

We are aware of the fact that in the majority of cases a comprehensive diagnosis like this would be useless for treatment, if not dangerous. When somebody has a cut that bleeds profusely the bleeding must be stopped first before any other measures can be thought of. It is the same, often enough, with all kinds of eye patients. Yet in the field of ophthalmology there are lengthy illnesses which afford the double opportunity of teaching the diagnosis of general human matters on the one hand and, on the other, of testing whether, with the help of extended diagnostic examinations complementary methods of treatment could not be explored with the specific patient.

We feel obliged to say a few words about the consequences for therapy which follow from our opinions. We do not feel justified or qualified to interfere with the specialist activities of the eye doctor. The achievements of this discipline are so great that they do not need to be given any further recognition. Yet since we believe that the eye does not merely exist for seeing but just as much for the avoidance of seeing, that it discharges numerous functions which are not connected with seeing since it has no separate existence from the microcosm, but is active as one of the most sensitive parts of the human being in all aspects of its own and other organisms and is influenced by all aspects of one's own person and one's own and other microcosms; as it is – on top of all this and in particular – a universal symbol, we also believe that ophthalmology has the right and the duty to pay attention to these facts and to act on them. Since we believe that sight is not merely a function of the eye, but of the whole human being, that sight is indissolubly linked with every other human function, that sight has become a generic term for everything that happens with the help of the mysteries of light between the internal and external world, we insist on asking for certain requirements in the training of the eye doctor which so far have not been fulfilled, in particular the requirement that he should be taught to serve the human being as a whole rather than merely the eye. The level on which the specialist works should be the same as that on which every doctor works, i.e. the human level. If he is sufficiently confident of himself to apply this specialist knowledge while using this basis, he should do this and it will be well. Yet as long as the theory of optics does not even know that it mainly obscures the world of the symbol which is the real life, as long as it does not know that so far every technical advance in the field of vision has to be paid for by a frightening increase in blindness concerning vital matters, we are inclined to the view that ophthalmology mixes up technology and art, that it does not strive for the light but for the dark. As it is at the moment we have to confirm Schweninger's statement that the specialist has to be a living tool of the doctor whose merit is judged merely by the technical execution of a medical task. – The danger is particularly great for ophthalmology because it essentially bases itself on physical knowledge, on optical laws. Optics tried again and again to supplement its theory by integrating the second factor of vision, its human element, the light which a human being radiates. Unfortunately it has not succeeded in this and consequently the medical practice of the eye specialist has been removed even further from the human condition.

In daring to make some remarks here we want to emphasise from the outset that we are amateurs in this specialist field, and thus ask for allowances to be made for this fact.

When we amateur eye doctors treat the eye we are struck first by the fact that this organ has a very high liquid content and yet its most important parts carry no blood vessels, that in other words the eye has comparatively little use for the heart's driving power. The general practitioner is thus faced with the primary task of supporting, in the case of illness, the liquid circulation in the eye which probably determines the chemical processes. This is a question neither of the vascular nor of inter-cellular circulation, but of the movement of liquid between the cells. At first we are aided by the eye's activity, the change between methodical movement and rest, while movements which are not habitual are given preference (upwards movement). This 'voluntary' activity can be strengthened by passive pressure (almost all eyeballs which are examined are very tender when pressure is exerted on the closed eye from above to below, and simultaneously the open eye has to look up, the upwards glance is that of venerating the higher powers, this veneration is almost completely lacking in our lives). Further one can massage the tangible nerves in the closer or remoter environment of the eye.

The heavy weight of the inter-cellular liquids can be made use of by resting with the head lower and the legs higher. Use of damp heat in the form of eye baths and head baths has proved effective. Attention to breathing, removal of obstructions in the inter-cellular circulation – they are usually in the digestive system; breathing exercises with heavy pressure on the belly. Artificial change of liquid distribution by deviating to other parts (hot bathing of certain parts of the body). Alteration of light and dark, removal of all spectacles, if this is impossible a reduction in their wear to the shortest possible time. Training of all senses in order to ease the sense of vision.

In giving these instructions as to the physical treatment of eye patients we want to give more emphasis to the treatment which is usually called psychological. It seems to us advisable here to apply Bates' prescription to train the imagination as an active measure. Perhaps Graf Wieser's therapeutic exercises with overstrong lenses might be of use, too; we do not have any experience of that. We would place most value in the treatment on the stabilising of the eye's repressive activity and there, again, on the study and use of the symbol. Automatically treatment turns into a mutual exchange of conscious and unconscious forces in which the human aspects of both partners reveal themselves. If the partner physician pays attention to all the signs of resistance in himself and in the patient, all may be well in the end and it may perhaps turn out to be best if specialist knowledge is used in the process.

Yet the physician should and will learn one thing when he is an explorer: when there is a cure, it is not his merit, when there is failure, it is not his fault.

6

The Meaning of Illness*

Sickness and health appear to be opposites. They are not, any more than heat or cold are, for instance. Just as the latter are effects of different wave lengths, so illness and health are effects of one and the same life. Illness does not come from the outside; it is not an enemy, but a creation of the organism, of the It. The It – or we may call it the vital force, the self, the organism – this It, about which we know nothing and of which we shall never recognise more than some of its outward forms, tries to express something by illness; to be ill has to mean something.

It is impossible to find a general and universal meaning, impossible because there is no definite boundary between sick and healthy, because we cannot say illness starts here, health ends there, not even theoretically, as we can with the zero point in measuring temperature. Finally, as with everything else, we can only determine the meaning which illness has for human beings, or the even more restricted meaning which we individually give it; an ant or an oak tree gives a different meaning to this expression of life than human beings, and Miller's meaning is different from Jones'.

And yet the question about the meaning of illness is of value, of practical value, of value for the physician, and everybody is a physician who treats illness, be he a consultant or a country doctor, a shepherd, faith-healer, wise old woman, or simply a mother, for the medical licence has to do with the titular aspect of the doctor and not with the concept. It would be good if general attention were drawn to this question of the meaning of illness, and if an attempt could be made to find at least a provisional answer to it. It is rewarding to take one of the innumerable forms of illness and look at it as impartially as pos-

* 'Der Sinn der Krankheit. Der Leuchter', *Jahrbuch der Schule der Weisheit*, ed. H. Graf Keyserling, VI, 1925. Reprinted in *Psychoanalytische Schriften zur Psychosomatik*.

sible in its context of life and find a meaning for it.

Somebody walks from the bathroom to the sitting-room, he stumbles at the doorstep, falls and breaks his right lower thigh. To find out what this event means in my view I look at the consequences. The first thing I can observe is fear, a double fear; on the one hand, during the fall, in the form of 'now I am falling, physically and morally', and then, after the fall, 'now I have got hurt'. Not all people are frightened when they fall, nor are they frightened every time; very small children, if our observations are right, never get frightened at all. It seems that one must have experience of falling to feel frightened, and also a certain frame of mind, for adults are not always frightened when they fall. In my view this frame of mind is a feeling of guilt. While falling is nothing but the sudden loss of one's temporary foothold, an experience of fear while falling indicates that the foothold was important, that it was rash to give it up, or to intend to give it up, in spite of internal and external prohibition, and that there is danger and punishment in store. To fall is to confess: 'I have forfeited the right to the upright position, the right to be considered a full person, I am not strong enough for it'; it is a request: 'fate, God, do not judge me as you judge human beings, look at me, I am a child, that has not yet learnt to stand, I am unworthy of your anger. Do not punish me, look, I am lying there, powerless; hold me, I cannot stand up by myself.'

The second thing that strikes the observer is the expression of pain. It could easily be seen as a form of punishment, and with this we are in the midst of the hocus pocus game of life, in the confusing game of appearances and deceptions which the It, man's unconscious, plays with our reason. For the intensity of pain immediately represses the feeling of guilt that rises up from the depths during the fall; we believe we have been punished enough, perhaps too much; the feeling that one has got what one deserved disappears, and in its place there is now indignation about the treacherousness of fate. Only the warning is still there, 'don't ever do something like this again', a warning which is repeated at every attempted movement. Yet the knowledge what the 'something like this' is has already been drowned by pain. 'Be careful' is the only warning left. And louder, more distinctly: 'I am helpless, help me, you, who are grown-up. Have sympathy, help me, ease my pain. I am suffering innocently. You are obliged to do it. Look here, I am lying, I am a child; you are standing up, you are walking, you are obliged to help the child.'

The warning to be careful becomes compelling with the fracture of the bone, which makes it impossible to go on walking in the normal way. The meaning of this is: 'since you would be doing even worse than you have already done if you went on walking, as the direction in which you were walking would have brought you close to mortal danger and would have made you fall into the unfathomable abyss of hell, I, your It, by virtue of my absolute power, am making you lame, for some weeks temporarily. Retreat from life, stay in bed, be a child and you will find a mother who will care for you.'

If the premises and assumptions that I have suggested so far are right – and they are right for me – then we can draw some conclusions about the meaning of illness now. In the first place – I claim the validity of this sentence for all illnesses, every form of illness and at any age – the meaning of illness is the warning 'do not continue living as you intend to do'; this warning increases, could become a compulsion or lead to arrest and ultimately even to death. The It interferes with the various quarrelling and centrifugal drives of the organism, makes them less dominant, and ends the quarrel with illness and reconvalescence, or allows it to continue in narrower confines as a chronic condition, or destroys the fight of the factions with death. In the illness we hear the It's commanding voice ordering soul and body, organs, tissues, and cells, and all its creatures: 'So far and no further! I gave you far reaching independence; since you want to abuse it in internecine quarrels I shall restrict it, and if that does not stop you I shall destroy it and you.'

The It can be imagined in a different way; a different role can be ascribed to it, for instance the role of reasoning in the following way: 'This cannot go on. I do not want to bear the responsibility for what is happening with and in this man, my creation, I shall become a child again, hand back the responsibility to the mother, or give it to those who are boasting that they can take on responsibility: the doctors, the nurse, the persons who consider themselves grown-up, wise, strong.' Then illness is the expression of the wish to be small, to be given help, to have a mother, to be blameless. This wish could increase and become a longing for prenatal conditions, in which no consciousness, no reasoning thought, existed as yet, a longing which to my mind seems to be present in all fits of fainting and unconsciousness. There are innumerable gradations in the force and the aim of this longing for the past, which can be gauged more or less correctly by observing and weighing the forms and the symptoms in which they express themselves. It is difficult to say how far an illness expresses the confusing and confused feeling of guilt whose origins are a mystery; yet I do not doubt that it contributes to illness, at least after the first months of life, and perhaps even earlier, and that it expresses itself at a very early age in illness. This, the wish to punish oneself, to do penance, is the meaning of certain kinds of illness.

If it is true that the meaning of illness is among other things a warning of danger, then the question is what is this danger that is common to all mankind. Everybody will think of the inescapable danger, death. Thus illness would be an expression of the fear of death. That might be so. Yet at once a new mystery presents itself. If there really is a fear of death and it exists universally, then there must also be a longing for death universally; for fear is a wish, a repressed wish, in most recent terminology. Could this be possible? Could it be that man, every man, has a longing for death? The Greeks, who were better at understanding the symbolism of the It than we are, gave the God of Death the same features as the God of Love: to them love and death were more or less the same. And it is the same with us: with us, we merely do not want to know about it any more. In reality we die when we love; our personality is wiped out in these rare moments of life – for it must be said at once that only for seconds can man love in the way in which it could be equated with death –, death and love are the same for us, too. And the longing for love is the longing for death, the longing for death the longing for love.

This sounds somewhat mystical – it is and should be mystical. This does not make it any less true or any less clear in its meaning. We possess a religion which still seems to us the symbol of our human existence. This religion makes the God of Love die on the cross, be buried and rise again. Yet the man, male existence, dies in the woman in direct proximity to the *os sacrum* (the *Kreuz* = backbone in the woman), for after the union the man is no longer male, but child; he buries himself in the woman's lap, as the corpse is buried in the bowels of the earth, and he rises from his grave as the son of his mother. The truth is: man has a longing for death because he longs for love, and a longing for love because he craves death, the mother's womb. And illness, the meaning of illness, is this death wish and love fear, love wish and death fear.

The meaning of illness is elucidated further by the symbol of Christ. Christ dies on the cross; the backbone (*Kreuz*) is called the *os sacrum*. Labour pains start from the backbone, the death of foetal life and the resurrection start in the womb; the cross (backbone) is the mother herself. On this cross dies the son of man, the all-loving. Suddenly I am confronted with the question: 'isn't it perhaps the unattainable longing to become one with the mother – unattainable because the son is nailed to the cross on the outside, turned away, his back to the mother – isn't this longing perhaps the deepest meaning of illness? or does it merely mark a certain depth of meaning and there are still others, even darker, unrecognisable meanings?' It may or may not be too presumptuous and impudent to follow Faust into the realm of mothers.

The example I chose shows some details which help to explain the meaning of this specific case and which will have to be taken into consideration during treatment; thus it is significant that the right thigh was fractured, for right is different from left. The lower part of the lower thigh is different from the upper part of the upper thigh. The place where the accident happened, the threshold between bathroom and sitting-room, the sensory perceptions of the patient before, during, and after the fall, his experiences and the predominant mental preoccupations of the It at the time of the accident, all this and more needs to be taken into account if one wants to get the meaning of this illness approximately right. Yet the person who does the interpreting should no longer be the physician; only the patient himself can supply the necessary information about his It and its intentions and activities. For every It has its own thought processes and ideas concerning symbolic meanings. The role of the therapist is restricted to that of making the recalcitrant It talk and, even more significantly, being as open as possible in order to allow the patient's It the least possible excuse for mistrusting him.

I want to point out in a few words what meaning the symptom has in the interpretation of illness. Here, too, one must proceed without prejudice, I would like to say in a child's way. Man has legs to walk with. The meaning of a leg fracture, of any complaint located in the lower limbs, is thus as follows: the It considers it better not to walk for a while. A complaint on the hands presupposes an order by the It not to use the hands, perhaps because there is a danger of stealing, or of masturbating, or of violence, or some other kind of action, some fantasy which the high-handed It considers unreasonable. Illnesses of the orifices or their surrounding areas can be interpreted to mean that there is something which the It does not want to come in or to get out. The meaning of a rash is repulsion and – attraction. For there is a law that every activity of the It has a double meaning, has meaning and counter-meaning; perhaps it may even have a thousand meanings. The examples are plentiful, yet I have said all I want to say. That this search for meaning is a human universal, that there is a compulsion to attribute meanings, is only doubted by those who do not want to and cannot see. It is thus superfluous to bring in the Greeks who imagined Homer blind and Hephaistos lame. They gave the former an It that prevented the disturbance of the wealth of his visions by destroying the world of the eye, to the latter an It that took away his freedom of mobility and forced him to stay near his anvil.

The route which I have sketched out briefly here is worth following and offers many interesting views.

7

Clinical Communications*

That disease of every kind is susceptible to psychotherapeutic treatment cannot be proved; it can only be a matter for trial and experiment. My only aim in making these communications is to induce as many physicians as possible to make the trial.

The first case I shall deal with is that of a lady who came under my care in 1921 suffering from general oedema, the result of non-compensation in heart disease. The first three weeks of combined physical and mental treatment produced good results, but things came to a stop in the fourth week, and then there was a serious relapse. I therefore decided to take certain action which I had often found beneficial, though only when taken at the right juncture in any treatment. I explained matters to the patient as follows: 'You know you have been up and about and have had no pain these many years, although the condition of the heart has been the same. That you are now ill and have oedema cannot therefore be due to the heart trouble, but to some disturbance between the action of the heart and the opposition of your organism to this action. The attempt to strengthen the power of the heart has failed, as you know. The attempt we have made during the first three weeks to diminish the resistance against the heart's action led to improvement, yet during the last eight days, although apparently the treatment has not changed, we have first come to a standstill and then lost ground. That shows, if we like to understand the message, that something in the treatment has changed so that it no longer is effectual. All treatment includes two factors: First, what is prescribed, and second, the personal influence of the doctor. Since no change has been made in the regimen prescribed for you, the

* This chapter is translated by V.M.E. Collins, and is reprinted from Georg Groddeck, *The Unknown Self* (London, Vision Press, 1951). Groddeck gave the paper originally before the Psychotherapeutic Congress of 1928. The German text, 'Klinische Mitteilungen aus einer 20 jährigen psychotherapeutischen Praxis', was first published in *Psychoanalytische Schriften zur Psychosomatik*.

disturbance must concern my personal influence. I would ask you to think over what it is that you have against me.' I received the usual reply, the patient had nothing at all against me. At last, as I remained obstinate in my belief and the patient equally so, I resorted to cunning and asked her, without warning, to repeat one of the commandments. At once, without stopping to think, she repeated the commandment against adultery. 'Why do you think that I have committed adultery?' I asked. 'I have been told that you were divorced, and although your first wife is still alive, you have married again.' 'That is so,' I replied, 'but you forget that I am a Protestant, and so my faith does not prohibit a second marriage while my first wife is alive. But when did you hear that my first wife was still living?' 'Eight days ago.' 'Then that was when you first began to get worse. I must now tell you something else if we are to get any good from all this. You have made a charge against me which cannot be justified, and this you did knowing that I was a Protestant. Now unjust charges are only made when the accuser has committed the fault with which he taxes another, I know, then, quite certainly, that you yourself have broken your marriage vow.'

Greatly moved, my patient then told me the following story: 'It is not the vow of earthly fidelity that I have broken, but a far more sacred pledge. As a young girl I longed to be a nun, but my parents set themselves against my desire and I gave it up, making a secret and inviolable oath to myself that I would remain a virgin for the whole of my life. This vow, made to God, I have betrayed, for, as you know, I am married. Since my wedding I have had bitter struggles with my conscience, always renewing them as soon as they die down. I have spoken of it in confession, but although the priest has assured me that no validity can attach to such a vow, and therefore no mortal sin is committed in breaking it, still I never lose my burden of anxiety nor find any peace of mind.' After this confession I had a further conversation with the patient, and advised her when she returned home to discuss the situation with a priest, not in confession, but in his private capacity. What she had told me showed that she did not trust the judgment of the priest as her confessor, and so that could only increase her sense of guilt. This she promised to do.

After I had gone from the room she started to urinate, and in such quantities as I have hardly ever experienced with any patient, certainly not with any suffering from incapacity to urinate like this patient. Within four hours her weight had gone down by five kilograms, and the next morning by another kilogram. From the moment she told her story her condition grew better every day, and in a short time every sign of defective compensation had disappeared. Some idea of her condition may be gathered from her loss of weight, which amounted to four kilos in the first four weeks of the treatment, and in the week following her confession to twenty-five kilos. The patient returned to her home quite recovered. Six months later her husband wrote, asking me to come to her, but I could not answer the summons, for the distance was great and I was tied by other duties in Baden Baden. A week later he wrote again to tell me his wife had died from dropsy. He added that severe symptoms had made their appearance after his wife had been to confession. She had then told him of her belief that she had broken a sacred oath and said that in her last confession she had again included this sin and the priest had once more assured her that such a vow made by a young girl was of no importance, but she could not believe this.

From my way of relating these events it will be clear that I am inclined to believe that the disturbance of the circulation was, in fact, overcome through the patient's talk with me, and that accordingly the treatment of a conflict in the heart – and religious belief in common parlance is an affair of the heart – may well be included in the treatment of heart cases. This cannot be proved, at any rate not at present, but after all it is not the duty of a medical practitioner to furnish proofs, although, of course he will always think he is in the right. But it is surely permissible to regard an indication arising out of practical experience, such as I have given, as sufficient grounds for scientific investigation.

I give a second case which illustrates anew the importance of the fundamental principle in all medical treatment, 'See that you do no harm.'

A lady with chronic inflammation of the joints of both upper and lower extremities sought my help after trying many fruitless treatments. She had already been about six weeks in Baden Baden under the care of a doctor in this town, and had been taking the baths on his advice. Instead of improving she got worse, for a severe pain in the upper part of her spine made it impossible for her to lie either on her side or on her back, so she was forced to sleep lying face downwards. This pain began on the first day of her treatment in Baden Baden, and had got worse and worse. Before examining her carefully, I gave her the following explanation:

'If we like we can regard an illness associated with increasing pain as a self-punishment. In your case, assuming this to be so, it would be easy to get an answer, not a learned, but still, perhaps a useful one, to the question as to why your arms and your legs are affected, for it is with arms and hands that evil is done, and legs and feet may wander into ways of sin. But this unscientific though practical explanation gives no reason for the pain in your spine. Can you tell me of any incident which may have led to the punishment of your spine where inflammation is rarely met with?' 'Yes,' replied the patient, 'I can. The doctor whom I have been under in Baden Baden threw me into a state of excitement the first moment that I saw him, and of this I am deeply ashamed, for he has not the slightest inkling of the effect he has on me, and my feeling seems to me a proof of my vileness. My excitement and at the same time my feelings of guilt rose to an almost intolerable degree when the doctor helped me to prepare for his examination by unfastening a button at the back of my blouse which I was unable to reach with my bad arm. I do not ever remember feeling so deep a sense of shame as I had when I felt his hand on my back. And as far as I can judge, the painful place is exactly where his touch produced in me this strange confusion.'

Not until after this conversation did I make any searching examination of the patient. The remarkable swelling and sensitiveness of the fourth vertebra led me to conclude that there was inflammation there. I discussed very fully with her the question of her excitement and feeling of guilt, and the unconscious sources of her transference. On the following day the swelling and the pain had disappeared and did not return. The patient has come for several years in succession to spend six weeks or so in Baden Baden. In the first year I treated her with massage, baths, dietary and psychoanalysis, but subsequently only with analysis, and the result may be considered as a complete cure.

The analysis led to the conclusion that the illness had arisen through the 'double sex' of the patient, that it was what Adler calls a masculine protest. The most noticeable somatic phenomenon was a strong growth of hair on the upper lip, and that has not altered. Her deep, manly voice has quite gone, and she has lost all swelling and stiffness of the joints, symptoms which in my opinion are symbolic of the masculine protest. However, I am not quoting this case to justify these views, but to show that without any blameworthy action on the part of the doctor, even without his being in the slightest degree aware of what he has done, great harm may be suffered by the patient in the course of a necessary and unavoidable examination. To observe any harm when it occurs, and to rectify it as far as possible, is the most difficult task in the whole of psychotherapy.

Another case, taken from the surgical field, is a further example of the masculine protest. In 1911 an English lady came for treatment because of severe abdominal pain. Four years before, she had had her first operation for hysteroptosis, and the womb had been firmly stitched in place. The following year floating kidney had been discovered, and a second operation was performed to put that right. The third year the stomach was stitched in place because of gastroptosis. This last operation did nothing for the patient, while the first two had at least for a time ameliorated her many pains. I only treated her by psychotherapy, from which it emerged that from the time of her earliest childhood she had been dissatisfied with her fate of being a girl and had tried to imitate the peculiarities of boys in all sorts of ways. When eight years old she was put in charge of a governess whom she loved passionately, and who with some success tried to wean the child from her playing at being a boy. An apparently trivial incident changed the little girl's tender love into overwhelming hate. She had been accustomed, through her desire to be a boy, to stand on the closet when urinating. One day the governess surprised her in this act, and there was a stormy scene in the course of which the child's love was altogether destroyed. In her conscious mind she now abandoned the attempt to be a boy, but the desire appears to have been reinforced in the unconscious through repression. The patient at least accepted my suggestion that her sufferings, this continual sinking of the abdominal organs, were due to the attempt to press out of the body the masculine organ which must there be concealed. All pain disappeared and had not returned three years later, but the outbreak of war prevented my hearing anything more from this patient. Her treatment lasted three weeks.

From this and other cases in my experience I am inclined to think that there is some causal relationship between the 'double-sex' of a girl and multiple enteroptosis, but this is merely a subjective opinion of little practical value. At the same time I hope that the history of this case makes it clear that psychotherapy has a special significance, hitherto unfortunately quite neglected, in surgical cases.

In conclusion I will relate a case from another department of medicine. Many years ago a working man whom I had learnt to know and to respect told me the story of his life. He had grown up in a mountain village far from civilisation, and had never been to school, but had spent his childhood as a shepherd boy. Only when he left home in later years did he learn to read and write. At fourteen he was taught shoe-making by the village shoemaker, and from morning till night he had to sit silent at his work, his only distraction being the conversation his master had with passers-by. Among those who came to the shop was a certain blind man whom all the village people called a blasphemer of God. They were ignorant enough to believe absolutely that he had been made blind by God as a punishment for not going to church.

This man had made an unforgettable impression on the boy. After some time he gave up his shoe-making and took to wandering, for he was suffering from retinal haemorrhage, and the doctor warned him he must find some other work less trying to his eyes. Years later he came to consult me, for his eyes had gradually got worse and the oculist had told him nothing more could be done for him. The retinal haemorrhage was continually starting anew. The very day he came to me his oculist had discovered a fresh bleeding. He told me that autumn was the worst time for the haemorrhage, and also he suffered from great depression in autumn as now – in October. When I asked him how he explained the outbreak of bleeding in October, he said it might be connected with the dying of Nature. The fall of the leaves made him sad, and it might well be that his eyes grew weaker on this account. Moreover, on this occasion he knew of another reason for the haemorrhage: his little daughter had struck him in the eyes while playing. At that time I was still a little bold in my associations, and I told him that while there must be some connection between autumn and his retinal haemorrhage, it was obvious that it was nothing to do with the dying of Nature, since Baden Baden in October gives no impression of death, but rather of glowing, fiery life. I asked the patient whether anything serious had ever happened to him in October, but he said there was nothing. As I was not convinced, I asked him to name any number, and he gave me 'eight'. To my further question whether anything had happened to him when he was eight years old, he again replied in the negative. At that moment it occurred to me that he had told me how the blind man was called a blasphemer of God, so I asked him whether he had ever blasphemed God. He laughed and said he had been very pious as a child, but for many years now he had ceased to trouble himself about these things. God and the Church, they were only bogies used to deceive the common people. Suddenly he stammered, grew pale and fell back in his chair unconscious.

When he came to himself again he fell weeping on my neck, saying: 'Doctor, you are right. I am a blasphemer of God, just as the blind man was, of whom I told you. I have never told a single soul about it, not even in confession, and now when I think of it, I find it almost unbearable. And you are right too about the autumn, and about my being eight years old. It all happened in autumn in the year I was eight. In my home district, which is strictly Catholic, there are wooden crucifixes on the borders between one village and another. At one such crucifix we, my brothers and I and a few other boys, were throwing stones, when I was so unfortunate as to knock the figure of the Christ from the crucifix so that it fell and broke in pieces. That is the most terrible experience in the whole of my life.'

When he had calmed down a little, I told him that I could not associate today's haemorrhage with the blow in his eye he had had from his little daughter. There must be some other connection, and he must think about the preceding day and name any hour to me. He said, 'five o'clock,' and to the question whether he remembered where he was at that time, he replied that he knew exactly, for he had got into the tram at a particular spot at five o'clock. I asked him to go again to that spot, and when he came back, he told me with some excitement that immediately opposite the place where he had mounted the tram there stood a crucifix.

I explained to him that it is possible to look upon every illness as a measure of protection against a worse fate, so one cannot escape the idea that retinal haemorrhages arise in order to prevent the sufferer from seeing something – in this particular case, so that the patient might not be reminded of his blasphemy by the sight of the Cross.

It is a matter of indifference whether this suggestion has any justification or not, and I know full well that it is not a complete explanation of the problem of disease, but it does not matter to therapy whether the doctor's action is correct or not. All that matters is that the patient should make use of this action in order to get himself well. I must conclude that this patient did so use my observations, for he had no further haemorrhages for a couple of years, although he gave up his outdoor occupation and settled down to sedentary work which required a great deal of writing. Two years later he had a fresh attack, which proved to be associated with the sight of an iron cross worn by an ex-soldier. This cleared up, and from that time, thirteen years ago, no haemorrhages have occurred. Yet he is now a book-keeper and must use his eyes more than most people.

Everyone of these patients had consulted specialists before coming to me, and the diagnoses were made by them. For myself, I believe that errors are not infrequently due to the striving after exactness in naming diseases, and that a different type of diagnosis will be developed which will not be satisfied with names, nor even with the findings made by examining the patient, but which will attempt to understand his situation in regard to his environment. I should like to repeat once more that these communications are made solely in order to persuade other doctors to test my conclusions for themselves in their own practice.

8

Some Fundamental Thoughts on Psychotheraphy*

When I use the expression psychotherapy I must define my meaning of the term; it is somewhat different from what has so far been considered psychotherapy.

I shall leave out the word psyche for the moment; it seems to me more important to find out first what therapy means. Originally therapy meant service, not treatment. The person who serves acknowledges the person he serves as his master, the person who treats works an object with his hand (German *behandeln*) – in its literal and its figurative meaning. The doctor's fate is to serve and to treat patients: his activity is ambivalent. Yet there is a great, a decisive difference if the emphasis is on the serving or the treating, and I do not consider it accidental that the word therapy combined itself almost automatically with the word psyche. As soon as the word psyche is defined more accurately one can see that psychotherapy means something different from psychological treatment. I shall come back to this later, here I merely want to emphasise that behind the two expressions therapy and treatment hides the inner conflict of our profession, that they express the fight every doctor has to fight daily and hourly, and that the two words express the specific tendency that has predominated in medical theory and practice during the changing course of time. The doctor who treats patients believes that he practices medicine only with part of his personality, be it his knowledge or his ability, according to his philosophy he will call his activity a science or an art, or even – if his professional ethos, which partly promotes and partly hinders modesty, allows it – a craft that is rooted in experience, yet he always activates only a part of his human personality, and the word treatment will always mislead him into believing that he should guide and could or should direct

* 'Grundsätzliches über Psychotherapie', 1928. Printed in *Psychoanalytische Schriften zur Psychosomatik*.

211

the processes under consideration. A person who serves knows that he has to do what his master says; he knows that he is in service with his whole being and not just with his knowledge or with his skill, that he is obliged to guess at the wishes and needs of his master, that he has to adapt himself in everything, in his deepest nature to his master's nature, and if he cannot do this he has to admit it quite openly and leave it to the master if he can and will put up with his servant's idiosyncracies willingly and without resentment, or not. He can try and execute his individual services in a way that surpasses his master's expectations a thousandfold, yet he will always remain aware of the fact that he is in service with his whole being, his strength and his weakness, and has to ask forgiveness and forbearance for every action done against his master's will, for every idiosyncracy of his nature that offends the taste or the mood of his master.

To illustrate the meaning of all this I shall now turn to the word psyche. As things are at the moment psyche, for us, means consciousness and the unconscious in Freud's meaning of the term, no more and no less; unconscious is what was once conscious and was repressed into regions which are either retrievable or not retrievable to consciousness. Everything that is outside consciousness and the unconscious and what I call the vegetative aspect does not belong to the psyche.

Before I continue I must say two words about an expression which I originally added to the theory for my own use, the expression 'the It'. This expression, which means nothing else but the whole of all the life forces that make up an individual from the moment of his conception, is used by Freud in a different sense; he uses '*Es*' (Id) to denote the hitherto unknown parts of living matter and juxtaposes (*setzt*) – the word (*setzt*) is typical of his way of using the term – the Id and the Ego. He thus does something which is the exact opposite of what I intended with the choice of the word '*Es*' (It); because for me the Ego is one of the many outward expressions of the It. The consequence is that my *Book of the It* is incomprehensible to all those people who adopted the later, Freudian meaning of the word. I repeat that I see the It as the sum of all the life forces making up an individual, and believe that the It is something absolutely different from what I have just called the vegetative aspect of human life.

Having thus defined the psyche as the whole of all the conscious and unconscious or repressed forces of the individual, and therapy as service, it has become easier to say what psychotherapy is. Yet there are still a number of difficulties which ought to be discussed.

To sum up what we have said so far: the person who wants to practice psychotherapy makes it known that he wants to serve with his psyche, with the whole of his conscious and unconscious being. Now it will be easily understood that only something which is conscious can be used for the purposes of treatment. The unconscious cannot be used for treatment; it serves, but the doctor does not treat with its help; it is outside his intentionality, it is effective but only recognisable in its effects.

This requires the doctor to expand the range of his consciousness as much as possible and to limit the unconscious of his psyche as much as possible; he ought to make unconscious matters conscious. He should at least increase his store of preconscious matter, that is, of matter lying close to the surface of consciousness and easily reached by it. He has to acquire a knowledge of the unconscious. How can he do this? There is only one sure way, by service. One has to put oneself fully in the service of the patient, observe every conscious or unconscious or vegetative expression of his, and make these the guidelines of one's medical activity as order or reprimand. The patient alone knows how he has to be treated, of course, neither his consciousness nor his unconscious suffice for this, but his It knows and utters its wishes and requests clearly, clearly for those who want to and are able to serve it, clearly in its conscious, unconscious, and vegetative processes.

Whoever wants to serve a human being whose language he does not understand must try and interpret the signs which are made by the foreign language speaker. Whoever wants to help a mute person must try to get into the sign world of mutes. He will soon find out that the mute mostly uses the same signs that the servant would use if he were mute; signs are the same everywhere. A person who deals with mutes, with the mentally ill, or with delirious persons learns their language merely by being with them. When one involves oneself in the personality of the individual patient – or of the healthy person, it does not matter

213

–, in the wish of becoming like him, one learns about human universals, there is no doubt about that. Yet this is not enough: the doctor, as well as understanding the language, ought to speak it himself, to speak it consciously. Then he will also acquire the ability to talk to the patient in the language of the unconscious and the vegetative, not as a patient but as a doctor, as a human being who has learned to speak such a language and yet remain healthy with it.

To enter into the patient's personality is a demand that has to be made of the doctor. The doctor must try and sympathise with what may have gone on in a patient's mind before he decided to produce a high temperature with the help of some germ, to make tumours grow, to allow certain microbes to enter his body and stay in his brain for years so that they will be able to destroy this brain sometime; what might have caused him to torture himself with pains, anxieties, compulsive worries; he will find an answer in himself for all these and a thousand other things. And if it is not the right answer, at least it was the right question. To put the right questions is very important.

The concept of service implies that the master – in this case the patient – is always right. In considering this relationship between doctor and patient as established at the start, the doctor can expand his conscious psyche and train his unconscious. Whoever makes a habit of always remaining true to the idea of responsibility, no matter what happens, an idea which is certainly wrong yet has to be adhered to and which one must never abandon – whoever can entertain the belief, full of the miracle of man, that the tendency to cure exists everywhere and would win through if the professional helper, the doctor, had not made mistakes, will soon acquire an extraordinary knowledge of his own unconscious by constant attention to the smallest sign of deterioration and by repeated attempts at tracing these deteriorations to his own mistaken service, and – it sounds like a joke – he acquires this knowledge almost without effort.

So far I have talked only of the psychotherapeutic instrument and its most favourable construction. Yet it is also a question of using this instrument. What is the object the doctor has to serve psychotherapeutically? The answer is self-evident: the patient is the object. I have no doubt – and I believe this

214

holds true for most doctors – that psychotherapy, that is, the putting into service of the doctor's psyche in its conscious and unconscious aspects, should be practised always and everywhere except when the patient is completely unconscious. This lone exception teaches us the way psychotherapy has to go, where this instrument of the doctor's psyche has to be applied. This can always and only be the patient's psyche, and again both parts of his psyche, the conscious and the unconscious. But this is merely the way that leads to the effect. It would be a fateful error to assume that psychotherapy works only on the psyche. On the contrary one can make sure of the fact that the patient uses the doctor's psychic services for his vegetative system as often as for his psychological system, for better and for worse, for convalescence or for continued illness.

Here I am faced with the strange turning point where the relationship of doctor and patient is reversed, where the patient becomes the doctor and decides himself what he is to do with his servant's services and even whether he wants to accept them at all. To be sure, the doctor can offer his service in a different way too, if he realises that it does not please, and must if need be make the patient accept his service by cunning. He can do a lot in that way. When the patient's It deigns to use what is offered to him, then the doctor's activity is over; he has no influence on what the patient will do after that. He has to wait in the antichamber, inactive, but always on guard, ready to jump as soon as there is an order, or a piece of misfortune, deeply convinced that it is not the master's mood that spoils the healing effects of the service but that he, doctor and servant, has offered misguided service.

So far my argument is easy to understand, yet I admit that it might be wrong. I merely maintain that it is easy to follow. For his psychotherapeutic activity the doctor's instrument is his more or less well-functioning psyche. He applies this instrument to the patient's psyche. As soon as he has done this he stops leading. Then the doctor becomes the patient's instrument.

Before we can continue the argument I must stress a peculiarity of the patient's, the ambivalence of his intentionality. Two forces in constant flux and obscurely interdependent are at work in him, the tendency to recover and the tendency to remain ill. During treatment both tendencies are active without interruption, both make use of the doctor for their contrasting purposes. The fact that the patient is ill reveals a wish to be ill, going to the doctor's – it must not be forgotten that in the patient's terms anybody he asks for help is a doctor, no matter whether he has an official licence or not – is an expression of the will to get better; this sees the doctor as a friend, the will to be ill sees him as the worst enemy.

In saying that the doctor becomes the patient's instrument the moment he starts his psychotherapeutic activity – and that is the moment when patient and doctor meet up for the first time or often the moment when the patient (without having seen the doctor) thinks for the first time that he wants to go to a certain doctor or to any doctor at all – I want to say that from this moment he is going to be used by the patient in a double sense, namely for better and for worse. Both tendencies can make use of the three psychological aspects of the patient: consciousness, the unconscious and the vegetative, and it is possible and even usual that consciousness is used by the will to get better, while the will to remain ill uses the unconscious and the vegetative for its own purposes. Yet quite often the opposite happens, or the two tendencies interchange their methods in the course of treatment. In the same way, for better or for worse, both tendencies can make use of the doctor's three psychological aspects, his consciousness, his unconscious and his vegetative forces.

Having discussed – I hope with reasonable clarity – the patient's ambivalence, I can now examine the question of what the physician treating the patient has to do, while emphasising again that treatment is different from service. The answer seems to be easy: he has to help, for instance somehow intervene purposively, perhaps write out a prescription, make a cut somewhere, check on diet, breathing, bowel movements, sleep and waking hours, give advice, etc. This is usually called 'treatment'; this is essentially what we were taught at university and what we perfect more or less successfully in the course of our medical practice to a personal technique. We have a duty to support the patient's will to get better directly; it is the first thing we have to do, yet the question is whether it is the most important thing. In the majority of cases by far, in my experience more than three quarters of all cases one comes across in one's whole medical practice, it is quite sufficient to give direct support to the will to get better. The doctor who sees this as his task will have numerous successes and, if he has the talent, will bear the honourable name of doctor with justification because he has not only got a licence but has become a doctor by his own efforts. Yet something will disturb his own self-esteem: that so many patients get well without him, with the help of some other perhaps very stupid and incompetent doctor or quack, a change of climate, an intervening event or some mysterious unknown factor. Gradually he will understand that the essential contribution to a patient's recovery is not his effort but the patient's will to get better. Automatically and more and more often his attention will be drawn to those cases where his help is no use, where the patient stays ill or gets worse. And gradually his deepest interest will become concentrated on the individual's will to be ill; he will recognise that the most difficult part of his duties is not direct help but the prevention of damage. From this insight it is only a step to the understanding that damage is unavoidable since the patient – in the ambivalence in which the will to be ill predominates – wants to be damaged; that the will to be ill can always and easily or not so easily transform the doctor's best efforts even into a damaging force. Nil nocere? Often damage is unavoidable. Often, very often, it is only by the continuation or deterioration of an illness that we can tell whether the patient has used the doctor in order to become more ill, and sometimes the doctor manages in such a case to transform damage into cure – rarely by treatment but by service. And at this point something starts that can properly be called psychotherapy.

The doctor becomes the patient's instrument, I said: the premise is that this instrument is prepared to be used in the wrong way for purposes of falling ill and that it automatically prevents this, or at least makes amends for the damage it has done. Psychotherapeutic activity could be demonstrated by comparing it to a well-known party game in which a person is blindfolded and told to find a needle that is hidden somewhere in the room; the only help he is given in his search is that he holds hands with somebody who is concentrating on the hiding place, and that he can lead this person about the room. Since the person whose hand is being held is forced, by thinking of the hiding place, to stop the searcher from going in the direction of the hiding place, the needle will be found in a short while even by an inexperienced player if he follows the involuntary resistance of the other player. The stronger the resistance the closer the needle. To transfer this to the doctor's activity: at first the doctor has to direct the patient's attention squarely to the will to be ill and the hide-and-seek activities of this tendency, and then he has to trace the resistance which expresses itself in the patient's infinite big and little symptoms, in his consciousness, unconscious and vegetative systems, in his healthy and in his diseased parts.

This allows us to formulate a clear proposition: the fundamental task of all psychotherapy is the tracing and dissolving of resistance. Often enough, of course, one is forced – mainly because one wants to get to one's goal more quickly – to make the service more effective by conscious treatment with the help of the technical skills a doctor can muster from his knowledge, ability, and experience. Yet in the small percentage of cases which absolutely need psychotherapeutic treatment patient, unflagging attention produces good results more certainly and thus faster than does the most carefully worked-out treatment. In cases as difficult as this, treatment should be reserved for moments of danger. There is no doubt that as a doctor one has to be able to master every kind of technical treatment or be in a position to call on specialists using other techniques. Yet it is advisable to be economical in this respect. This applies only to that quarter of patients who require the help of the best qualified doctor, and one should add that not a quarter but at most a tenth of patients are involved. 75 per cent of patients get well by themselves and by some kind of treatment, 15 per cent do not get well under any circumstances, this leaves, at the most, 10 per cent who need the doctor's most intense efforts.

An example will show what I mean. Let us assume that a cut in the skin has to be made for some reason and that the cut is stitched up and bandaged. The chance is a thousand to one that the wound will heal smoothly, yet on the one thousand and first case the wound will not heal, even after all precautionary measures have been carefully observed. Why is it that the wound does not heal? Because a cure is never brought about by the doctor, but by the patient. The fact that the wound does not heal proves that the patient does not want to be cured and prevents cure by one or more of his life forces – the conscious, unconscious or vegetative systems – the patient puts up resistance. What shall the doctor do? He has to realise that the patient resists. And then, like the blindfolded player who tries to find the needle, he must trace the reason for the resistance with the help of every word, every movement, every sign of life from the healthy or sick person, and make the patient verbalise all the resistance in his consciousness, make conscious what is unconscious and retrievable to consciousness of his resistance, and get the patient's interpretation of everything that is unconscious or vegetative. If it can be avoided, the doctor should not attempt the interpretation himself; his interpretation is almost always used as a new means of resistance, is rarely useful, and often does so much damage that it destroys any hope of a successful service by the doctor; he has to be prepared to be sacked from service.

I said above that the patient's will to be ill considers the doctor its worst enemy. If this is true – and I consider it to be true – then one can imagine that the will to be ill is constantly on the look-out to find fault with the doctor – be it something that is conscious, unconscious or vegetative. It uses this justified or unjustified objection – the unjustified objection is much more useful for the will to be ill because it forces the patient to feel guilty and thus helps to keep him ill, in order to persuade the patient to use the doctor's service as a ploy to stay ill or to get worse. The will to be ill is not satisfied only with finding reasons for resistance in the doctor; it fashions an image of the doctor and his whole life environment in order to make certain, and this image corresponds to reality only in a few, perhaps only in a single detail. Brush and paint for this picture are taken from the patient's experiential world in which it is active, the conscious, unconscious, or vegetative world. It transfers certain things on to the doctor which are from totally different experiential spheres and have nothing to do with the doctor's personality, in the same way in which the will to get well transfers and fashions an image of the doctor in order to strengthen itself with its help. This fact is important for treatment as well as for service.

Since the will to be ill resists recovery, sees and has to see the concept 'doctor' as an embodiment of the will to get well, since this latter tendency makes the doctor serve, the patient's resistance will always be directed more or less against the doctor; I say always, yet this is merely a personal conviction which is prompted by the fact that I have never seen an exception to this rule in my practice. Thus as a person treating the patient I possess a starting point from which I can trace resistance, for of course it is easier to find a resistance towards my person than a resistance about which I know nothing at all. To search out and make conscious this personal resistance is one of the important means of psychotherapy or really of every therapy. This is the place from which it is easiest to root out the will to be ill.

Yet this is not the only or even the most important reason why I have insisted constantly and for decades that the personal resistance has to be discovered. I have experienced in my own person that this is the most certain, I almost said the only, way to learn how to serve. In order to be able to serve, one has to know one's own idiosyncracies, try as much as possible to get rid of them, and admit frankly what cannot be got rid of. The servant-doctor can only make one fateful mistake: that of hiding things, of hiding them from others and, even worse, from himself. Yet the patient clearly says to those who have ears to hear consciously, unconsciously, and vegetatively: 'you are like that: I know you, it is stupid to hide'. And this clear and audible language of the patient, this resistance in the patient, makes the doctor serve better and better from year to year. Slowly and gradually he will grow in his whole being – conscious, unconscious, vegetative – from a person who treats patients into a servant, a real doctor. Yes, it could even be said that by following this path he comes closer to becoming a full human being. For the wonderful thing about the medical profession is that it can lead one on to being a full human being, and more so and better than any other profession. Yet at the same time it can lead one away from this goal more easily than any other profession. This is certainly true.

I have to correct what I said earlier on: I said – with a definite reason – something that is incorrect. I said the will to be ill invents unjustified objections to the doctor. In the deepest sense of the word these objections are never justified; they are always rooted in the doctor's character, are not idiosyncracies of the fictional image but of the doctor himself. The patient helps the doctor make his unconscious conscious. This is why I believe that the doctor should be grateful to his patient. The patient is the doctor's teacher. Only from the patient will the doctor be able to learn psychotherapy.

9

Treatment*

While the ideas discussed in the previous lectures can be traced back to the influence that Freud exerts on me, the following investigations into medical treatment derive from a doctor the like of whom I have never encountered again in forty years of medical practice: Ernst Schweninger. All my knowledge and all my skill I owe to him. I do not claim that what I am going to say today is a faithful reproduction of what Schweninger thought and taught but what my brains made of it. I know of no shorter and clearer way to present the aims of our profession than by using the expressions into which he cast the articles of the belief that he held on to with the naivety of genius.

'Man is the product of his living conditions in the broadest sense of the word: if the product is to be changed then the factors which produce it have to be changed'; this statement was the guiding line Schweninger followed in his therapy. As a young man I did not understand the profound meaning of it; in those days I confused the term living conditions with another term, namely living environment, which Schweninger never used; I believed that one should change the patient's circumstances of life, his environment, if one followed Schweninger's doctrine. But this was just what Schweninger did *not* want; he said and meant living conditions, and conditions always require at least two things that are related to each other. A change in somebody's living conditions can be effected in three ways: either by changing the external world, the environment – this is the way which is shown to students at the universities and which the physician usually takes, and believes he takes even when his unconscious, his demon leads him a different way; or by changing the human being – as psychoanalysis does – and

---

* Fourth lecture in a series of four, given at the Lessing Hochschule, Berlin, Autumn 1926. Overall title 'Das Es' (The It); titles of individual lectures: 'The It and Psychoanalysis', 'Everyday', 'Illness', and 'Treatment'. First published in *Die Arche*, II, 17 (17.12.1926). Reprinted in Georg Groddeck, *Der Mensch und sein Es*, Wiesbaden, 1970.

thereby the product human being-environment-patient has to change; or thirdly, by changing the environment sometimes or the inner human being sometimes, or, if necessary, both at the same time; this alone, in my opinion, was the meaning of Schweninger's dictum. In any case I do not know what else the word 'living conditions' could mean.

The sentence assumes a strange meaning if one remembers one fact which Schweninger emphasised again and again, which almost nobody noticed, even though it is obvious and can be observed by everybody. Schweninger said: The majority of all illnesses cure themselves, no matter how they are treated or whether they are treated at all; if I am not mistaken, he said 75 per cent, a figure I consider too low; he quoted the drastic words of the surgeon Nussbaum who used to say: Most wounds heal even when you bandage them with cow dung, but a certain number of them will only heal when treated with the utmost care. A further number, perhaps 15 per cent will never improve, no matter what treatment is given. Then there is the remaining 10 per cent for whom the kind of treatment they get really matters. – It is of no importance whether these figures are right or wrong, the fact remains that treatment rarely decides whether the patient recovers or remains ill. It may be a pity that people do not know this; it may also be a good thing: human beings seem to need fear in order to allow themselves to be saved. Without doubt the question of the choice of treatment acquires a different weight with the knowledge that it has to be asked very rarely.

If one continues the game with percentages and bears in mind that in most illnesses treatment is unnecessary, it becomes apparent that most of the cases which do need treatment are favourably influenced by a change in external living conditions; nothing else is needed. This is the reason why treatment generally consists in a change of environment. What remains to be achieved is a change of heart by the individual, or a combination in which the attempt is made to change both environment and personality. My professional experience of the last two decades makes me prefer the combination. The result seems to me, as far as I am able to perceive, so successful that I am inclined to assume that it might be possible, with this combination, to treat some of the patients who belong to the 15 per cent of incurables. But this is an assumption which may be occasioned by wishful thinking.

Like all intelligent people whose intelligence and humanity is great enough, Schweninger had a tendency towards self-irony, a consequence of which was his use of bon mots – for all his aversion and hatred of clichés – in order to emphasise the views he presented to his students. He maintained among other things that the easiest way of discussing the question of medical treatment was by using the formula which used to be the basis of Latin essays written at school: quis, quid, ubi, quibus auxiliis, cur, quomodo, quando; in other words: who, what, where, by what means, why, how, when. And in fact this tired old formula really helps to elucidate a number of things.

Who does the treating? The answer to this question seems to be simply this: the physician. Yet we start from the fact that the human being is an It, that the effective principle of treatment is not simply the physician's Ego nor a combination of his consciousness and his unconscious, but his It which is sometimes active in his consciousness, sometimes in his unconscious, sometimes in areas beyond these two systems. If the doctor wanted to find out who really does the treating he would have to know and judge himself, and nobody can do that. Thus the question, who does the treating?, is answered very imprecisely when people say: the physician. It is even doubtful whether the answer is correct; it is not. This becomes apparent if one goes on to ask: who is being treated? The patient, of course. But again there is the unpleasant fact that we know very little about the patient, that we can only know a small part of his Ego, his conscious and unconscious systems and what lies beyond these systems, namely no more than what is revealed by the patient's It and what our It wants to perceive. In treatment two independent yet voluntarily communicating entities meet; the physician wants to change the patient according to certain ideas which are only partly known to him, by means of certain measures which again are only known to him as far as his It allows him; the doctor's It without his own knowledge adjusts itself, however, in its activities to the reactions of the patient's It, its actions are to a large part unconscious, even beyond retrieving into consciousness. The patient's It, on the other hand, which is apparently the subject of treatment has an interest in being ill since it reveals itself in illness, it wants to remain ill, and therefore tries to mislead the physician's It, changes it to such an extent that it is incapable of describing the advantages of being well to the patient's It and making the latter want to be well again. The question: who does the treating? cannot be answered, the doctor treats the patient – that is only one side of the process – there are always two simultaneous, interacting treatments and therefore two persons who do the treating: the doctor treats the patient, the patient at the same time treats the doctor. It could be said that there is a fight between two treatments, one of which tries to strengthen the will to get well in somebody else while the other, the treatment by the patient, is out to test every one of the doctor's measures for its usefulness towards its object of remaining ill. Treatment will only be successful if the doctor is able to change the capacity of the diseased It to interfere, in such a way that it either gives up its resistance or gets too exhausted to continue its resistance.

To say it again and emphatically: in dealing with patients there are two treatments which cross each other and possess opposite aims. Thus there are also two 'Who's' treating each other; the physician treats the patient and is simultaneously treated by the patient. Obviously for a successful outcome it is more important that the treatment of the doctor by the patient should fail than that the doctor should act on the basis of scientifically prejudiced or unscientific principles. The saying: Nil nocere – damage nothing – is the alpha and omega of all medical activity; unfortunately this principle is much more difficult to follow than is generally believed. While the question of who is doing the treatment is very confusing because there are two persons doing the treating and two being treated, the question What is being treated? can be answered in one word: the resistance. Yet at once question and answer split in two, since there are two kinds of resistance against getting well, one emanating from the patient, the other from the physician's It. The resistance that emanates from the patient is comparatively easy to sum up: it is essentially the patient's unwillingness to get well. In order to simplify things (though this alone is far from making them simple) the patient can be imagined as an individual with dual motivation: on the one hand his will, the will of his It, is bent on being ill otherwise the patient wouldn't be ill, he is so

225

because of a mostly unconscious act of will; on the other hand, he wants to get well – unless he is one of those patients who are undergoing treatment merely to obtain proof of being cleverer than their doctors, i.e. than their parents whose representatives the doctors are – otherwise he would not allow himself to be treated. In treatment it is fairly useless to support the will to get well because it is always present, even in those who are dying, as is often proved by the final upsurge of strength. Since the strengthening of the will to get well is an exercise of medical technique which can be taught, this is essentially what is being taught at the universities and, if fortune smiles, also being learnt. How to treat the resistance is not teachable, it has to be learned, and can only be learned by treating patients; this explains the perplexing fact that the young doctor, for all his talent and eagerness, initially bungles his work; he cannot help it and no improvement of teaching methods will ever change this fact. It is sad that exams can at best only tell us that the young doctor has mastered the unimportant aspect, the techniques, of his profession. Yet it is true. Admission to the medical register is no certain measure of medical ability, nor is the lack of admission a certain sign of somebody's unfitness to practice the medical profession. For technical ability can always be obtained everywhere, though it has to be admitted that the easiest way of learning this technique is to go to university. – To put this aspect of medical practice into other words: the doctor's task is to liberate the patient's will to get well from all obstructions, traps, and snares, then recovery will come about automatically. This needs careful attention: at the slightest sign of deterioration, of a slowing-down of convalescence, and even of a minute strain in the emotional relationship between patient and doctor the doctor will have to tell himself: I have made a mistake; what matters then is to find out what kind of mistake it was and to discuss it honestly with the patient; without any embarrassment or attempt at apology. – And with this I have returned to the most important part of treatment: the treatment of the doctor by the patient. I have already mentioned that apart from the patient's resistance to treatment there is a resistance in the doctor's mind to the measures necessary to effect the patient's cure; it would take me too long to describe the conditions and expressions of this internal resistance which is so often dangerous; as a simple example I shall only mention the battle which the doctor has to wage against his own vanity and the megalomania fed by the public, by the facts of life, and by the self-adulation innate in man. One could say that the doctor should believe the conscious and unconscious expressions of everybody absolutely as long as he takes some notice of the various ways in which the It expresses itself, but he should never believe in anything unless a favourable reaction on the part of the patient confirms it. In other words: the doctor has a yardstick with which to measure his It in the behaviour of the patient he is treating. The doctor's profession alleviates man's essential duty – know thyself – in a way unrivalled by any other profession. The doctor is the person who can in all events derive profit from the treatment, inner profit. It is not the patient who should be grateful to the doctor, it is the doctor who must be grateful to the patient. It is never the doctor's merit when the patient gets well; but it is his fault, the fault of his foolishness and dishonesty, if the patient does not get well; the doctor, however, can always get well during and through the treatment which he gets free of charge from the patient, and if he doesn't it is due to the fact that he does not want to get well, and often consciously; because a precondition of this is a renunciation of ego-worship, and this renunciation is more difficult for the doctor than for other people.

Thus the question of who is to be treated is also split up into two lines which permanently cross, then withdraw, reapproach and cross again. Only one thing is clear: the doctor continues to be under treatment as long as he practices his profession; yet the people who treat him change; the results can be found in his being rather than in an increase of medical skill; they are, however, never complete. The patient, on the other hand, is always treated by one doctor, or rather by a figure from his unconscious which does not really change in spite of the succession of personalities attending to him but always bears the features of his mother. Since he goes to the doctor for a specific complaint, treatment for him also comes to an end with recovery; it is possible that the events of illness and treatment have brought about changes in his personality, but it is also possible that they haven't. This should not be the aim of the treatment anyway, it should concentrate on breaking down the It's resistance. What the It does after it has given up its resistance lies outside the domain of medical practice. If a person can come to realise that one cannot have any more power over somebody else than that other person allows, then this person should be the doctor, and he should be well aware that he is no prophet, that his treatment is tied to the moment, that a preconceived plan can be a hindrance and, finally, that he has to leave the outcome to God and is thus not in a position to say anything about this unknown outcome without being presumptuous. Diagnosis and prognosis, what is and what shall be, these are things the patient and his family would like to know, yet the doctor does not know and therefore should not offer any opinion on them. The fact that a doctor agrees to treat a patient indicates that the doctor is hopeful of achieving something. This should be sufficient for the patient, is usually sufficient for him. The family is not satisfied, but the family come into the category of 'resistance'. Their curiosity has to be treated.

With the word 'family', the terror of every doctor, I have arrived at the question of where the patient should be treated. If it is at all possible the patient should be treated wherever he happens to be at the moment in question. This is such a general statement, yet how can it be put into practice? The doctor and his patient have to stay in close touch otherwise the treatment cannot be properly conducted; for it implies that the doctor knows the patient's living conditions in order to change them if necessary. Once more the emphasis is on the word 'living conditions'. The important factor in a successful treatment is not the environment, but the patient's reactions to his environment. Keeping this in mind, the question of where treatment should take place loses its importance. I do not have to mention that the environment in which somebody is ill deserves our attention: everybody knows that, daily life teaches us, since it has invented hospitals, convalescence homes, spas, and health cures of various kinds and in various places and these are successfully used; it is even taught at university where in other respects one learns very little about treatment, probably in the legitimate knowledge that essential things cannot be taught, that only technique can be taught and learnt. When I said that it is not very important where treatment takes place, provided the doctor has the opportunity of quickly discovering the patient's areas of resistance, of examining and if possible re-moving these, I meant that the patient does not bring his exter-nal environment with him, but that he find his attitudes to life and the fundamental aspects of these everywhere; for these fun-damental aspects are contained within himself. Man is not the product of his environment, he constructs his environment him-self; by adopting attitudes towards the world around him, by accepting or rejecting it he creates the environment, at least the environment, in which his life is to be conducted. For man there is apparently (a word I use advisedly since I do not know any-thing for certain) a law that his behaviour towards his environ-ment is determined by his past experience, that he tries to approximate his present and future environment to a picture which he formed in the past and which essentially does not change after the completion of the third year. Man's environ-ment – one could say without too much distortion of the facts, without which nothing can be said – is a figment of his imagin-ation, is his very own, self-created artifact. Since this is so and since all his life man works away at nothing else but this artifact and has no time for anything else, he always and in the true sense of the word lives in the same living conditions. If these are to be changed – the idea borrowed from Schweninger with which I started this argument – they have to be changed at the spot where they were formed, and thus the doctor, if he wants to conduct a proper therapy, must take the patient back to his childhood, to the age of three years. In doing so he merely imitates the course of nature, for illness, as I tried to argue earlier, is a return to childhood. Nature or, if you want, life is as Christ described it; unless you become children you will not enter into the kingdom of heaven.

The patient has to be treated in his past by his past. I must add, however, that I do not count technicalities like the setting of an arm, the dressing of a wound, the prescription of medicine or diet, medicinal baths or massage as being part of treatment, for these are practices the mastery of which does not give anyone the right to call himself doctor.

If I weren't afraid of being misunderstood, of people taking literally what is meant to be metaphorical, I would say: every now and then man finds himself confronted with his environment in ways which remind him – or perhaps only his unconscious – of the image he formed as a child of his environment and of how as a child he behaved vis-à-vis certain situations and events. Then his It managed to master every difficulty with the help of the imaginative and logical tricks peculiar to all children, and the more easily so since he still possessed then the far-reaching possibilities of repressing insoluble problems; there was above all ample opportunity for putting the responsibility and thus the blame on others since the adults, parents, teachers, and so on believed they had a right, arising from human necessities, of persuading the child to give up its sense of responsibility and barter it away. So this was an easy thing, and it is not surprising that the It, whose unconscious harbours such images of innocence created in childhood, should return to the artifact, to poetry. Now it merely lacks the means of blaming mother; neither the mother nor the recognition of irresponsibility are there: they have to be invented and invented in a way that they really participate in the spectacle of life. Both factors, mother and irresponsibility, are there with the illness, but unfortunately at the expense of inner truthfulness, and a poem which is made up without necessity, purely as a personal affair, and is not spontaneously created to fill a need, is not born, when pregnancy is over, is a failure in terms of the poet's conscience even if the world accepts it: it is a lie, not a poem. In order to escape this new guilt which originates in the untruthful rather than poetic irresponsibility, the It continues on the course of illness, hiding more and more behind the illness. Anyone who wants to help then – it is a question only of illnesses that cannot be tackled by medical technology – would do best to re-establish, re-invent childhood as it really was. This may be difficult in certain conditions, but it is usually possible since every human being is at bottom still the child he was and has remained so in all important matters such as breathing, eating, drinking, sleeping, acting, feeling etc., even thinking. The treatment should take the patient back to his past, confront him with the former decision which he evaded by untruthfulness, and make him see that what is important is not to be without guilt but to accept that one is a miserable human child with not even enough power to feel guilty. 'God have mercy on me, a poor sinner' – this ultimately is what it's all about.

The question quibus auxiliis, by what means all this can be

achieved, answers itself from what I have just said: 'The doctor who wants to conduct therapy, proper therapy, has to be childlike; the more of a child he is, the more successful his work will be'. In order to accept this statement one has to understand first that the child is the wise person. To anyone who cannot appreciate this the statement must seem nonsensical. I would like to think that many people among my audience share my opinion of the child's superiority over the adult and are themselves convinced of it. In order to make myself understood by everybody, however, I can choose the formula that the whole personality of the doctor constitutes the means of therapy, the whole personality to wit such as only the child possesses or is regained by individuals in moments when they are children again. Such moments occur daily with every human being, but we do not recognise them because we know so little about ourselves. It is worth our while to realise consciously how often we live and think and act in the simple manner of our childhood; this methodical attention will automatically establish a rhythmical pattern of those moments and, in addition to this, a great expansion of the personality which learns to open up and understand human worlds which were formerly unknown and closed to it. I might as well have said: to be a doctor one has to extend one's personality so far that it consciously plays on many human strings, that it masters human concerns better than other people. The doctor does not need a knowledge of people but a knowledge of the human heart. That such knowledge can be acquired is proved by psychoanalysis. It is the path which, before Freud, only children and childlike imaginative adults knew and which is now open to everybody, even though not everybody gets very far on it. In any case one can already say that the doctor who takes no notice of psychoanalysis or who even rejects it deprives himself of the best means of treating his patients with his whole being, and such a doctor acts like somebody who on principle treats haemorrhages with boiling oil.

Cure? Why does the doctor treat patients? Because he has to, for no other reason. He is like the pregnant woman: when her hour has come she has to give birth. It is the same with the doctor's treatment. When his hour has come he has to give birth to what is inside him, no matter whether it is a beautiful child or a freak, and since he is always pregnant and almost always in labour, he is constantly being fertilised since his profession forces him to self-knowledge – he will go on treating patients because he has to. I would not have gone into the why if there wasn't so much wrong and damaging talk about the doctor's profession, in particular the statement that he chose his profession out of love for mankind or even that he sacrifices himself. Such talk we can leave to those curious parents who tell their children that they made them out of love for them, their as yet unborn children, or the mothers who consider it legitimate to talk of sacrificing themselves when a moment's thought can prove to them that loving children is an immense joy and never a sacrifice. The doctor does not sacrifice himself, he has his inner urge and he has no more love of mankind than anyone else, the only difference being that his profession makes it easier for him to love people and to grow out of the habit of hating. The fact that there are so few misanthropists among experienced doctors is a favour their profession bestows on them.

Quomodo, how shall the doctor conduct his treatment? is an old question which is asked again and again; he is to treat causally, that is, find the cause of the illness and remove it or render it harmless, then the illness will disappear automatically. Perhaps it does; I do not know and I do not believe that anyone knows, and I think that this sort of talk is pure nonsense. For to know the cause of an illness means to be like God, and this is impossible. In order to believe in causal treatment one has to believe in a juggling trick of life, which is not, however, to be wondered at in view of the human propensity – it is called a law of human thought – to look for causes everywhere. For this purpose one has to assume that the illness starts from outside, which is the exact opposite of what actually happens. A dose of poison, the kind and number of respective agents, something can be said about this, yet it is at most a part of the affair, an unimportant part; the *cause,* the cause is man himself, is the way in which he relates to those external processes, and since this relationship changes constantly, nothing can be said about the cause unless one knows the individual completely, and that would mean knowing the universe. – It is perhaps superfluous to mention these things; I do it because I have the feeling that the unfortunate search for causes, and the belief that causes could be found, has got into psychoanalytic thinking, too, and is causing a lot of confusion there. In contrast to this I declare that I do not share the view, and that psychoanalysis does not share the view, that repressions are the cause of illness and that the treatment of repression is a causal kind of treatment. It is rather – as all treatment always was, is, and will be – symptomatic, guided by the symptoms, starting from the symptoms, and using them as the guiding principle. The notion of the symptom does not apply only to the temperature, the pulse beat, the various signs of specific illnesses, but to everything expressed by the patient's It and perceived by the doctor's It, from the shape of the chin to the deepest emotions, from the present situation to the remote past. But we always treat a picture, a living picture and never a cause, always the individual human being, the cause, never the environment. Whether anything in the symptoms shown by the individual patient is important for treatment or not cannot be judged beforehand, it only emerges in the phenomenon which Freud called resistance. Since resistance, the proper object of all treatment, becomes only gradually recognisable in its various expressions, it is comparatively unimportant how the treatment is begun, yet it is important that it is conducted patiently and attentively; patience and attention are aids which one can almost say make every treatment a proper treatment. The doctor who bears in mind that he is the tool with which the patient tries to get well, and that it is thus the doctor's duty to be a good tool and not a good conductor, best corresponds to the views I have of the doctor's function.

Finally to conclude these superficially structured views on treatment, for now there remains the question of when the doctor should treat a patient. The answer is not easy for me, yet it contradicts everything that is customary. The doctor should give treatment only when the patient asks him. This simple sentence contains a sharp break with the general demand that the doctor has to look after the hygiene of life and that his foremost task is to prevent illnesses. I am of the opinion that this is the task of the health officers, not of the doctor. If he is interested he can occupy himself with it, but then he must know and should not forget that, by occupying himself with general hygiene and specific prevention of illnesses, he strengthens in himself the biggest enemy of his medical talent, i.e. megalomania, that he feeds the one flaw of character which doctors in any case are horribly prone to, arrogance, and thus reduces his efficiency in his proper field, the treatment of patients. The doctor is there for the patient, not for the healthy. He is an instrument with the help of which the patient recovers. The more sensitive the reactions of the doctor's It to the actions of the sick It, without imposing his own ideas, his own imperfections, the more he merits the highest title which mankind can bestow on somebody, the title of doctor.

Massage and Psychotherapy*

The mutual relations between massage and mind are so complicated that in the nature of the case it is impossible to sum-
marise them in brief. Moreover, the processes of endocrine
action and the effect of massage upon certain systems to which
we are compelled to assign some intermediary function between body and mind (e.g. the autonomic nervous system) are
entirely unknown to us. My treatment of the subject is therefore
inevitably incomplete, and I shall only attempt to discuss isolated sections.

A certain harmony of feeling on the animal level between
doctor and patient is the fundamental basis of medical treatment which is, in essence, a reciprocal activity between doctor
and patient, patient and doctor, wherein the doctor undertakes
the duties, difficult to understand as well as to carry out, of servant responsible for the well-being of his master. The term
'animal' is meant to indicate that this important factor in treatment has, to begin with, nothing to do with the knowledge and
skill of the physician, but arises from the contact of two human
worlds and from their mutual human sympathy and antipathy.
One does not need a great deal of experience to find out that the
influence of this factor in healing is almost entirely dependent
upon physical contact. The unconscious realisation of this
truth is shown by the custom of submitting every patient on the
first interview to a physical examination, although in most
cases this procedure might be postponed without any ill results.
Skilled physicians of long standing have learned that, given certain circumstances, examination may do irreparable harm, for
one cannot always predict the result of bodily contact, and so,
often enough they renounce the momentary advantages of a

---

* This chapter is a translation, by V.M.E. Collins, of 'Massage', a paper
contributed to the Psychotherapeutic Congress at Dresden, May 15, 1931. It
is reprinted from *Exploring the Unconscious* (London, Vision Press, 1950).

diagnosis and the consequent immediate resolution of the extremely delicate relationship between two colliding human worlds. This is not to say, however, that, generally speaking, the speedy conquest of the patient is not of great advantage in his treatment, indeed it is not seldom demanded by the exigencies of his case. All that is here claimed is that this question of the appropriate moment for making physical contact is intensely important in treating with massage, since by its very nature the exercise of massage compels a closer physical contact between doctor and patient than does any other form of treatment, surgery not excepted. And just as the first treatment by massage consistently and invariably affects the patient both pleasantly and unpleasantly, so does every succeeding treatment; hence we can say with full justification that massage, in whatever way it is carried out, must have some psychical influence upon the unaccustomed organism, and that it is an important, though incalculable weapon for psychotherapy. What we call transference and resistance appear during the course of the massage to help or to hinder.

Massage can be of service both in diagnosis and in treatment. The physician who himself treats by massage thereby gains a most excellent instrument for investigation. That his sense of touch develops a greater refinement is too obvious to need mention, were it not that our methods of work make little use of the feeling-sense, although for our predecessors it was the most important means of arriving at a diagnosis. Vision, too, is sharpened through massage. Not only does one notice changes in form and colour due to the distribution of warmth, changes which might otherwise easily escape observation, but also the patient's changing expressions reveal hidden secrets of his soul that in no other way could come to the knowledge of his doctor. Unconscious impulses and deeply buried traits of character betray themselves in his involuntary movements, so that a massage treatment can hardly ever be given without enriching the doctor's diagnostic knowledge of his patient. His sense of hearing also improves in such a way that he can follow specific changes in breathing and tone of voice well worthy of attention. But most important of all is the part played by the sense of smell. There is a general neglect of this sense, too, although our forefathers attached great importance to it in forming or correcting their diagnosis, but no one who gives massage can avoid noticing remarkable changes of smell, and even though he may be unable to communicate his own impression in any convincing form to other people, the fact remains that by this means he can detect changes in the course of the disease sooner than he would otherwise do.

It is not only the physician, however, to whom the diagnosis is important; the patient's anxiety to know it is a proof of its significance for him, though here we are faced at once with a diametrical difference. One may take it on the whole that the physician is able to construct a more or less accurate picture of the real state of affairs when he gives his diagnosis, but it is absolutely certain that for the patient the diagnosis at best is but an empty phrase, while in some cases, it gives rise to a completely false idea of the situation. Lack of medical knowledge and the resultant wild fantasies over what will or what may happen in the near or the remote future, often prove a great hindrance to recovery, not seldom, indeed, they give rise to conflicts which invade both family and professional life. The absurd superstitions about medical matters which one finds in all social classes, have become in their half-knowledge a general danger. In certain circumstances, however, this can be obviated through the mental effects of massage. At the first touch the patient's thought and attention are diverted into other channels. He gets some insight into his own condition and wants to find out something more about himself than can be given by the phrase which for him is purely fantastic. Thus he gradually begins to realise that in a diagnosis, e.g. in the term 'heart disease', there is included a number of different things which are more important for treatment and recovery than the anatomical condition, that the sick man, his functional capacity, and his return to a useful career are the real objects of medical treatment, that his state is more important than the name of his disease, and that in disease we are dealing with a changing situation, since illness is an organic process of life, not a thing that is fixed and dead. As day by day he is faced by new problems arising out of his changing sensations in massage, his awakening desire to learn then becomes so intense, that generally, after a very short time, in the company of his doctor, he is exploring new physical and mental fields which would otherwise only be discovered by the greatest of good luck. Together with this change of attitude on the part of the patient towards his illness and his doctor, there goes what is still more important, the widening of the doctor's horizon. A doctor who gives massage cannot help evolving, stage by stage, his own methods of psychotherapeutic treatment. The very nature of his work makes him a psychotherapist. Certainly his methods are often tortuous, crazy, even dangerous, but that does not alter the fact that the practical experience of the medical masseur gives him a far better foundation for the doctrines of the new psychotherapy than can be obtained through the best theoretical instruction about mind and disease.

Another aspect of the mental effect of massage must be mentioned, an important one though unfortunately almost unrecognised, in its full significance certainly unrecognised. In the course of time human life brings about certain functional disturbances and anatomical changes which have little importance to the healthy man, but which retard the recovery of the sick, and nearly all of these can and should be put right at the cost of some trouble and care in massage. In the first place their removal at once releases energy, though for present purposes nothing need be said on this point: at the moment we are chiefly concerned with psychotherapeutic influences. The mere discovery of these almost universal injuries has an invaluable effect upon the patient's conscious and unconscious will to be healed, and hence upon the strengthening of the mysterious forces which make for health, the eternally insoluble X of medicine. One or two examples may perhaps make this clearer.

The exigencies of life are such that the four extremities, the legs even more than the arms, hang downwards almost the whole day long. The only effect usually noticed is that the influence of gravity sets up small disturbances of the blood-circulation which have little importance in view of the strength of the heart-beat. But other fluids are circulating in the body as well as the blood and the movement of these is to a great extent dependent upon the force of gravity. It is remarkable that this other type of circulation hardly appears in medical theory or practice. The fact remains that certain lower parts of the adult body always contain an excess of fluid, with some reserve one might say, they always contain oedemic tissue. Chief of these parts are the feet, the hands, and the joints. In the case of the feet, boots and shoes play a special part since they put out of action a good part of the machinery of their special circulation, which is of importance also to the whole economy of the organism. A number of different movements are prevented by the wearing of boots and so it comes about that the adult nearly always stands with his legs a little bent, that he seldom makes any fully extended stretching movements and that with certain joints (e.g. at hip and neck) he either does not bend at all or makes only limited movements in bending.

This water-logging of particular regions of the body goes unnoticed because it comes about very slowly over a period of years. It is at once revealed to the masseur, however, because he observes with all his patients that the toes, the finger-tips, the great nerve of the sole of the foot, the neighbourhood of the knuckles, certain parts of the region round the os sacrum, particular points in the shoulder-blades, and the neck, etc., are painful under pressure. Usually it needs only slight pressure to establish this fact, in no case such a pressure as that exerted by the weight of the body as it bears down upon the foot. Extended stretching and bending of the limbs and spine are also remarkably painful to the average European, even to the trained athlete. A great part, a very great part of our unconscious mental energy is used up merely in warding off pain from these waterlogged places. As has already been said, the diseased conditions are slow in developing, but for that very reason they can be quickly got rid off by massage, at least partially and for a long period, and that is why they must be brought into any discussion on the relation of massage to psychotherapy. From the moment that it no longer becomes necessary to devote a great deal of unconscious attention and mental energy to the avoidance of pain, the power thus set free can be used for other purposes, for the task of recovery. This can be done all the better because the patient's conscious mind is able to recognise and follow up in his own experiences the using-up of power and its subsequent release. This not only increases to a marked degree his confidence in his doctor, but also the healing power of his own organism, and brings about a transformation of conscious, unconscious and vegetative mental characteristics of great consequence to psychotherapy.

One example may be given which shows how the masseur, without any further effort, discovers a way which may remain unknown to others their whole life long. The particular instance might of course be paralleled in other regions, and more especially in diseases of the breast and abdominal organs. The value of breathing as a means of psychotherapy is already widely acknowledged, although the physical effects have been made more of, perhaps with some justification. Nevertheless it must be emphasised here that breathing provides and releases an incredible amount of mental energy; it only needs to hold the breath to the point of exhaustion to be convinced of this. Breathing, indeed, is the chief driving-force of the circulation of fluid which we have been considering. It is hardly necessary to mention that the indirect mental effect of massage in this territory is important, and in the abdomen also. That is the boggy region of the body, since it is the most capable of expansion and, being crammed with spongy organs, offers continual opportunities for collections of water. In this connection attention may be drawn to the fact that the abdominal muscles above the navel, are painful under pressure, owing possibly to our habits of eating, but that this condition can be easily got rid of, together with fantasies of serious disease in the stomach or appendix. For this it is necessary, however, to take the muscles actually between the fingers and this is something of a strain for the masseur. In every adult the eyeballs are sensitive, and in the effort to avoid the irritation which is particularly associated with looking upwards, there is a useless expenditure of power, mental power. The tongue, too, the gums and special parts of the nose, show the same sensitivity. In other words, with every glance we give, every word we speak, every mouthful we chew, everything that we smell, we are wasting mental power which by the help of massage we could at least in part and for a time divert to useful purposes.

All things considered, we may perhaps be allowed to contend that massage and psychotherapy can be usefully employed together.

The Human Being, not the Patient, requires Help*

When one has reached 60 years of age it is advisable to gather together and communicate what one knows or believes one knows. If one is lucky one finds a suitable form for this: for some this means donning the solemn robe of serious aspiration, others will recite their wisdom with a raised index-finger to emphasise its importance, others again chat and instruct in an entertaining way; I cannot help but talk to myself, this is the way in which I have expressed myself ever since my childhood.

What happens inside me when I am confronted as a doctor by a human being who is a patient? Nothing else than what happens to other doctors: I try to find out what kind of a person is asking me for help. With this I am already deep into examination and treatment, the decisive thing has happened already: for it is decisive that I am dealing with a human being, that this human being is suffering and demands help from me. Whether this person is ill in the accepted medical sense or not has nothing to do with what happens first; it is unimportant whether I, the doctor, consider him ill or not, he does not expect knowledge from me but help. It is not the illness but the human being that needs help. As a doctor I am not concerned with the illness but with the human being.

The idea that the doctor has to make a diagnosis in order to be able to help is still predominant in medical practice, though gradually other approaches are gaining ground. But the general public cannot understand that a doctor could do his work without caring about diagnosis, about categorising a specific illness; even the amateur doctor, the quack in common usage, reinforces the public's wish to consider illness as something of importance. It will be decades before the diagnosis of the human being will be a general custom. The mistakes of the

* First published in *Die Arche*, III, 2 (26.4.1927). Reprinted in Georg Grod-deck, *Der Mensch und sein Es*, Wiesbaden, 1970.

expert – and our kind of diagnosing constitutes an expert's mistake – continue long after they have been recognised as such by experts; they are tough, inert masses and difficult to get rid off. This is why the doctor who takes his profession seriously and enjoys it will have to repeat to himself again and again: to diagnose an illness is of little use, can often be dispensed with and is often very, very damaging. To recognise the human being or rather to make guesses about him – since recognition is hardly ever possible – is what is needed. The doctor has nothing to do with illness, this is the pathologist's affair, the doctor as doctor has to deal with a specific individual that has come to him for help, everything else is of interest to him only insofar as it can be used by him for treatment. There are three things only which have to be observed on starting treatment: the human being who is to be treated, his request for help, and his relationship to the person from whom he asks help. These are the materials of diagnostics, everything else is of secondary interest in comparison.

One would think it is easy to follow this instruction; but it is not. On the contrary, one could say that this kind of diagnosis is the doctor's most difficult task and that this task cannot possibly be solved completely. That it is so difficult is explained by the fact that these areas of diagnostics are usually neglected. Almost always the doctor's attention is first focused on establishing the nature of the illness – he examines and decides what measures to take, how to fight it. The fact that the individual human being is to be discovered by all available means, with every effort, if possible in all his vital concerns, that the doctor is not dealing with illness, not even with ill or suffering people but rather with people in need of help who are often, mostly, not ill or whose illness is of secondary importance, that at the moment when the person who is seeking help encounters the helper something totally new happens, namely the most important aspect of diagnosis and treatment, a relationship is established between the person seeking help and his helper and vice versa, this is known only to a few and those who know are rarely able to use their knowledge for they are not gods, they harbour the enemy of all doctorhood and godhead, vanity.

I hope it is understood that I was talking of myself, when I was being so critical. Who else would I be talking of since I know so little, in fact nothing, about others? I am old enough – I said it before in order to be allowed to talk about myself, exclusively about myself; I beg you not to forget: what I am writing here is a soliloquy.

Do not forget that this is a human being who comes to you here. Remember what you know of human beings, and the first virtue of doctors, humility, will be yours automatically; for you know how little you know. Of course you might say here is somebody who is neither chair nor carpet, neither animal nor flower, neither stone nor wood. Yet is what you are saying true? No. This person is in reality animal and flower, stone, wood, carpet, and chair, too. Beware, if you attempt to pry him away now from his connection with the universe, do not forget how many mistakes this attempt at isolation brings about and must bring about, mistakes which, perpetrated thousands of times, have heaped up so much debris around you that it requires all your strength and all your greatness to lift up your eyes over the pile. If you isolate man and deny that he is animal and flower, stone, and wood, then you are like a person who does nothing else during his whole life but look through a microscope: he is in danger of denying heaven, earth, the stars, since he cannot look at them through a microscope. Remember that the human being in front of you is an arbitrary figment of your lack of imagination, that he certainly is not what you believe you can see in him, that you give expression to a miserable probability when you state: this human being is like this or like that.

Of course you cannot help making this inevitable mistake when you want to treat somebody, but you should be aware that it is a mistake otherwise you will have less understanding than the simplest Indian. You should, moreover, accept scientific errors; life is strong and will not let you founder because of your ignorance. Yet you have to be even more honest and admit to yourself that you are violating this isolated piece of world if you regard it as an entity by itself. This is not true. You know that this entity set up by you artificially is a thousand million-fold multiplicity, is a conglomerate of innumerable and immeasurable multiplicities which are independent and yet conditioned by the whole of man. Every cell, every cell nucleus, every tiny particle lives its own life. Are you so foolish that you want to know what cannot be known?

Yes, I am bold enough to know, in spite of this, like everybody else, bold enough to err, yet I err knowingly, I remember sometimes that I err. And this remembering is important. Man's danger is his vanity, it is his danger and his greatest strength. It is difficult to help those who cannot understand this.

The human being should be diagnosed in as many of the breadths, depths, flat and narrow bits of his nature as possible, in all the elements which all human beings share and those which seem peculiar to individuals alone, but which to the gaze of the old keep shrinking: his shape and the shape of his limbs, his external and internal parts, and all his functions from breathing, sleeping, moving, digesting, heart beat to speaking, thinking, feeling. The It talks to us in a thousand languages, loudly and mutely, hesitatingly and cheekily, in well-composed, easily understood paragraphs and in quick interjections, and occasionally in a kind of gibberish which sounds childish or even mad and yet makes sense if patiently listened to. Occasionally we need some physical or chemical test, an X-ray, a check-up of the heart, an examination of the chest, a screening of the hidden cavities, and whatever else there may be in the way of possible medical investigations. Yet all these things which seem to make up the doctor's work are only occasional necessities, they do not mean very much in terms of the whole of medical business, they can mostly be dispensed with and should never be uppermost in medical practice, let alone be its whole content. Not everybody who goes to a doctor demands help against his illness, most people are simply seeking help of any kind, and most of them are not helped much when they recover from their illness.

The human being, not the patient, goes to the doctor, the human being not the patient asks for help. Certainly the shortest and easiest way to help is often to tackle his illness, yet not necessarily, for illness is merely a form of expression used by the suffering It which vociferously emphasises its illness in order to be able to hide its deepest secret the better.

To study man is ultimately the most important duty of the doctor, and our researches of the past century have been very little concerned with that. One can even say without qualification that we have forgotten a lot of what our ancestors knew and what is of urgent importance to the doctor, and also to the scholar – though I would not be so bold as to pass judgment on that strange human species.

Man is not always the same, everybody knows that; he changes constantly, yet who remembers that he changes constantly? Who would therefore shy away from making a diagnosis and yet we all know of this uninterrupted change in man's nature. – Of course we follow the course of the illness and change our diagnosis when the symptoms force us to use a different nosological label for the case, to give the illness a different name. Yet the doctor's function consists in discovering not the illness but the person who is seeking help, and we do not follow his changes or not enough. Thus inevitably all the essential things about the people who come to us remain hidden from us; they are patients, ill people not human beings; to be ill to us is still something essentially different from being well, we still do not acknowledge life's ambivalence, we still pretend that illness is an evil, as if the It weren't as sublime in the language of illness as it is in the language of painting or writing poetry or researching. We still do not understand that in the illness the It expresses thoughts as deep as in the gospels and that it announces in both forms the very same thing: Behold the greatness of God and the miracle of man!

Man changes; there is no doubt; and yet he always stays the same; that, too, everybody knows. Nobody will mistake a human being for a dog or a gnat. Yet we forget this, too, when we come to diagnosis. Otherwise it would not be possible that two fundamental facts which are a part of every honest diagnosis are rarely ever mentioned in medical literature, firstly, that man's It is bisexual, that every human being is a hermaphrodite, that never has there been a creature that is only man or only woman; secondly, that man's It is timeless, that it is never child, or adult, or old man but always all three simultaneously, and that adulthood and old age are as nothing compared with being a child if one weighs the three evolutionary stages according to their importance for the individual. The sentence: If you do not become like children you will not enter into the kingdom of heaven, can safely be changed to: since you are all children you are all in heaven. Unfortunately nobody takes easily to the fact that he is a child; the twenty-year old and the sixty-year old is as obsessed as the six-year old by the wish to be a grown-up, and as this seldom comes about, at least act as if he were; which is ridiculous, of course.

Since it is my intention to flavour these soliloquies with occasional examples I shall tell a story here. It is about a maid servant, she complained of violent pain in the area of the heart, she was examined, found to have a defective cardial valve, shown the cardial enlargement on her X-ray, discovered to have severe pain in the seventh inter-costal nerve; swelling from the feet up to the calves was observed and used to make the diagnosis: mitral insufficiency – a closure defect of the valve. Rest, careful nursing, digitalis taken internally. There is nothing to object to either in the name of the illness or in the treatment. Only the treatment doesn't work and the diagnosis, the name of the illness, is wrong. At least this is the conclusion I draw from the further course of the illness.

The girl had a faint black fluff on her upper lip, something that is quite common and seems to be particularly attractive to certain men, I am told by those who know. After a while, when she had become more trusting, she told me that the moustache had to be shaved from time to time otherwise her mouth looked too ugly. Wouldn't it have been advisable if the doctor had taken account of this obvious sign of the girl's masculinity before he decided on the name of the illness and digitalis treatment? He might then perhaps have noticed that the right index finger was stiff as the result of an ulcer. Moreover, if he had noticed that this decidedly shy girl had a page-boy haircut, that her hair was parted like a boy's, that her first name was Friederike, he might have decided to learn a little more about the masculine aspects of this woman's personality. Soon guided by the girl's evidence and behaviour – he would probably have begun to doubt whether the absence of the menstrual period for over a year was really due to the assumed heart disease or whether it might not be seen as an expression of masculine wishes. Perhaps he would have been heretical enough, against all the rules of medical science, to take the swelling of the feet and the stiffness of the finger as an erection symbol and not as a consequence of defective cardial activity. In short, he would have felt bound to explore the human being and, since this is a true story, he would soon have found out that this girl was in the grip of a hopeless homosexual love that tortured her heart and conscience. She would have told him gradually as she told me; if only he had remembered that one of the fundamental principles of diagnosis is to establish how much masculinity there is in female patients and how much femininity in male patients. Finally a new X-ray, the disappearance of water from the feet, the sounds of the heart, the recurrence of menstruation and the cessation of pain would have taught him that there was no question of a defective cardial valve. In particular – and this is why I mention this case – he would have learnt that this girl had chosen her illness because illness and even death would have been easier to bear for her erring and badly informed It than the unfulfilled longing for women which seemed unnatural to her mind.

This may be sufficient for today.

12

Language*

I hope you do not expect me to give a comprehensive picture of our time in these lectures. You will even be disappointed if you expect me to tell you something new. What I have to say is obvious and everybody can see it, in a way that is perhaps better than I can, certainly different. Yet it is well worth looking occasionally at what is familiar through the eyes of a stranger, and if nothing else is achieved but a lively conflict of opinions, that is quite enough for me.

With this I have come to the theme of today. One has to speak in order to exchange opinions and I want to talk to you a little about speaking.

Daily and hourly we use an instrument, I mean language, and we take it so much for granted that we hardly ever think about it and what kind of a tool it is, just as we use a handkerchief without asking how old this custom is and where it comes from. This is the fate of everyday things.

That much is clear: language is the vehicle of culture. It is the precondition of human communication. Language has created religion and art, built streets and conducted trade all over the world. In truth it is the means by which thought turns to action and, eternally fertile, it produces new thoughts. Agriculture is as unthinkable without language as is philosophy; the comforts of the house and even the house itself were made by it; all action, thought, emotion, even love and hatred, God and nature are dependent on language. All this is obvious. Yet I beg you to look around once more and with eye and mind find all the concepts which make up language. I would like you to devote at least a short while to the contemplation of this miracle. The bolder your imagination, the quicker its survey of this world, the better for our mutual understanding.

* 'Von der Sprache' (*Hin zu Gottnatur*, Leipzig, 3rd ed. 1912). Reprinted in *Psychoanalytische Schriften zur Literatur und Kunst*.

For now I beg you to consider the opposite, the culturally inhibiting effects of language, the invincible claims by which language enslaves our thought and action. There is the well-known saying that man was given language in order to hide his thoughts. You may think what you like about this. But it is quite another thing to ask whether language is capable of expressing thought. We all know from experience that it isn't, that it is incapable particularly of expressing the most cherished and deepest thoughts. Nature has been wise in this, for the individual alone should know about his innermost and deepest thought. Man's most personal thought is speechless, subterranean, unconscious, and the struggle of the creative forces with mute nature constitutes man's innermost life. The inner muteness is the real human personality whether one chooses to call it soul or spirit or anything else. It is common to us all, the common factor, the basic human entity. Yet creative ability is a human being's most valuable gift. The degree to which he can communicate vividly and effectively what goes on inside him, and the value of these communications, is a distinguishing mark between great and small minds, between the poet who remains the greatest of all mortals and the common people. Yet even the most marvellous poet can express no more than a fraction of his thought in words; his best ideas remain as mute as with everybody else, and he would be committing a sin if he revealed them. It would amount to being unchaste. He would lose himself and cease to exist as an individual if he could completely expose himself. Here, as I said above, language acts as a fetter which wisely holds us back. Nature shies away so much from showing itself as it really is that it does not allow the inner life to be conceived in words, not even in silent words. Suddenly there is something, nobody knows where it came from. Life is an abyss of impenetrable darkness, from which strange shapes rise up like butterflies which lose their beauty when the finger touches them, and so would our thoughts if they had to be cast into words. When something has to be communicated from the innermost soul as happens particularly in relationships between men and women, then it is done by gesture, touch, by the light of the eyes, perhaps by a louder sound, perhaps even by music, but never by language. The barrier is ihsurmountable.

There is one thing: man does not manage to express his innermost self in words; his capacity to speak does not enable him to say the truth. Going one step further, it can be recognised that speaking as such already contains the distortion of truth. We speak of a piece of bread, a glass of water, a picture, a star, as if they were self-contained objects with defined frontiers. This is wrong. They do not exist as separate objects, we do not perceive them as separate. When we perceive a glass of water we also see the table on which it stands, the hand which holds it, the room in which the table is placed, or the person to whom the hand belongs. Or another image: a piece of bread is certainly a piece of bread. Everybody knows what it is and calls it that, too. Leave it lying about, for two days only. Then it is still a piece of bread for us, but in the meantime it has changed; even with blunt senses one can see the transformation. It is hard and dry now, and has started to go mouldy. And yet we all say: this is a piece of bread that was left lying about. But is this true? No. One only has to touch it or bite into it to know that it is no longer the same. We resort to excuses and say: it is old now. But what does this mean, 'it is old'? When did it grow old? Today? Yesterday? No, it grew old gradually. Gradually? When did it start? one might ask, and the answer ultimately is, it never started to grow old. It changed constantly, without interruption, was never constant, not even the smallest fraction of a second, not even the moment when we held it in the hand, but changed constantly with the help of certain forces which are active inside it and preserve it in the context of the whole. We immediately understand: the piece of bread only exists as a separate thing because we name it, because we arbitrarily and dishonestly tear it from its context, because we talk of it.

We are thus faced with the fact that every word in our language is a lie whether it is uttered by our mouth or remains mute in our brain, a lie which violates facts, which makes us look at the world from a false perspective and think falsely. For it is the same with water as it is with bread; it does not for a moment stop evaporating, getting colder or warmer; dust continually falls into it and so does light and electric current. We take a drop and put it under the microscope and ask with astonishment: is this really the same water, the water I drink? there are thousands and thousands of animals in it which quarrel, love each other, breathe, feed, die and are born. Or let's take a picture. We stand and look at it. How dark it looks! The painter messed it up, it's all blurred, without contours, without life. Here a line is too hard, there we see a lump of shapeless flesh. And now from the window a beam of light falls on the picture. It is still the same picture. But what has happened to it? Suddenly it is different, glowing, colourful; triumphantly art asserts itself. A little bit of sunlight proves that the picture did not exist by itself, that it exists in the context of the world, that only our language has lied to us. Or the star. We see it shine up there in the sky. Yet we know for certain that it changes constantly. Millions of years ago it was a speck of mist, in millions of years it will be extinct. Maybe at this moment already it is no longer a shining star, we merely see the light which thousands of years ago was sent out by it when it still existed, was still shining.

Language lies, it must lie; this is due to its being part of human nature. And the answer with which Christ agreed to what the Roman had said, 'Truth is neither in heaven nor on earth nor between heaven and earth', is clear to everybody. It is in the nature of language to be imprecise, to distort, it is in the nature of man. Yet it is also in the nature of man the more sophisticated he is the more to correct this imprecision of language and the more truthful to be. This holds true in particular for silent speech, for talking to oneself, for thinking. We Germans have produced a man who was exemplary in all things, who recognised and defined this phenomenon clearly: Goethe. There is a statement which he made repeatedly in talking and writing and which he tried to live consciously, perhaps the only human being ever to do so: Every thing should be considered as part of the whole. See the whole in the part, see in the whole the part. – This is how one should go about doing research. Grip the object in front of you tightly, look at it and touch it on all sides, yet when you have done that remember that this apparent whole is merely a part, a dependent link in a chain. When you want to investigate an arm, forget that it is attached to a body and try to see and understand it as an entity. Then you must remember that this arm is nothing without the human being to which it belongs and that this human being is a part of its parents and that these parents have come from the flesh of animals and the fruit of the forest and that the ray of sun awakens the fruit and the animals and that the sun is revolving around other suns in the universe and owes its existence to other stars.

Now you'll say these are well-known stories; everybody knows that and there is no need to call on old Goethe. We all know. Of course we all know. Yet we do not live as if we did. And to live in the awareness is the aim, the unattainable and yet necessary aim. To experience everything as a part, to experience one's self as a part – nobody can do that. And yet it is the way to the truth, the only way and the way we have to take and shall take. It is not easy. Which of us looks at this moment at a cup or the tablecloth or the neighbour or me and sees in this cup, this cloth, this person the whole of the world? Nobody. Nobody even tries to. And yet it is necessary. And yet this attempt will transform the whole of the world, the inner world, religion and science. And Goethe made this attempt.

Goethe's reputation as a scholar had a curious fate. His contemporaries rejected him as an amateur, as a troublesome amateur even, and for half a century his scientific studies were considered nonsense. Then it became fashionable to praise him as a precursor of Darwin, yet one placed him on a considerably lower rung than that occupied by the English master. Gradually people are beginning to understand that he was not merely a precursor, and the statement made against universal mockery by the physiologist Müller in the Thirties is taken seriously: Goethe was greater as a scientist than as a poet. We can foresee now that in centuries to come people will rightly say that he was one of the greatest thinkers of all times. He showed science a new approach, namely the approach of seeing the part in the whole, of taking the apparent whole as a symbol of the universe, of seeing the whole world symbolised in a flower, an animal, a pebble, the human eye, the sun; and to construct the world from this flower, this pebble, that is to create it anew and to investigate things not by analysing but by placing them in the context of the whole. He opened up this approach to science which will achieve undreamed-of results in fields which have so far been untested and unknown, for, hardly have we started on this approach, it turns fairytales into truth, confirms with its theory of radiation the old Old Indian legend about different kinds of light which emanate from all creatures, and fulfils the alchemists' and goldsearchers' dreams by transforming metals into other metals. Goethe opened up new avenues to life. The old concept of the world which regarded man as the crown of creation will disappear, and a new life with a new religion will come about. What we now call Christianity, the doctrine of man's sin and salvation, is fading away. For man is nothing by himself, he only exists as a dependent part.

Again one can say that all these ideas about seeing the whole in the part or about man being nothing by himself are not new to Goethe and have been taught by thousands of men before him, and yet the world continued on its course. Goethe's wisdom is ancient, older than the walls of the Assyrians. For sure. Thousands of people have thought it before him, yet nobody tried to put it into practice, to make it happen, to live it. And now take any bit of Goethe's life, any day, any word, any poem or idea of his. Everywhere you will find the attempt to make the part suggest the whole and to represent the apparent whole as a part. He never forgot that he was in the world and, as its creature, affected this world. In all his utterances and innermost revelations one comes up against the imperative: be objective. One is sometimes tempted to think, when one comes across this recurring word which demands the highest degree of self-denial, that he is related to the Indian thinkers who strive for the same goal of objectivity, of self-distancing, of dehumanisation. Yet the Indian strives to get away from the world in order to reach his goal. Goethe, however, threw himself into the world in the fullness of life and tried to objectify it; he was not at all a renouncer of the world, but a human being who was very much alive, perhaps the most alive personality of all times.

You must not be surprised when you hear me talk so enthusiastically. My intention is to present trends of our modern times, and in this context the first word has to be about this man in whom the modern aspiration for objectivity is embodied, and the striving for a new world view which does not see man as a God; this man in whom the coming religion is embodied. For it is certain that it is coming and not too far away.

Of course I do not want to suggest that Goethe was an objective human being. This is totally impossible, every man is subjective, nobody can forget himself, yet one should at least make the attempt. And whoever tries, if only for a moment, will realise at once how infinitely difficult it is, how such an attempt can well purify a man with a thousand flames and change him inside out. For not only the artificially bred arrogance of man, which is expressed in the belief in immortality and eternal happiness, but all our habits, our thoughts and feelings, our whole life and particularly our language are in contradiction to this aspiration.

And this brings me back to the statement that language hinders culture. You must recall that language possesses the word I, a word which we hear everywhere and which determines and dominates our whole life. And then you must try and understand what kind of an I this is. Try and understand this I, separate it, grasp it as an entity on its own. You will see that this is impossible. There is no such thing as an I; it is a lie, a distortion, to say: 'I think, I live.' It should be: 'it thinks, it lives'. It, that is the great mystery of the universe. There is no I. Science has long since proved even to the pedants that this I is made up of millions of smaller I's; every day brings more scientific proof of the fact that the blood that circulates inside us is as independent an entity as is the I in which it circulates, and that the human being is as dependent on and inseparable from the whole as is the blood from the human being. Daily, science adds more proof to the notion that every organ, the brain, the heart, every gland in the body, every cell is an entity with a will and a mind of its own, and yet that it is nothing but a part which has come about through the whole and affects the whole. Everything is in flux. Quite certainly there is no I. This is one of language's untruths and unfortunately a fateful one. For nobody can free himself from this single word I.

We are confronted by one of nature's deep mysteries which cannot be fathomed. The awareness of being an individual, an I, is a primitive and completely internalised awareness. Reason, science, religion may prove irrefutably that it is an illusion, yet man would rather be skinned and live on in suffering than stop conceiving of himself as a whole, as an individuality, an I. It is in man's nature, it is one of his characteristics, like the roundness of his head or the shape of his hand. And we all know, too, that man's self-confidence is a great strength; one could even say that life's whole purpose lies in the effort to assert oneself in this world, in the struggle for the recognition of individuality. The more man separates himself from his environment the more he will achieve, the higher he raises his self above others the more energetic he will be, the more strength he will draw from others.

Yet the consciousness of self, this natural instinct, is like all other human instincts. Like the sapling of a plant that runs to leaf it has to be held down, cut back, otherwise it will destroy man's equilibrium. Thus the desire for happiness is the innermost impulse in a woman's soul; that she does not succeed in taming it is the ultimate reason for woman's sufferings. The instinct for self-preservation is the protector of life yet, left to itself, it degenerates into fear. The power of instinct is immense, elemental, and to further it artificially is to destroy the whole in favour of the part, an important insight which throws light on the mistakes of our education and is a warning of imminent danger. Life defends itself against this danger, not least against its tool, language. Next to the hunger for happiness it puts hysteria; the names gourmand, rake, drunkard, coward are given to those who blindly follow the forces of nature. Honour, obedience, industry, spirit of sacrifice, all these words stand for a specific fetter which has been applied to these primitive forces. To tame the consciousness of self, has also been attempted many times; selfishness and egotism are strong insults in our language. Yet how little they achieve against the single word I. They disintegrate when confronted with it; man's soul is sated with the consciousness of his own personality, the belief in himself and his own importance. This is his nature. Mankind is conscious of this most dangerous of all linguistic lies. Everywhere self-denial is considered the highest virtue. It was planted wherever man tried to ennoble himself.

In the two highest of the world's religions, in Christianity and even more in Buddhism, self-denial, disregard of self, is considered the aim of all our strivings. Now Buddhism, which I have called the wider-reaching vision of the two – it does not stop at man but also includes animals – Buddhism, or at least its fundamental ideas, is gaining more and more ground among Europeans. Yet Christianity is still the leading belief of our time and with it the dogma that gradually developed from the envious, basic moods of suppressed man, the dogma of the immortality of the self and of the heavenly reward and eternal punishment to which this I is subject. This is a fateful doctrine. It does not tame the elemental forces of the I; it has allowed them to grow into a terrible force, and there is reason to fear that it has undermined the innermost strength of European nations. I shall come back to this perhaps in a different context, since the idea of man's central position is still a pivotal concept of all action and thought with its implications of a God who is only concerned about man's well-being, of man's world domination, of God's sacrificial death for man. Here the few words I have just uttered will be sufficient to explain my position with regard to these problems; my attitude of contempt towards the insane arrogance of the human Ego.

Only one thing I want to point out. One of the fundamental differences between the modern age and antiquity is the attitude of religion towards nature. The Greeks saw God everywhere. Nature to them was something venerable, something fearful. We moderns with our naked unscrupulousness are unable to understand why the Greeks of the classical age practised so many strange customs when they cut down a tree or hunted an animal. We smile about superstitious fear. Unfortunately with the fear we also lost our holy awe; the only attitude towards nature we have is that of the exploiter vis-à-vis the exploited. For the sentimental love of nature which we harbour is a luxury feeling shared by the aesthetically educated; it is not a sacred feeling of awe, but importunate staring and touching governed by clichés. For us nature has lost its godhead. To this we owe all our progress in technology, in civilisation, yet we have lost much in inner culture, in inner values. In antiquity man did not presume that he was the centre of the world, the ruler of earth, rather the contrary. And now you must consider the strange fact that the classical languages express the Ego only by means of verb endings. For us the I has become an almost insuperable linguistic obstacle to recognising the unimportance of the human individual and to endowing life, religion, poetry with the sacred awe felt towards nature. Whoever looks at modern Europe carefully will be horrified about our lack of culture, no matter how highly he may value the sophistication of our civilisation. The

Renaissance, the only movement which can be considered to have been an approximation to culture, originated with a nation that is still steeped in antiquity and for which the word *io* is almost unknown. And even now the dead and totally degenerate Italian people have an attitude towards nature which we Germans might consider crude, barbarous, contemptuous, yet it still has traces of an awareness of God Nature.

Again I am using a word by Goethe – God Nature, *Gottnatur*. I have returned to this man deliberately. For our relationship to nature is beginning to change. A new world is opening up for us, a world in which there can be a growth of culture, in which Godhead Nature will be experienced with awe, a feeling we hardly know the name of. If anything can reconcile us to life, which takes away our breath with all its haste and greed, it is the sight of this gentle current of respectful veneration of God Nature.

But one must not underestimate the obstacles, the rocks, deserts, and swamps which obstruct the stream. Above all one should not underestimate the power of linguistic tradition. It is not only the lie 'I' which stops us. As I have already said, this lie is in man's nature. It cannot, does not have to be overcome completely. For what belongs to the nature of man is legitimate and must be respected. Yet we have inherited words which are the patent lies of ignorance, which we know to be lies, and which are yet so firmly rooted in language that we cannot do without them, so that we are astonished when we notice by chance that they are lies. Think of the word sky. How many educational, moral, and vital values are associated with this mendacious word. Impressed on the mind of the child, it remains ineradicably in our innermost being, never to be destroyed, always sending up new shoots. Or even the word soul, a word that tears man in two, a terrible heritage, a continuing curse of our life. I can hardly think of a greater achievement than to write the history of this word soul. It is impossible, as I well know. For just as nobody can see their own eyes, so nobody can get to the bottom of this word soul. But we can probably say: the belief in a soul, that is the belief in something which at most exists in the imagination, this belief is the basis on which all modern life is built. This has not always been so. In antiquity people thought otherwise. The people of Asia think otherwise. But it will be in vain if we try to rid ourselves of this nightmare. For language has secured it for the eternity of our existence.

Do you want more examples still? Then take the word atom on which our science is based. Quite certainly it is a lie, quite certainly a foolish idea which cannot even be entertained, for how should anything be indivisible? Or the word life. Something lives, yes, and we know that there is nothing that is not alive, that the stone is as alive as the bird that sits on it. We talk of death and are afraid of it; yet we know that there is no death. We talk of the five senses and have known for quite some time that there are rather more than five. We talk of settled nations and yet we can see that the Europeans are a nomadic people. We call ourselves Germans and our neighbours Austrians, Swiss, or Dutch, and yet we speak the same language, come from the same tribes, are cousins and brothers. One can already predict the tragic consequences of this ridiculous folly of calling ourselves Germans. And now take a name like Belgian or Russian. The fact that we do not understand what goes on in the Tsarist Empire is largely due to the fact that we conceive of the Russians as a uniform people because we are seduced into thinking this by our language. In reality there is even more variety there than in the Roman Empire of Augustus, a veritable chaos of races and peoples, a Babylonian confusion of languages.

You may wonder what this dry and rather problematical argument on language has got to do with the trends of our modern age. But I have tried to establish a base for myself on which perhaps one can continue to build. I have already expressed my view that we are on the threshold of a real cultural revolution, the attempt to reinstate the harmony between man and nature which was interrupted for a thousand years. There are many signs of this. The question is merely whether Europe has enough energy left to develop the budding forces. Not to answer – it is not yet possible – but to consider this question is of sufficient interest to justify our meetings. And if it is to be considered, then the first thing is to test the tool with which this new age will be built and this, as I said in the beginning, is language. The spirit of language is one of the signs which betray the direction of the trend and is almost the most accurate. Unfortunately it does not prove very favourable as far as the possibility of a strong cultural development in Europe is concerned. Again I shall have to take you into the confusion of words a little longer in order to help you understand what I mean. That I choose the German language will not be held against me. As far as my knowledge of foreign languages goes, I consider that the same is true for them, too.

A moment ago I mentioned the word German. Isn't it strange that the Pole Kantorowicz is considered German while Gottfried Keller or Karl Spitteler or Boecklin call themselves Swiss? It is at the very least inaccurate. Kantorowicz is and will remain a Pole and he is at the most a subject of the German Empire, yet never a German; Keller is German through and through and only secondarily a citizen of Switzerland. To use Germany and German Empire synonymously is a grave linguistic mistake which will lead to errors of thought and action in the course of time. Negligence of speech opens up an artificial abyss which, after a time, will be difficult to bridge.

In this particular case language is thoughtless. And immediately we remember that there are thousands of cases like this. We say that the sun rises and the moon rises. This is simply stupid. There are two completely different processes at work. The moon really rises because it rotates around the world. Yet the sun is standing still and we are rotating around it. Only a thoughtless language can describe with the same words two events as different as these. Small wonder that Copernicus' discoveries have still not penetrated people's minds. It struck me recently that I had told an acquaintance that I had gone from Dortmund to Amsterdam. This is stupid. Never in my life have I gone (*gegangen* = walked) so far. Or a patient tells me that he had a terrible (*schreckliche*) night and it emerges afterwards that he was lying awake for an hour. Bad if that frightens him (*wenn er darüber erschrickt*). Fear and anxiety, what a frightened breed of people we would be if we believed our language. Today people enjoy themselves awfully, they find a new dress terribly pretty!

We no longer know what words mean, our language does not think any more. Dear friend, somebody says to me, a double lie and disparagement of the highest ideals, of love and friendship. The man neither loves me nor am I his friend, he even uses the expression mockingly. One's heart could break when one considers what thoughtless uses the word love is subjected to. I tell my wife that I have seen Herr Müller talk to Frau Schulze. Nonsense, neither of them was talking, talking is something totally different from speaking. With almost every word I have to tell myself 'stop, you are merely talking nonsense'. There have been as many thoughtless remarks as there have been sentences in my talk tonight. And this is the same everywhere and with all human beings. Try just once, pay attention to what others say, to what you are saying yourself; every third word is an error of thought. Or take something printed, not a newspaper since everything is wrong in newspapers anyhow, but perhaps the works of a great poet, let's say Keller or even Goethe, not to mention the great stylist Nietzsche. You would simply laugh because you would find so many stupidities on the first page. This is a disquieting sign in terms of our ability to develop. When a language has become thoughtless through and through, when words no longer express what they mean, then it can hardly hope to have a future. This is the childish babble of old age. We are no longer able to distinguish words carefully from one another; they flow into each other, there is no strength and vitality in them any more.

This aging process can be detected in other peculiarities of our speech. We exaggerate because words are hollow, no longer have resonance, the sentence shall be made to sound. Observe how many superlatives we use in our daily speech. How often we have experienced the most marvellous thing! How often we have found something unspeakably stupid! How many thousands of times we have found some miserable talent or enviable piece of luck. For shame, in a decent language nothing should be enviable. And how about all the things we call wonderful! And yet, alas, we do not believe in wonders. Because we are surrounded by them.

All this is very sad, and the saddest thing is that it is the most valuable feelings and impulses of man that are devalued by language. I have already mentioned love and friendship, but let's return to wonder (*Wunder*). We *bewundern* (admire) a beautiful woman, a marvellous view, a perfect painting, a festive table, cold champagne, and a leather wall-covering. Things have gone so far that there is nothing we can marvel at (*bewundern*) any more. We have altogether become so indifferent and blasé that we are no longer capable of admiring though we could learn something from every blade of grass or flea. We do not possess this most marvellous of human characteristics, the ability to admire. We only imagine that we do. We are really quite dominated by the pseudo-wisdom of *Nil admirari*. We may not have gone quite as far as the Englishman with his 'very fine indeed' or the Italian with his 'bellissimo', his 'stupende'. But we have to admit that a language which uses concepts in this way is childish, senile. We no longer have any youthful sensations, and this is why we have to get intoxicated artificially with words. Where this will lead us is obvious. First to wrong-headed thinking, gradually to mistaken vision and learning. You only have to establish how few people can see or hear, how they cannot distinguish round from angular even when they try, how many applaud bad music merely because it exaggerates, how many buy bad works of art merely because they exaggerate, how many take a bad person for a good one because he is articulate. One has to be very trusting to hope for a good future.

The individual word has become devalued. Unfortunately this is not all. The individual dialect too has become devalued, and all the world is trying to destroy it completely, first the state and then educated people. Sometimes we remember that we perpetrate a sacrilege when we deprive a region of its individuality, and yet we go on enthusing about elementary schools and general education for all. This is a trend of the times, a trend which goes all out to blur distinctions, hierarchies on which, if not the world, then at least all culture is based. It is indeed a sad spectacle. In the same way in which the sober dress of our time gradually drives out all national dress so that only poor cranks continue to keep it alive, language works towards uniformity, more slowly yet more certainly, and one can work out the time it will take until the Saxon bureaucratic language* will be spoken everywhere, diluted and stripped of all the ideas which Luther expressed in it; for the few good

* Standard German is based on the language of Luther's translation which was developed from the German used in the Imperial offices of Saxony at the time.

minds and poets will not be able to stop the process once every trade and professions and particularly every school starts spreading Standard German (*Schriftdeutsch*).

School, education, and above all our mothers. One does not stop at destroying the dialects, one tries hard to destroy the mother tongue itself, in all innocence of course, in a stupid innocence. What is better in the modern view than to be able to speak foreign languages? Yet the German already finds it difficult to express his thoughts accurately in German. In a foreign language he never succeeds. In the foreign language he speaks even less accurately than in his own; there the use of words often does not correspond to the concept he is thinking of. When we cannot think of an expression in our mother tongue we take another one without hesitation, and the more often we do the more fluent we are. It does not matter in the individual case. So rarely do our educated people have anything original to say that ultimately it doesn't matter whether they repeat parrot-fashion pre-processed ideas in German, in English, or in French. The more common it becomes to talk in foreign tongues, the greater the danger that thoughtlessness will spread to those circles which still have a spiritual conscience, and that thinking men will be seduced into sloppiness of language and thought. Already it is considered a disgrace for decent people not to be able to speak fluent English or French; yet to speak fluently is the more difficult the more one is in the habit of thinking. This is a well-known fact; Goethe, though he tried hard from his earliest childhood, never managed a conversation without difficulty in French and Italian, not to mention English, and Nietzsche was not even able to do that, although he lived in Italy and France for years. People like them would nowadays have to write sloppily in order not to become a laughing-stock. Now I believe that one single mistake of Goethe's or Nietzsche's against their intellectual conscience would have done more harm than could ever be offset by the usefulness to our young girls of the ability to converse with a foreign suitor. It is said that thoughtlessness is not in the nature of woman but merely a consequence of their spiritual slavery. If this is true then the learning of foreign languages is a certain means of keeping women in their sphere of spiritual slavery. This is quite all right with us men. Every thoughtless word produces in us thoughts and actions provided we love the mouth who speaks it.

I could re-inforce my doubts about the probability of a cultural renaissance with a few more characteristics of modern linguistic usage, but I shall rather try to find out whether there are any comforts to be had in this usage. Two points strike me. The first ties up with what I said above; it is the attempt at inventing a world language and making it accessible to everybody. Clearly it would be much better for our spiritual education and, I would like to say, for our morality, if there were only one foreign language to learn and one which did not possess as many shades and nuances as modern languages. It would be less difficult to speak the truth. Unfortunately such a development is opposed by the strongest force in our age: the vanity of woman. Since she wants to prove that she is our spiritual equal, she will not give up the only field in which she is without doubt superior to us, namely chattering in foreign tongues.

The other point I would like to make which makes me hopeful is the use of foreign words. A language like German which is able to digest and incorporate and thus Germanize lots of foreign words cannot well be called senile. I do not share the modern aversion to foreign words. An excess is certainly harmful. Yet I am glad about every foreign word that is a genuine gain for the language. And I cannot see why '*Nation*' or '*Mikroskop*' should not be considered good German. A comparison with former decades or centuries is very instructive. A word which sounds alien in Goethe is not offensive when it is used by a contemporary. And if one considers what kind of German was spoken before and after Goethe, German interlarded with French sounds and interrupted by French sentences – it must have sounded like modern Alsatian – then one can say that in this respect we have come a long way.

In this respect and in something else. Whoever has followed the development of literature in the last thirty years must admit that some writers, at least the better writers, have recently become more conscientious in their use of language. It is a certain fact. And with this increasing conscientiousness in the use of language artists and writers have achieved almost spontaneously an increasing accuracy of thought, and greater care in the composition, the choice of ideas and materials. It would be rewarding to study this advance in the arts, and the reasons for it, in a separate talk.

To sum up my rambling discussion in a brief formula, which may be thought of as a conviction, I offer the following statement: We are barbarians, yet we have the possibility of producing a genuine culture in future. But language, the most important tool with which to further this, almost entirely fails us. Perhaps other means will appear later which are more useful for the spirit and for truth.

Select Bibliography

ENGLISH TRANSLATIONS

The Book of the It (*Das Buch vom Es,* 1923), translated by V.M.E. Collins (London, Vision Press, 1950; New York, Vintage Books, 1961).

Exploring the Unconscious, translated by V.M.E. Collins (London, Vision Press, 1949).

A compilation of addresses and articles by Groddeck taken, for the most part, from *Die Arche,* the journal which he circulated privately between 1925 and 1928. One chapter, 'The Body's Middleman', formed the first section of *Der Mensch als Symbol* (1933).

The Unknown Self, translated by V.M.E. Collins (London, Vision Press, 1951).

A selection of lectures and papers taken partly from *Die Arche* and partly as follows: five chapters from the course of six lectures on 'Das Es' (The It) which Groddeck delivered in Berlin in 1926; the 'Clinical Communications' reprinted in the present volume (Chapter 7); and 'A Sermon for Christmas' which Groddeck wrote for his children in December 1910.

The World of Man, translated by V.M.E. Collins (London, Vision Press, 1951).

A compilation of extracts arranged round Groddeck's last completed work, *Der Mensch als Symbol,* dealing particularly with pictorial art and language.

GERMAN EDITIONS

Hin zu Gottnatur (Towards God Nature), Leipzig, 3rd edition 1912. Partial reprint in *Psychoanalytische Schriften zur Literatur und Kunst* (1964).

Nasamecu, natura sanat medicus curat. Der gesunde und kranke Mensch (The healthy and sick person), Leipzig, 1913.

Der Seelensucher. Ein psychoanalytischer Roman (The Seeker of Souls. A Psychoanalytic Novel), Vienna, Internationaler Psychoanalytischer Verlag, 1921.

Das Buch vom Es. Psychoanalytische Briefe an eine Freundin. Vienna, Internationaler Psychoanalytischer Verlag, 1923; new edition, Wiesbaden, Limes Verlag, 1961.

(Trans.: *The Book of the It.* Archives of Psychoanalysis, published by the Psychoanalytic Institute, Stamford, Conn. Vol. I, Part 1, 2, 3, 4, 1926/7. *The Book of the It,* London, 1935 (Daniel); new edition, London, 1950 (Vision Press); paperback edition, New York, 1961 (Vintage Books).

Die Arche. Halbmonatsschrift im Selbstverlag (Fortnightly House Journal). Vol. I (16.5.1925–13.3.1926); Vol. II (12.4.1926–28.3.1927); Vol. III (14.4.1927–14.12.1927).

Der Mensch als Symbol: Unmassgebliche Meinungen über Sprache und Kunst (Man as Symbol: Unauthoritative Views on Language and Art), Vienna, 1933. Partially reprinted in *Psychoanalytische Schriften zur Literatur und Kunst.* Re-issued by Limes Verlag, Wiesbaden, 1973.

Psychoanalytische Schriften zur Literatur und Kunst (Psychoanalytic Papers on

Literature and Art), Selected and edited by Egenolf Roeder von Diersburg, Wiesbaden, Limes Verlag, 1964.

Psychoanalytische Schriften zur Psychosomatik (Psychoanalytic Papers on Psychosomatics), selected and edited by Günter Clauser, Wiesbaden, Limes Verlag, 1964.

Der Mensch und sein Es; Briefe, Aufsätze, Biografisches (Man and His It; Letters, Essays, Biographical Notes), Wiesbaden, Limes Verlag, 1970.

Index

267